MULTILITERACIES IN WORLD LANGUAGE EDUCATION

Putting a multiliteracies framework at the center of the world language curriculum, this volume brings together college-level curricular innovations and classroom projects that address differences in meaning and worldviews expressed in learners' primary and target languages. Offering a rich understanding of languages, genres, and modalities as socioculturally situated semiotic systems, it advocates an effective pedagogy for developing learners' abilities to operate between languages. Chapters showcase curricula that draw on a multiliteracies framework and present various classroom projects that develop aspects of multiliteracies for language learners.

A discussion of the theoretical background and historical development of the pedagogy of multiliteracies and its relevance to the field of world language education positions this book within the broader literature on foreign language education. As developments in globalization, accountability, and austerity challenge contemporary academia and the current structure of world language programs, this book shows how the implementation of a multiliteracies-based approach brings coherence to language programs, and how the framework can help to accomplish the goals of higher education in general and of language education in particular.

Yuri Kumagai is Senior Lecturer of Japanese in the Department of East Asian Languages and Literatures, Smith College, Massachusetts, USA.

Ana López-Sánchez is Assistant Professor of Spanish, Haverford College, USA.

Sujane Wu is Associate Professor of Chinese in the Department of East Asian Languages and Literatures, Smith College, Massachusetts, USA.

Language, Culture, and Teaching
Sonia Nieto, Series Editor

Visit **www.routledge.com/education** for additional information on titles in the **Language, Culture, and Teaching** series.

MULTILITERACIES IN WORLD LANGUAGE EDUCATION

Edited by
Yuri Kumagai, Ana López-Sánchez,
and Sujane Wu

Routledge
Taylor & Francis Group

NEW YORK AND LONDON

First published 2016
by Routledge
711 Third Avenue, New York, NY 10017

and by Routledge
2 Park Square, Milton Park, Abingdon, Oxon OX14 4RN

Routledge is an imprint of the Taylor & Francis Group, an informa business

© 2016 Taylor & Francis

Library of Congress Cataloging-in-Publication Data
A catalog record for this book has been requested

ISBN: 978-1-138-83218-3 (hbk)
ISBN: 978-1-138-83219-0 (pbk)
ISBN: 978-1-315-73614-3 (ebk)

Typeset in Bembo
by Swales & Willis Ltd, Exeter, Devon, UK

Printed and bound in the United States of America by Publishers Graphics,
LLC on sustainably sourced paper.

CONTENTS

FOREWORD

Multiliteracies in World Language Education presents an important paradigm shift in both the theory and practice of teaching world languages. This edited collection shows what can be gained by applying the New London Group's (2000) *pedagogy of multiliteracies* and new sociocultural theories of literacy (Gee, 1990; Heath, 1983; Street, 1984) to modern languages education.

This comes at a time when the field is still dominated by communicative language teaching (CLT), despite calls for change by the Modern Language Association (MLA). The Association's 2007 Ad Hoc Committee report argued for the importance of "translingual and transcultural competence" that "places value on the ability to operate between languages" and produces students who are not only "educated to function as informed and capable interlocutors with educated native speakers in the target language" but are also "trained to reflect on the world and themselves through the lens of another language and culture" (MLA, 2007, pp. 3–4; see also Chapters 1 and 9, this volume). Here language learners' plurilingualism is seen as a productive resource for denaturalizing all cultures and considering them critically in relation to questions of power and diversity. While these goals have support in the MLA community, the report is silent on the means for achieving them. This book addresses that silence.

Modern languages educators wanting to explore this paradigm shift will need to understand the work of the New Literacies scholars (Barton, Hamilton, & Ivanic, 2000; Heath, 1983; Street, 1984). They construct literacy as a situated cultural practice, which differs across sociohistorical contexts and languages. In addition, as the communication landscape has changed with the use of digital technologies, texts have changed. Language is one among many modes of meaning-making and texts are increasingly multimodal (Kress, 2010). The authors of this book have taken great care to make these theoretical shifts accessible to readers, to explain the key concepts, and to provide excellent analytic reviews of the literature; all with the aim of teaching languages in new, exciting, and productive ways. Chapter 1 explains the history of multiliteracies and Chapter 3 provides a clear account of multiliteracies pedagogy.

A focus on genre is apparent in Chapters 2, 4, and 5. Genres are conceptualized as textual designs that match texts to their social purposes. As these designs have stabilized over time they offer language students a repertoire of designs that they can find, analyze, and master in the target language. An analysis of the linguistic choices enables learners to understand the meaning effects of different choices. The same is true of other semiotic resources and, as different genres combine modes in different ways, students are given the opportunity of understanding how the modes work together to produce meaning. Because genres are not fixed and static they also offer possibilities for redesign as students become more fluent in the language and as they gain a better understanding of the sociocultural context. Chapter 2 provides a good understanding of genre pedagogy as conceptualised by the Hallidayan linguists, known as the Sydney School. Chapter 4 is rooted in Bakhtin's theory of genre as used in Socio-Discursive Interactionism, developed in Geneva. Having two different accounts of genre pedagogy makes for stimulating reading and Sagnier provides a useful comparison of the two approaches.

The use of digital multimodal genres is central to some of the courses discussed. Chapter 6 focuses on students' video production projects, Chapters 7 and 9 make use of film, Chapter 8 describes how students produce an online dictionary with the use of a Wiki, and Chapter 9 describes how poster production was used for assessment. All of these produce extremely high levels of engagement from the students.

A critical literacy dimension is evident in three of the chapters. Chapter 5 explains what is meant by critical multiliteracies with a detailed account of Japanese and how different scripts and languages encode different social relations. Here sociolinguistic variation as markers of status, formality, familiarity, and so forth are manifested not only in spoken varieties but also in written forms. The description of what is entailed in learning Japanese is fascinating. This chapter centers on a comparison of reports on the same incident in two different languages, in order to understand how the incident is reported from very different cultural perspectives. Chapter 7 invites students to consider how they are positioned as non-native speakers of Korean. Understanding how linguistic othering works enables students to consider the range of second language identities in the class and to consider how they might position themselves more agentively.

Alongside the discussion of the theory are detailed examples of practice. The authors share their innovative courses and approaches in ways that make them easy to copy or adapt. They also provide enough insight for teachers to imagine how they might experiment with a multiliteracies approach on their own.

These examples provide carefully scaffolded sequences that make the steps in the teaching and learning transparent and they offer examples of the work produced by their students. It is clear from the data provided of students' responses that they find the courses very interesting, that they are encouraged to assume agency for their own learning, that they benefit from collaboration, and that the use of different modes enhances their language learning.

There is no doubt that this book will breathe new life into the teaching of world languages. While the focus is on teaching these languages as foreign languages, the book will be equally useful for what used to be called "second" language teaching. What this new paradigm offers in fact is a way to think about how to use the range of students' linguistic repertoires and transcultural knowledges in the learning of any language at whatever level using a multiliteracies perspective. It marks an exciting moment in language education.

Hilary Janks
University of the Witwatersrand, Johannesburg, South Africa

References

Barton, D., Hamilton, M., & Ivanic, R. (2000). *Situated literacies*. London: Routledge.

Gee, J. (1990). *Social linguistics and literacies*. London: Falmer Press.

Heath, S.B. (1983). *Ways with words*. Cambridge, UK: Cambridge University Press.

Kress, G. (2010). *Multimodality*. London & New York: Routledge.

Modern Language Association (MLA) Ad Hoc Committee on Foreign Languages (2007). Foreign languages and higher education: New structures for a changed world. *Profession 2007*, 234–245.

New London Group (NLG). (2000). A pedagogy of multiliteracies: Designing social futures. In B. Cope, & M. Kalantzis (Eds.), *Multiliteracies: Literacy learning and the design of social futures* (pp. 9–37). New York, NY: Routledge.

Street, B. (1984). *Literacy in theory and practice*. Cambridge, UK: Cambridge University Press.

PREFACE

The contributors to this book all subscribe to the view that, in the 21st century, language learning and teaching can no longer be solely (or mostly) concerned with language per se. In today's highly digitally mediated world, language is often combined with other semiotic modes (visual, aural, etc.) to make meaning, and has moved from its role as "*the* medium of communication, to a role as *one* medium of communication" (Kress & van Leeuwen, 2006, p. 36). World language education, accordingly, needs to move beyond current communicative and "language-focused" approaches, and into those that prepare students to be effective producers and consumers of multimodal texts. One such approach is the *pedagogy of multiliteracies* (Cope & Kalantzis, 2009; New London Group (NLG), 1996) advocated by the contributors to this book. The *multiliteracies* framework emphasizes the multiplicity of languages, genres, and modalities present in any given social context, and advocates a pedagogy that puts this multiplicity at the center of the curriculum, while also honing learners' agency, all with the goal of generating active and dynamic transformation (Cope & Kalantzis, 2009). In addition to better equipping learners for today's world, a multiliteracies framework and pedagogy can help overcome the "glass ceiling" (Byrnes & Maxim, 2004) that has resulted from current language pedagogies and the structural dichotomies of world language departments that have contributed to the separation of language from content. Furthermore, this framework, as recent scholarship has proposed, can bring coherence to departmental curricula and help to realign world language/cultural studies departments to their humanistic mission (Byrnes, Maxim, & Norris, 2010).

Committed to a post-secondary world language education that emphasizes a broad range of multimodal meaning-making resources, in classrooms that are oriented toward a critical appraisal of these resources, we, the editors, as well as the authors in this book offer an array of curricular innovations and classroom projects based on the multiliteracies framework. These include chapters that focus on visual and multimodal literacy, multilingual/plurilingual literacy, critical literacy, genre-based instruction, and computer-mediated vocabulary instruction. The curricula and pedagogical practices presented cover all levels of instruction, from beginner to advanced levels, and have been implemented within a variety of institutional contexts in tertiary education, from large public and private universities to liberal arts colleges. The book uniquely brings together instruction of European and Asian languages, thus further highlighting similar as well as different aspects of multiliteracies and meaning-making that can be realistically and meaningfully implemented in the pedagogy of different languages.

Coming from diverse academic fields, including language education, applied linguistics, literacy studies, literature, and anthropology, the editors and contributors to this volume bring a wealth of perspectives, informed as they are by somewhat different learning goals and personal philosophies, their work a proof of the multiple affordances of the multiliteracies framework. It is our hope that, in the diversity of proposals and perspectives presented, practitioners and educational planners find ideas to inform their practice in productive ways. It is our hope that the ideas presented in the book can contribute to the transformations, big and small, in current language education, and can enable and foster student transformation as well.

Overview of the Chapters

The book opens with an introductory chapter setting forth the theoretical concepts underpinning the pedagogical proposals and practices presented. The eight chapters that follow are divided thematically into two sections: "Designing Multiliteracies Curricula" and "Implementing Multiliteracies-Based Projects." Part I (Chapters 2–5) showcases curricular innovations that draw for their articulation upon varied interpretations of the *multiliteracies* framework, while Part II (Chapters 6–9) presents various *project-based activities* whose goal is to develop some aspect of multiliteracies. The chapters in these sections can be read independently and out of sequence.

Chapter 1, "Advancing Multiliteracies in World Language Education," by Kumagai and López-Sánchez, presents the theoretical background and development of the pedagogy of multiliteracies, and argues for the adoption of this approach in the field of world language education, positioning the book within the broader literature of world language education.

In Chapter 2, "Developing Multiliteracies Through Genre in the Beginner German Classroom," Warren and Winkler explore the principles of a genre-based curriculum—as interpreted and operationalized by the Georgetown University German Department—and its application in the design of a beginner-level German course. The authors discuss the theoretical and pedagogical basis for selecting, developing, and implementing genres appropriate for this level, and guide the readers through an instructional sequence (based on Rothery, 1996) that leads to completing both a written and a spoken task.

Chapter 3, "Redesigning the Intermediate Level of the Spanish Curriculum Through a Multiliteracies Lens" by López-Sánchez, identifies appropriate textual and multimodal genres for the intermediate level of the Spanish curriculum, and explores practices that are commensurate with the NLG's knowledge components, to help students gain control over linguistic and schematic meaning resources (*Available Designs*) of those genres. The proposed curriculum ensures that language is learned in connection to sites, identities, and Discourses (Gee, 1990), and puts students on the path to achieve translingual and transcultural competence (MLA, 2007).

Sagnier in Chapter 4, "Multiliteracies and Multimodal Discourses in the Foreign Language Classroom," discusses the design and implementation of an intermediate-level French course ("Reading Images") that seeks to develop visual literacy. Through a focus on a series of visual-written genres, and a pedagogy based on the notion of the "didactic sequence" (developed from Socio-Discursive Interactionism (SDI) theory), the course engages students in critical analysis and interpretation of multimodal discourses.

In Chapter 5, "Reading Words to Read Worlds: A Genre-Based Critical Multiliteracies Curriculum in Intermediate/Advanced Japanese Language Education," Kumagai and Iwasaki introduce a *Genre-Based Critical Multiliteracies* curriculum designed for intermediate/advanced-level Japanese language learners. They describe the materials and instructional sequence, together with a depiction of the actual classroom implementation of one unit of the curriculum. The curriculum is designed to help learners relate the authors' purpose of writing (i.e., genre) to their language choices (e.g., orthography, vocabulary, structures, styles), and understand the effects of such choices. Such understanding, the authors contend, allows learners to become critical readers and writers of words and worlds.

Chapter 6, "Fostering Multimodal Literacies in the Japanese Language Classroom: Digital Video Projects" by Kumagai, Konoeda, Nishimata (Fukai), and Sato, discusses two video production projects conducted in first- and third-semester Japanese language classrooms. The first project, a vodcast project, sought to make novice learners use multimodal design elements to communicate in a more complex way than they could not have otherwise done with their limited language; the second project, a digital storytelling, aimed at developing students' multimodal literacy as a specific goal by carefully designing an instructional sequence based on the NLG's four pedagogical components. Drawing on the analysis of classroom discussions and students' video products, the authors demonstrate the students' development of "multimodal communicative competencies" (Royce, 2007) through these projects.

In Chapter 7, "Implementing Multiliteracies in the Korean Classroom Through Visual Media," Brown, Iwasaki, and Lee describe the use of films to develop multiliteracies in a third-year college Korean program. The films are used to explore discourses surrounding different categories of foreigners in Korean society and how foreigners (as the "other") are represented through multiple modalities in Korean popular culture. The authors propose activities to develop the learners' (critical) multiliteracies and discuss the potential of those activities for empowering learners (themselves members of the "other" category) with the capacity to resist and transform the status quo.

Chapter 8, "Empowering Students in the Italian Classroom to Learn Vocabulary Through a Multiliteracies Framework" by Spinelli, discusses the implementation of multiliteracies principles for L2 vocabulary learning within a Web 2.0 environment to increase learner autonomy and develop the learning process as "a process of design." Specifically, Spinelli demonstrates how using an instrument such as Wiki helps develop students' multimodal communicative competence and invokes the learners' agency. The chapter discusses the results of a qualitative study based on a classroom project that was developed over four years with intermediate-level Italian language students, focusing on the participants' perception of multiliteracies and on the strategies adopted during their collaborative learning process.

In Chapter 9, "Creating an Effective Learning Environment in an Advanced Chinese Language Course Through Film, Poster Presentations, and Multiliteracies," Wu describes a poster project focusing on film implemented in an advanced-level Chinese course. The chapter, designed to emphasize multimodal meaning-making, critical engagement, and the negotiation of meanings with a culturally and linguistically diverse audience, details the sequence of activities leading to the design of the poster.

In the final chapter, "Afterword," we offer a brief summary, with implications of using a multiliteracies approach in world language teaching.

Yuri Kumagai, Ana López-Sánchez, Sujane Wu

References

Byrnes, H., & Maxim, H.H. (Eds.) (2004). Advanced foreign language learning: A challenge to college programs. Boston, MA: Heinle & Heinle.

Byrnes, H., Maxim, H.H., & Norris, J. (Eds.). (2010). *Realizing advanced L2 writing development in collegiate FL education: Curricular design, pedagogy, assessment.* Monograph Series, *Modern Language Journal, 94* (Issue Supplement), s1–s221.

Cope, B., & Kalantzis, M. (2009). "Multiliteracies": New literacies, new learning. *Pedagogies: An International Journal, 4*(3), 164–195.

Gee, P.G. (1990). *Social linguistics and literacies: Ideology in Discourses.* New York, NY: Routledge.

Kress, G.R., & van Leeuwen, T. (2006). *Reading images: The grammar of visual design* (2nd ed.). New York, NY: Routledge.

Modern Language Association (MLA) Ad Hoc Committee on Foreign Languages. (2007). Foreign languages and higher education: New structures for a changed world. *Profession 2007*, 234–245.

New London Group (NLG). (1996). A pedagogy of multiliteracies: Designing social futures. *Harvard Educational Review, 66*(1), 60–92.

Rothery, J. (1996). Making changes: Developing an educational linguistics. In R. Hasan, & G. Williams (Eds.), *Literacy in society* (pp. 86–123). London: Longman.

Royce, T.D. (2007). Multimodal communicative competence in second language contexts. In T.D. Royce, & W. Bowcher (Eds.), *New directions in the analysis of multimodal discourse* (pp. 361–390). Mahwah, NJ: Lawrence Erlbaum Associates.

ACKNOWLEDGMENTS

We owe a great debt of gratitude to many people who have helped us along the way to put this volume together. First and foremost, we thank Sonia Nieto, the series editor, for her unfailing encouragement and warm support. Without her help, this book would not have been possible. We are extremely grateful to Hilary Janks who has graciously agreed to write the foreword for this book. Her work has been a great inspiration for all of us who believe in the power of literacy in educational and social transformation. We would also like to express our thanks to two anonymous reviewers for their comments on the proposal and sample chapters. Special thanks go to Naomi Silverman and the editorial staff of Routledge for their guidance and assistance in bringing this book to publication. Our gratitude goes to Smith College Connections Funds for providing us with financial support at the initial stage of this book project. Last but not least, we would like to thank all of our students, present and past. Their aspirations for learning languages have kept us motivated to seek ways to better our teaching practices.

1

ADVANCING MULTILITERACIES IN WORLD LANGUAGE EDUCATION

Yuri Kumagai and Ana López-Sánchez

Globalization has been a "game-changer" bringing unprecedented change at unseen speed to all arenas of life. In the past decades, the conditions it created, together with the climate of accountability and economic austerity in education, placed significant pressure on the humanities. World/foreign language[1] academic programs were not spared and, in fact, have been subjected to these changes and pressures—some seeing their budgets drastically reduced or the entire program cut, while others (in the so-called "critical languages") have expanded greatly. Adding to these pressures, the publication, in 2007, of the MLA Ad Hoc Committee on Foreign Languages special report heightened the profession's long-existing internal tensions—tensions stemming from its intellectual and structural bifurcation—and generated further questioning of departments' missions, creating, in turn, increased attention to curricular and pedagogical issues. This re-examination of departments' academic goals and missions, brought about by the compounded effects of internal and external factors, could ultimately bring about profound transformations in the profession. One major area where this transformation may be felt is in the restructuring of curricula.

The current division between the so-called "language" courses at the lower levels and the so-called "content" courses at the upper levels of instruction can be traced back to the middle of the 20th century, when—encouraged by national security needs—second language acquisition (SLA) developed with an emphasis on oral communication with a total disregard for the textual and interpretive concerns of the traditionally philologically inclined foreign language (FL) departments (Matsuda, 2001). With the appearance of communicative language teaching (CLT) in the 1970s, the ground was set for an even greater separation between instruction at the lower and upper levels of the curriculum. In fact, the adoption of CLT in the lower levels of the curriculum resulted in an unbalanced focus on oral communication, especially on functional and transactional language use, that undermined the role of reading and writing and, more generally, of literacy practices in the lower levels of the curriculum. In CLT classrooms, when reading did take place, it emphasized information retrieval, and it served as an excuse for vocabulary and grammar practice and as a pretext for oral communication (Homstad & Thorson, 2000; Kramsch & Nolden, 1994; Matsuda, 2001). Writing was completely neglected.

In contrast, in the upper levels of European language programs, reading and writing were traditionally at the core of a curriculum that focused on national literatures, their canonical texts, aesthetic appreciation, and critical interpretation. With the "cultural turn" of the 1980s, the focus on the interpretive remained but now expanded to include "new" types of texts (including "minoritized" literatures and other forms of cultural production, such as film). A disregard for the medium (i.e., for language and language development), however, remained a constant through the shift in focus, perpetuating the familiar divide between upper and lower levels.

In Asian language programs, this situation was and still is more extreme. While reading literature and other types of texts indeed is at the core of the upper-level curriculum, the focus of instruction has often remained at the surface level of comprehension, rarely including aesthetic or evaluative comprehension or interpretation practices (Iwasaki & Kumagai, 2008; Kumagai & Iwasaki, 2011; also Chapters 5 and 9, this volume). Moreover, reading and interpretation of canonical literature has mainly been done with texts in English translation, showing a disregard for language as a meaning-making system, and clearly marking a profound division between "language" and "content" courses. In writing instruction the primary focus has continued to be on accuracy (e.g., writing characters and grammar).

This continued separation of goals and practices resulted in the "schizophrenia with which the profession end[ed] the century," most notably perceived "in the tension between the traditional, humanities-based, reading-oriented study of belles lettres and views advocating functionality and oral proficiency" (Bernhardt, 1998, cited in Byrnes, Maxim, & Norris, 2010, p. 3). But, by the beginning of the 21st century, with CLT having fallen short of fulfilling its original ambitious agenda (Kramsch, 2006) and losing the central stage it has long occupied, with a revised conceptualization of literacy and the literary (Kern & Schulz, 2005) in place, and with renewed calls to correct the inadequacies of the current two-tiered system—most notably and forcefully articulated in the report published by the MLA Ad Hoc Committee on Foreign Languages (2007)—the time was ripe for a new construct to articulate and restructure world language curricula and pedagogical practices anew.

This construct is *literacy*, a *socioculturally conceptualized literacy* (e.g., Barton & Hamilton, 2000; Baynham, 1995; Gee, 1990)—i.e., understood as a social practice where the knowledge of reading and writing is "[applied] . . . for specific purposes in specific contexts of use" (Scribner & Cole, 1981, p. 236). The many scholars who have invoked the construct—most notably Byrnes and Maxim (2004), Byrnes et al. (2010), Kern (2000), and Swaffar and Arens (2005), but also others (e.g., Allen & Paesani, 2010)—have articulated their framework in distinct ways, but are informed by the same critical set of notions and assumptions. These are, namely, (1) a view of language as a socioculturally situated semiotic system (Halliday, 1978), and of language learning as a process of gaining access to meaning-making resources; (2) a curriculum that is "text"-based including written and multimodal texts; and (3) a pedagogy that emphasizes "*what texts do* and *how texts mean* rather than *what they [texts] mean*" (Bazerman & Prior, 2004, p. 3). The argument for this kind of literacy and its associated notions is that the continued focus on texts and textuality not only brings coherence to the programs, but also develops the learners' ability to "operate between languages" (MLA, 2007) by addressing differences in meaning and worldviews expressed in their primary language and in the target language; and that it hones the learners' critical thinking skills throughout the entire program. This, in turn, helps bring world language education in alignment both with the goals of the humanities and, more generally, with higher education.

The proposals put forward by the above-mentioned FL scholars can be said to generally align with Cope and Kalantzis' (1993), and the New London Group's (NLG, 1996) *pedagogy of multiliteracies*. This is a framework that emphasizes the multiplicity of languages, genres, and modalities present in any given social context, and advocates a pedagogy that puts this multiplicity at the center of the curriculum, while also honing learners' agency, all with the goal of generating active and dynamic transformation (Cope & Kalantzis, 2009).

In the remainder of the chapter, we discuss the notion of literacy and how it is conceptualized and operationalized in the field of language education. We pay special attention to the theoretical and practical underpinnings of the pedagogy of multiliteracies, as proposed by the NLG (1996) and as later revised by Kalantzis and Cope (2005) (also Cope & Kalantzis, 2009). The constructs and notions introduced in this chapter inform the curricular proposals and the pedagogical practices presented in the individual chapters in this book, and help situate these proposals within the field of (language) education and learning.

Notions of Literacy

Literacy can be a "catch-all term" and can mean different things to different people. In the traditional, most accepted sense of the word, literacy is understood as the ability to read and write. This understanding is informed and shaped by two main perspectives: linguistic and cognitive. The linguistic perspective of literacy is concerned with the linguistic features of texts such as orthographies, vocabulary, grammar, mechanics, rhetorical organization, and genres. The cognitive ("in the head") perspective of literacy—or what Johns (1997) calls a "learner-centered view"—is concerned with the learners' individual cognitive development and processing when they engage in a task of reading or writing (Kern, 2000). Neither the linguistic nor the cognitive view takes into consideration the crucially important contextual factors that mediate and shape how one engages in literacy practices: the social dimension.

Research drawn from anthropology, education, linguistics, and sociolinguistics, among other disciplines, and known as New Literacy Studies (NLS) (Cope & Kalantzis, 2000; Gee, 1990), incorporates the social dimension, also calling forth the cultural, historical, and institutional. It also proposes that, because literacy practices vary across discourse communities and through history, it is more appropriate to talk about *literacies* (the plural form) (Gee, 2010, p. 168). Within this "new" sociocultural conceptualization, literacy is understood as a dynamic process that encompasses reading and writing, and the meaning resources necessary to read and write, together with the social practices in which those meanings emerged (Baynham, 1995; Gee, 1990, 2010; Heath, 1983; Street, 1995). Accordingly, accessing the meanings in a text is not a simple exercise of decoding words. It demands that one is socialized into the practices in which that text emerged, which involve "ways of behaving, interacting, valuing, thinking, believing," or what Gee calls *Discourses* (capital D) (Gee, 1990, p. 143). As Gee put it, to be able to read and write a text of type X, we have to be socialized into the practice in which the text emerged, and for that we have to first be apprenticed into the social groups where the text emerged (Gee, 1990).

Multiliteracies

The pedagogy of multiliteracies was put forth in 1996 by a group of ten scholars from various disciplines who shared a concern for education and who came to be known as the New London Group. Their most immediate interest—as made evident in their theorization as well as the implementation of their pedagogical model in, for example, the "Learning by Design" project led by Kalantzis and Cope (2005)[2]—was to overcome the inertia in schools and disciplines and reverse the effects of the "back-to-basics" movements (Cope & Kalantzis, 2009, p. 182) that stifle true learning through, for example, the use of standardized testing.

But, more critically, the group was seeking to respond to the challenges and demands a world of rapidly changing social, cultural, economic, and technological conditions was placing on education. One direct consequence of the changes in these conditions, specifically resulting from the unprecedented levels of global connectedness due to migration and economic integration,[3] was increased cultural and linguistic diversity, and a multiplication and diversification of discourses. A second, equally important, consequence of these changes was the proliferation of communication channels and media, particularly influenced by new (social) media technologies and platforms (e.g., internet, Facebook, YouTube, smartphone, etc.). The new technologies have often resulted in multimodal meaning-making practices "where the textual is also related to the visual, the audio, the spatial, the behavioural, and so on" (Cope & Kalantzis, 2000, p. 5).

To capture the multiplicity of aspects involved in literacy and to highlight the centrality of the notion for their pedagogical model, the group coined the label "multiliteracies." The remainder of their proposal centered around the development of these multiple literacies (i.e., the "how to"). They contend that the educational space must evolve to account for these new multiple representational forms, forms that will only continue to increase and evolve, and to gain more relevance because of further globalization and further development of digital communication tools. "Effective citizenship and productive work," Cope and Kalantzis (2000) argue, "now require that we interact effectively using multiple languages, multiple Englishes, and communication patterns that more frequently cross cultural, community and national boundaries" (p. 6). Only if educators rethink and stop privileging the written text and standard forms of language and create opportunities for students to be exposed to a multiplicity of discourses, and to produce such discourses in the classroom, will the full participation of students in public, community, and economic life be ensured (NLG, 2000, p. 9).

To develop the needed competencies in learners, the NLG engages insights drawn from the field of *multimodal literacy*—itself advanced in major ways by one of the members of the group—which explores the multiple semiotic resources (i.e., linguistic, visual, audio, spatial, tactile, gestural) of a textual composition (Jewitt & Kress, 2003; Kress & van Leeuwen, 2006), and develops meta-knowledge about how these various resources are independently and interactively used to construct different kinds of meaning (Cloonan, Kalantzis, & Cope, 2010; Kress, 2000; Unsworth, 2010; Unsworth & Bush, 2010). Visual resources, which are particularly predominant in contemporary texts and thus particularly well researched, are paid special attention (Bazalgette & Buckingham, 2013). To develop *visual literacy*, questions about the color, perspective, framing, and composition of images, and how meaning is made when visual resources are combined with written texts (Kress, 2000; Kress & van Leeuwen, 2006), are posed in the class.

Multimodal meaning-making practices are strongly (though not necessarily) associated with digital media. Understood as "the myriad social practices and conceptions of engaging in meaning-making mediated by texts that are produced, received, distributed, exchanged, etc., via digital codification" (Lankshear & Knobel, 2008, p. 5), *digital literacy(-ies)* are a critical element of the multiliteracies pedagogy. Instructional modules featuring computer-mediated instruction (CMI) projects, that, for example, make use of Web 2.0 and other various multimedia tools, are considered essential parts of the curriculum; both multimedia and multimodal projects, indeed, have been incorporated in numerous multiliteracies-inspired pedagogical projects in various educational contexts.[4]

As mentioned above, the NLG also underscores in its initial proposals the multiplicity of languages and cultures. It, however, discusses this multiplicity mostly within the realm of a specific language—i.e., intra-language diversity (Lo Bianco, 2000)—(e.g., the proposal talks about attending to differentiated *Englishes*, rather than to a "standard" English) and not as much across languages; that is, while the NLG proposal acknowledges the need to use multiple languages (multilingualism), only some large-scale educational projects, mostly in contexts where the societal bi/multilingualism is acknowledged as a reality (e.g., Canada, South Africa), have made it a priority.[5] The general neglect of language diversity, which may also be seen as a paradoxical consequence brought about by globalization and the hegemony of English, could lead to "the greatest collapse of language diversity in all history" (Lo Bianco, 2000, p. 94), an effect that needs to be avoided: Lo Bianco (2000) argues that, within a pedagogy of multiliteracies, "true linguistic diversity" (p. 101)—"languages other than English, foreign languages, individual and social bilingualism, and more broadly global language diversity"—must be addressed (p. 105). The bleak scenario painted by Lo Bianco puts in perspective the questioning of world language/cultural studies departments, reaffirming their critical importance. Furthermore, it begs the question of whether the study of foreign languages should be, as Thorne (2013) proposes, relocated "from isolated positions on the periphery of academic content learning and to embed language learning and intercultural engagement throughout educational institutions, and further, into the realms of non-instructed social spaces" (p. 3).

Last, but not least, the NLG underscores the importance of critical analysis, and in fact identifies it as one of the four essential pedagogical components of the pedagogy of multiliteracies (discussed below). Such focus stresses the need to develop in students a critical stance in relation to texts, as proposed by the advocates of critical literacies: "Such a stance is predicated on students' access to and facility with the language and literacy tools they need to be both critical and creative, problem posers and problem solvers, social analysts and social agents" (Janks, 2010, p. 23). By developing this critical stance, in turn, learners can become agents of social change, "active designers—makers—of social futures" (Cope & Kalantzis, 2000, p. 7). In encouraging this stance, the pedagogy put forward by the NLG aims to create "paths to improvement in our human futures"; it is, in other words, a pedagogy that aspires to be emancipatory.

"Design" and Related Notions

To articulate a vision of a pedagogy that leads to the form of literacy they advocate, the NLG makes use of a metalanguage based on the concept of "design." The term "design" can refer to the internal structure or morphology of a "text" broadly conceived, as well as to the act of building or constructing texts, and evokes thoughts of creativity and transformative processes (Cope & Kalantzis 2009; NLG, 2000). This double denotation makes the term particularly felicitous as an organizing metaphor for the model. The group's proposal is to treat "any semiotic activity, including using language to produce or consume texts, as a matter of Design" (NLG, 2000, p. 20). Three elements are involved in the production of meaning: the *Available Designs*, the (act of) *Design*, and the *Redesigned* (p. 20).

The Available Designs are the resources for the act of Design, and include the "grammars" of various semiotic systems and "orders of discourse"—the ways in which diverse genres, discourses, and styles are networked together (Fairclough, 1992). The term Available Designs recognizes the multiplicity of existing languages and discourses—each with its linguistic, cultural, and subcultural diversities, each with its historically shaped conventions, styles, genres, and dialects.

Any act of communication and negotiation where the speaker/writer is re-presenting, recontextualizing, and transforming the Available Designs is considered *Designing*, or the process of Design. Designing transforms the Available Designs through the new use of the old materials and reproduces and/or transforms knowledge, social relations, and identities. The outcome of the Designing process is the Redesigned, the transformed resources for making meanings, which subsequently become Available Designs. As the product of both culturally available resources and human agency, these resources contribute to the future Designing.

The construct underscores the idea that "we are both inheritors of patterns and conventions of meaning while at the same time active designers of meaning" (Cope & Kalantzis, 2000, p. 7). That is, we have agency in the meaning-making process; we creatively adopt, revise, and transform meaning-making, rather than merely imitate authoritative (i.e., "native," in the case of world language education) conventions (Cope & Kalantzis, 2009). And we have the potential to impact and change the future of language and literacy practices. We are seen as the designers of our own learning and of social futures for equitable access and critical engagement. This view is in stark contrast with traditional education, where learners are considered as passive recipients of normative knowledge, whose task is to reproduce a sanctioned form of language.

The "How-To" of the Pedagogical Model

To achieve the goals of their critical educational project, the NLG proposed a pedagogy that attended to four different components: *Situated Practice*, *Overt Instruction*, *Critical Framing*, and *Transformed Practice*. Kalantzis and Cope (2005) later reformulated these components to reflect knowledge processes—modeled after the familiar (knowledge) processes identified in Bloom's taxonomy. The processes, now named *Experiencing*, *Conceptualizing*, *Analyzing*, and *Applying* (p. 17), respectively, are not hierarchical and linear (i.e., they do not necessarily follow any particular sequence); they are also not neatly segmented components (Kalantzis & Cope, 2005; NLG, 1996), and, in fact, should be seamlessly "weaved" (Luke, Cadzen, Lin, & Freebody, 2004). All four components/knowledge processes and their weaving are indispensable for the attainment of the desired outcome of the pedagogy. Below we explore them in some detail.

Situated Practice/Experiencing

This component of the pedagogy involves immersion in experience and the utilization of Available Designs, both from the students' "lifeworlds" (*Experiencing the known*) and from different, "unfamiliar" contexts (*Experiencing the new*) (Kalantzis & Cope, 2008, p. 206), and the weaving between them (i.e., the familiar and unfamiliar texts and experiences).

Overt Instruction/Conceptualizing

This pedagogical element seeks to supplement immersion by developing the learners' systematic, analytical, and conscious understanding; making tacit knowledge explicit; and generalizing from the particular. This is achieved through the use of a metalanguage (*Conceptualizing by naming*, e.g., drawing distinctions of similarity and difference, categorizing, and naming), and through concepts (*Conceptualizing with theory*, e.g., by providing scaffolding for learners to make generalizations and put the key terms together into interpretative frameworks, thereby making them active conceptualizers and theory-makers).

Critical Framing/Analyzing

This component aims to develop the learners' ability to be critical (i.e., "become aware of, and . . . able to articulate, the cultural locatedness of practices" (NLG, 2000, p. 32)). To get learners to stand back from the meanings they are studying and to view them critically in relation to their contexts, they need to *[Analyze] functionally*, that is, to reason, draw inferential and deductive conclusions, establish functional relations of cause and effect, and analyze patterns in texts; and to *[Analyze] critically*, that is, evaluate their own and other people's perspectives, interests, and motives—relationships of power—implicated in texts (the latter is what is fundamental in critical, emancipatory literacy).

Transformed Practice/Applying

This element entails "re-creating a discourse by engaging in it for our real purposes" (NLG, 2000, p. 36), implementing what was previously learnt, while simultaneously revising it. *Applying appropriately* entails the application of knowledge and understandings of the complex diversity of real-world situations and testing their validity. *Applying creatively* involves making an intervention in the world which is truly innovative and creative and which brings to bear the learner's interests, experiences, and aspirations. "This is a process of making the world anew with fresh and creative forms of action and perception" (New Learning, "Learning by Design" Knowledge Processes;[6] also, Kalantzis & Cope, 2005).

In the next section, we discuss how the notions of literacy and multiliteracies have been adapted for the purposes of world language education, preparing the ground for the work presented in the rest of the book.

Literacy and Multiliteracies in World Language Education

In SLA and the FL education field, in the last quarter of the 20th century, literacy was not a major focus on instruction at the lower levels of the FL curriculum. As is well known, the dominant pedagogical model applied in this part of the curriculum was communicative language teaching (CLT), which promoted an (unbalanced) focus on oral language, particularly of a transactional nature (Byrnes, 2006; Kramsch, 2006).[7] This is not to say that literacy was ignored or not part of the picture; in fact, it was often invoked and enlisted in the 1980s (Bernhardt, 1991). But, as Byrnes et al. (2010) point out, this was a literacy conceptualized in cognitive terms that understood reading and writing as merely encoding and decoding (p. 27), and that was based on a structural understanding of language. It regarded written texts as "language data" and mainly used them for language exercises (Bernhardt, 1991) and for literal comprehension (Wallace, 2003). The task of the learners was to decipher linguistic codes and uncover the meanings encoded by authors. Writing instruction did not receive much attention, and the little attention it did receive focused on the use of the correct conventions (spelling and punctuation) and on grammatical accuracy; the meaning-making process or social function of writing was totally ignored. Mastery in writing was equated with adopting and conforming to prescribed rhetorical structures. The social situatedness of language, as well as the meaning-making capacity of the learners, was not part of the discussion.

An orientation toward a socioculturally oriented literacy, then, does not make its appearance until the beginning of this century. Indeed, it only begins to take hold after decades of repeated calls to end the division between upper and lower levels of curricula, after the shortcomings of CLT had become evident, and amid the growing presence of technological advances. The publication of Richard Kern's book *Literacy and language teaching*, in 2000, put it squarely on the (FL) map and initiated what may be considered a paradigm shift in the field,[8] and Swaffar and Arens in *Remapping the foreign language curriculum: An approach through multiple literacies* (2005) argued definitively for rethinking programs and curricula around the construct, while identifying "multiple literacies" as the goal to be pursued by post-secondary FL institutions. Heidi Byrnes and other scholars associated with the Georgetown University German Department (henceforth, GUGD), who were particularly focused on the attainment of *L2 advanced capacities* (e.g., Byrnes & Maxim, 2004; Byrnes et al., 2010), also pointed to literacy "as a suitable overall framework within which to envision FL learning and teaching in multicultural and multilingual environments" (Byrnes et al., 2010, p. 9). The department, in fact, embarked between 1997 and 2000 on what is, to date, the most comprehensive effort to completely overhaul a curriculum reorienting it to develop "Multiple Literacies" (Developing Multiple Literacies, 2000). Much of the process and its outcomes are documented on the department's webpage, and in many publications. Byrnes et al.'s (2010) "Realizing advanced L2 writing development in collegiate FL education: Curricular design, pedagogy, and assessment" provides the most extensive discussion, and an ample bibliography discusses a wealth of details about the program (e.g., Byrnes & Sprang, 2004; Byrnes, Crane, & Maxim, 2006; Crane, Liamkina, & Ryshina-Pankova, 2004; Maxim, 2009; Ryshina-Pankova, 2006, among many others; see also Chapter 2 in this volume).

It is important to note that, while they present somewhat distinct views and engage different traditions, the above-mentioned authors, as well as a growing number of others (e.g., Allen & Paesani, 2010), as Byrnes et al. (2010) point out, all "enlist literacy in order to signal unequivocally that language in FL education contexts must be understood as socially, rather than individually, constructed and must take seriously its fundamentally textual manifestation" (p. 28). A view of language as socially constructed and an understanding of language use as inseparable from the contexts in which it emerges recast any language learning experience as a possibility for "heightened awareness of dynamic and shifting processes of meaning-making and the divergent cultural practices, values, and ideologies that are involved" (Thorne, 2013, p. 2). This, in turn, elicits a view of language/cultural studies departments as loci of apprenticeships for new meaning-making and, ultimately, for new ways of being in the world. By articulating entire curricula around the studies of texts, language/cultural studies departments can overcome the existing "narrow model" (MLA, 2007) and prepare students to become translingual and transcultural citizens.

The proposals by Kern and by Swaffar and Arens have in common a pedagogical orientation, identifying tools and techniques to teach texts, and (in the case of Swaffar and Arens) genres in particular. Swaffar and Arens (2005), for example, present the reading *matrix* and the *précis*, and Kern (2000) presents a vast array of reading and writing exercises. Neither one of the volumes, however, addresses programmatic issues; that is, they do not provide particular guidelines regarding what to teach, when, and what criteria to use to inform those curricular decisions. For a framework that presents both the pedagogical practices and a curricular perspective, we have to turn to the GUGD, where the genre-based framework informed by systemic functional linguistics (SFL) and the genre movement in Australia is adapted for FL education.

Genre-Based Approaches

The notion of genre can be traced back to Bakhtin's (1986) notion of *speech genre*. For Bakhtin, every social activity involves language that is not random but that instead relates to the contextual variables in which it occurs and to the activity's participants (Crane et al., 2004, p. 160). This idea easily finds its way into SFL, where the relationship of language and the performance of activities are perceived as symbiotic, such that "the very existence of one is the condition for the other" (Hasan, 1995, cited in Byrnes et al., 2006, p. 88). Thus, a communicative event that is tied to a particular social and cultural context, its micro- and macro-linguistic resources linked to that particular context, exemplifying in clear ways the connection between language and content, constitutes a genre. In Maxim's words (2014), genre encompasses "the broader array of written and oral texts that include any staged, goal oriented, socially situated communicative event (e.g., book review, eulogy, letter of complaint)" (p. 82), its meaning, clearly extending far beyond its use in literary studies (Martin, 1985, p. 250). In a curriculum that is grounded on genre, language and content come together, consequently eliminating the bifurcation that is at the base of much of the discontents FL departments face. This reason alone suggests adopting the construct for curricular purposes.

But there is a number of additional advantages to choosing genres as instruments for curriculum development. Because they are relatively fixed and recognizable forms——they advance through various phases or *moves*, both obligatory and optional——genres can be taught, their language and structure analyzed and made recognizable; and their textual properties and features can be identified and correlated to learners' abilities and developmental stages (Byrnes et al., 2010, p. 83). They are, then, particularly useful since, as Maxim (2014) states, they provide "a principled way to select and sequence language and content across the curriculum" (p. 83).

And indeed many authors have enlisted genres as pedagogical tools, including Warren and Winkler (Chapter 2), López-Sánchez (Chapter 3), Sagnier (through the concept of "didactic sequences") (Chapter 4), and Kumagai and Iwasaki (Chapter 5), in this volume. Swaffar and Arens (2005) not only enlisted genres as a pedagogical tool, but grounded their literacy model in the concept. However, as Byrnes et al. (2010) point out, Swaffar and Arens did not spell out "how those language abilities would develop formally in support of textual meaning-making" (p. 30); and they did not identify specific teaching/learning routes. This sequencing and articulation of genres into a full four-year curriculum can be found in the model put forward by the GUGD. We turn our attention to that model now.

The GUGD Curriculum

The redesign of the GUGD curriculum was sparked by the desire to make achieving advanced levels of development in language possible in its four-year program; for this, the integration of language and content throughout the program was seen as a necessity. To achieve these goals, the department needed a construct that would also provide clear criteria for articulation of the curricular content. The department found *genre* to be that construct.

The GUGD turned to the work of SFL genre scholars (e.g., Christie, 2002; Martin, 1985) for a classification of genres and to determine appropriate teaching sequences. These scholars had classified genres around different continua: a discourse-centered primary–secondary continuum, and a congruent–synoptic (or non-congruent) continuum. The first continuum draws from Gee's (1998) distinction between primary and secondary discourses, that is, discourses that are associated with the private sphere, mostly associated with narratives and orality, and discourses that are associated with the public sphere, and that can be described as expository. Linguistically, these discourses are realized through either congruent semiotic practices, which construe reality in terms of actors and actions, "and being verb-based, emphasize function, process, and flow" (Maxim, 2009, p. 174); or through non-congruent (or metaphorical or synoptic) forms of semiosis that "construe human experience as objectified knowledge, and are based on nominal patterns [that emphasize] stasis, structure and 'thinginess'" (p. 174). The curriculum[9] they devised was presented as a sequence of series of genres and corresponding tasks[10] (mostly writing tasks).

The curriculum:

> Begin[s] with recounting, reporting, and narrative or story genres that . . . focus on the congruent representations of everyday experiences in the verbal system . . .; move[s] gradually into genres found in the public sphere that [sic] tend to reference values, beliefs, and societal institutions through more non-congruent or metaphorical construals of the world; and . . . conclude[s], at the uppermost levels of the curriculum with genres in academic, public, professional, and institutional settings that feature both human and abstract actors that are used to create an entirely semiotic world realized in textual spaces. (Byrnes et al., 2010, p. 83)

In addition to identifying appropriate genres and tasks, the department had to didacticize them—i.e., establish pedagogical practices that would help students identify and replicate the formalisms that define each genre so that they could reproduce them. To establish such pedagogy, the GUGD once again turned to existing scholarship by genre scholars. It adopted the pedagogical procedures advanced by Rothery (1996): (a) Negotiating Field, (b) Deconstruction, (c) Joint Construction, and (d) Independent Construction. The procedures are presented as a circle and are meant to be used recursively (Rothery, 1996, p. 102; Byrnes et al., 2010). (For an illustration of the "teaching cycle," see Chapter 2, this volume.) The *Negotiating Field* stage involves the teacher and learners jointly building a shared knowledge of the subject matter of the text, including its context of production as well some of its language. Next, is the process of *Deconstruction*, in which students are guided through the analysis of model texts of the targeted genres in order to identify the genres' textual properties and communicative and ideological purposes (Byrnes et al., 2010, p. 124); this is accomplished by looking at the "context of culture" (i.e., the genre's users and purpose), "context of situation" (defined in SFL in terms of the configuration of the three register variables: field, tenor, and mode), schematic structure (i.e., the stages or moves of the genre), and the linguistic realization of those stages (Byrnes et al., 2010, pp. 124–135).

Deconstruction is followed by *Joint Construction*, a stage where teacher and students jointly construct a text, with the help of the metalanguage learned in the previous stage. The final stage, *Independent Construction*, comes typically after several iterations of the other stages, and here, as the name of the procedure suggests, students produce the text on their own.

The literacy enlisted by the members of the GUGD is "a language-based literacy" (Byrnes et al., 2010, p. 32), one which privileges writing and the written (alphabetical) mode. This orientation is doubly pragmatic: (1) it serves to affirm the unique, inalienable, space foreign *language* departments occupy in academic life; and (2) it derives from a strong concern regarding measurable outcomes, that the social science orientation of the language acquisition field (SLA) demands, but also from the climate of accountability in education. While this orientation might be justified and well intentioned, it is also somewhat detrimental to the development of certain capacities learners need in the current highly multimodal textual and communicative environment. A mono-modal language-based literacy does not adequately recognize the changing nature of communication and the increasing multimodal nature of meaning-making, and may be too narrow a framework to achieve the goals of transcultural and translingual competency advanced by the MLA. As Kress (2003) explains: "language alone cannot give us access to the meaning of the multimodally constituted message" (cited in Nelson & Kern, 2012, p. 49). We, however, agree with Nelson and Kern (2012) that:

> the goals of language learning and teaching in [this] era will most effec-
> tively, efficiently and ethically be served by an approach that is principally
> focused on processes of meaning-making writ large, and the roles that
> language plays in ... broader semiotic processes. (pp. 49–50)

Critical Literacy in the World Language Classroom

A genre-based approach—or, for that matter, any other approach of any semiotic system that is meant to familiarize learners with meaning-making resources—then, is particularly valuable, in that it gives important access to powerful resources (i.e., "cultural capital," to use Bourdieu's (1991) concept) that otherwise might be inaccessible for learners.[11] However, such an approach is not without its limitations since, as some critics have pointed out, it may lead to an uncritical reproduction of texts (Pennycook, 1996), and to naturalizing the status quo and inhibiting subversive or transformative meaning-making (Janks, 2010). Janks (2000, 2010) refers to this dilemma as the "access paradox" (2010, p. 24), a paradox that may be resolved by designing a curriculum that controls and balances the elements of "domination" (or power), "access," "diversity," and "design." A curriculum created such that it provides learners with access to dominant genres, dominant languages, and dominant literacies, while simultaneously engaging them in both deconstructing the very nature of their dominance and reconstructing (redesigning) them by using "diversity" (i.e., different discourses; different "ways with words" (Heath, 1983)) as a productive resource, Janks (2000, 2010) argues, will prevent reproductive and uncritical tendencies.

Specifically, what we may call a *Genre-Based Critical Multiliteracies* curriculum (see Chapter 5, this volume) creates the appropriate conditions for learners to analyze the production of texts as well as their own relationships to the texts; it seeks to "critique not just micro features of specific texts but attend to wider implications which relate to the circulation of dominant discourses within texts" (Wallace, 2003, p. 27); it encourages learners to become more agentive, both as producers and consumers of texts (e.g., Janks, 2010; Pennycook, 2001; Chapters 6, 7, and 9, this volume). To illuminate power relations, as created and enabled by genres, this critical framework enlists pedagogical practices and the tools of critical discourse analysis (CDA) (e.g., Fairclough, 1992) in the classroom. That is, instruction should include questions about the significance of the choices (lexical, structural, visual, etc.) made in various semiotic systems by writers/designers, and about how these may naturalize events and position the readers (Kern, 2000; Chapters 4, 5, and 7, this volume). Awareness of the effects specific resources produce, in turn, gives learners the ability to critique and possibly reject the discourses being produced, or to appropriate them to create their own meanings.

Digital and Multimodal Literacies in the World Language Classroom

As discussed earlier, in today's technology-mediated communication world, the ability to interpret and produce mono- and multimodal semiotic texts is critical. As Thorne and Reinhardt (2008) point out, for many individuals, and especially young adults and teenagers, "performing linguistically structured identities in second and foreign languages now involves digital mediation as often as, or more often than, non-digital forms of communication" (p. 560). Thus, the development of what has been called *digital literacies* (see section on Multiliteracies, above) needs to be addressed in the world language classroom. In addition to forming tech-savvy identities, the benefits of attending to and engaging in digital literacy practices like blogging, gaming, and simulations include access to complex and specialized language, immersion in situated meaning-making, and a productive stance on design (Gee, 2007; Lankshear & Knobel, 2008). But an equally important advantage to designing curricula that engage learners in digital projects where decision-making and problem-solving are involved is that it allows for "build[ing] bridges to learners' existing interests" (Lankshear & Knobel, 2008, p. 9). As Lankshear and Knobel (2008) point out, bringing this type of learning into the classroom can create "experiences of agency, efficacy, and pleasure" (p. 9) that are ultimately very powerful for learning. Additionally, digital and multimodal projects (especially gaming—see below) can correct the peripheral position into which learners are often placed into in SFL genre-based pedagogies (Reinhardt, Warner, & Lange, 2014, p. 166).

It is important to remember that meaning-making in these digital platforms increasingly involves the use of semiotic modes other than language (i.e., multimodal meaning-making). The pedagogical interventions designed for the FL classroom, thus, should aim to create the necessary competencies for understanding, interpreting, and creating a variety of multimodal digital texts.

One such case is the model proposed by Thorne and Reinhardt (2008) to develop in students the ability to interpret existing digital texts. In particular, the model targets students' critical language awareness of internet-specific genres (such as instant messages, synchronous chats, blogs, Wiki, and gaming) through "bridging activities" that compare those texts with school mainstream traditional texts. Some online genres, the authors point out, are similar to traditionally written ones, but many others are new forms that combine several semiotic systems, or that are simply novel and unique to internet-mediated communication and that are "much more elusive and difficult to identify and teach" (p. 561). They propose a three-phase cycle of activities made up of observation and collection, guided exploration and analysis, and creation and participation (p. 566) and inspired by the NLG (1996) four components' pedagogy. This cycle of activities, they argue, offers a "counterweight to the prescriptive versions of grammar, style, and vocabulary presented in foreign language texts" (p. 562) and "increases the practical relevance and contemporary currency of an institution's foreign language courses" (p. 563). This model also serves the purposes of Advanced Foreign Language Learning "by combining the best of analytic traditions of schooling with the life experiences and future needs of today's foreign language students" (p. 562).

Increasingly, class projects attend to the development of particular (multimodal) digital genres. We report here on a very small sample of projects and pedagogies for digital environments, focusing on the use of games and gaming technology, and digital stories. We have chosen to discuss these particular studies because their authors explicitly invoke the multiliteracies framework, and show a clear understanding of how the development of these particular genre literacies (i.e., gaming, digital narratives) engages and hones awareness of other semiotic systems and literacies, as well as of the connections between the learners' developing literacies and their changing social identities. These authors also point out the difficulties and hurdles that obstruct and challenge these projects in reaching their actual potential.

The first of these studies is by Reinhardt et al. (2014), who designed a two-week "gaming" unit, as part of a fifth-semester German genre-based course, to raise genre awareness and develop game literacies. Greatly inspired by the work of Gee (2007) (whose theorizing on gaming aligns well with his work in the

NLG), but also by other game-based theories, these researchers reasoned that "Applied to L2 learning, [game] literacies would potentially transfer metalinguistically to the awareness that language [*sic*], both familiar and those under study, are complex and dynamic, yet structured, rule-based systems of interrelated systems" (p. 164).

They had also hoped that the development of game literacies would create an awareness that "languages are made real through creative language use, and the awareness that languages, discourses and particular genres, as social practices, are systems *designed* by and for humans, as both process and product" (p. 164). The participants in the pilot project showed mixed reactions—some embracing gaming as a new, effective, and even pleasurable way of learning, others demonstrating resistance or skepticism—suggesting that, due to a clash between notions of learning and playing, FL education may need to further work on the implementation of games (see below).

In another project, Michelson and Dupuy (2014) implemented in their fourth-semester genre-based multiliteracies French class a "Global Simulation" project; that is, students adopted specific character roles in a culturally grounded, fictitious scenario (i.e., an apartment building in Paris) and enacted the discourse styles of their characters. The authors posit that adopting the characters' identities and attending to the simulation's attendant social demands fosters learners' intersemiotic awareness and develops their understanding of the interrelationship between language use and social identities (Gee, 2002). Their findings show that, while some students continued to hold a view of linguistic forms (i.e., vocabulary and grammar) "as primary conveyor[s] of meaning," by expressing desire to spend more time with explicit instruction, other students displayed "their budding awareness" (p. 41) that linguistic forms are only one system and that other signs such as "gestures, facial expression, body movements, proxemics, and images, are also resources that can be drawn upon to make meaning" (p. 42).

The studies by Reinhardt et al. (2014) and Michelson and Dupuy (2014) both showed that the learners' beliefs about language (as code) and language learning (as the study of the grammar and vocabulary) prevailed, mostly unchanged, at the end of their participation in the projects. The product of prior socialization in traditional FL education, the students' expectations and beliefs require that curricular practices be altered early on and across all levels to truly and definitively shift (Michelson & Dupuy, 2014, p. 43).

Oskoz and Elola (2014) report on the integration of digital stories in an advanced Spanish writing class to enhance learners' "twenty-first century literacies" (i.e., digital literacies). They discuss that the development of a digital story involves more than simply including multimodality such as images, music, and voice, and that it is the integration and combination of multimodal resources in complex layers that promotes learners' linguistic and writing development. Based on analyses of artifacts produced by the learners, the authors contend that creating a digital story pushed the learners to move beyond traditional oral and written presentational forms by making connections to other forms of expression (i.e., images and sound).

Pedagogical proposals and studies that seek to develop digital and multimodal literacies, such as the ones discussed here, are on the rise. A thorough review of all relevant CMI work is beyond the scope of this chapter, but readers interested in developing similar projects in world language instruction at the collegiate level are encouraged to refer to literature such as Belz (2002), Malinowski (2014), and O'Dowd and Waire (2009) for telecollaboration; Yang (2012) for multimodal composing; and Hampel and Hauck (2006) for audio-graphic conferencing.

The chapters in Part II of this volume also contribute to this literature, presenting pedagogical proposals that seek to develop digital and/or multimodal competencies (receptive and productive), while also addressing other aspects of the target language and culture. (See, especially, Chapter 8 for Wiki and vocabulary learning; Chapter 6 for digital videos; and Chapter 9 for poster creation.)

Additionally, a growing number of publications try to gauge the usefulness and learning outcomes derived from CMI projects (through the use of surveys and qualitative methods). A number of these, concerning the use of blogs (Jimenez-Caicedo, Lozano, & Gomez, 2014), telecollaboration (Kurek & Hauck, 2014), digital social reading (i.e., e-reading) (Blyth, 2014), and scrapbooking (Peters & Frankoff, 2014), can be found in a recent volume edited by Guikema and Williams (2014), *Digital literacies in foreign and second language education.*

A Multiliteracies Model for World Language Education

In this section we "translate" the principles and research discussed earlier into the practices of the classroom, in an attempt to present some very broad guidelines that practitioners can implement according to their needs and specific conditions, and in alignment with their own views/understanding.

A multiliteracies curriculum for the FL classroom is one centered around the analysis and production of texts, broadly understood. Texts give learners access to the meaning-making resources a language offers. These resources are simultaneously grounded and construing the social practices in which language emerges. Instruction, thus, should be structured to create opportunities for learners to gain control over these resources, to equip them to, potentially, participate in those practices, and possibly transform them. As said repeatedly through this introduction, meaning-making in the 21st century involves engaging with digital platforms that easily afford (and, in fact, invite) blending/integrating modes of communication. The multiliteracies-based classroom should be one that affords the learners opportunities to familiarize themselves with new and old kinds of genres, to critically analyze those genres, and to provide opportunities to produce those genres or alternative/hybrids of them that better express the learners' world. Ultimately, the FL classroom is one that encourages learners to become aware consumers, and possible change agents who make conscious design choices to engage/disengage with existing discourses and create new/alternative ones.

Below we spell out how some of those processes unfold in instruction and the curriculum, attending to the pedagogical elements of the NLG and of Cope and Kalantzis (see also Chapter 3, this volume).

Experiencing

The multiliteracies-informed or based classroom should seek to expose students to a wealth of Available Designs, encouraging reading, viewing, and listening to a multitude of texts of all sorts—"new" types of texts (e.g., online genres) as well as "old" ones, language-based, and multimodal texts. To prepare learners to engage with these texts of and from unfamiliar contexts, pedagogical practices that encourage the activation of learners' existing knowledge and resources drawn from their primary language(s) and literacy experiences of Designing (in and out of school contexts) (i.e., Available Designs) are also deployed.

Conceptualizing

This component of the pedagogy focuses on guiding learners' attention explicitly to various elements of language and other semiotic systems (i.e., the Available Designs), with the goal of achieving conscious control of those elements. This can be achieved with scaffolded learning activities (rather than drills and memorization) and through the development of the students' metalanguage.

Primary among the "designs" that should be targeted in FL education are genres (written as well as multimodal, print as well as digital) since, as explained, they are the nexus of language and culture, and they can serve as organizers for the instruction of other Available Designs (e.g., grammar, and vocabulary/ lexicogrammar) (see Chapters 2, 3, 4, and 5, this volume).

Analyzing

This element involves reflection on the learners' own and other people's "perspectives, interests and motives" (Cope & Kalantzis, 2009, p. 186) as reflected in the Designed. Learners need to be scaffolded (through the teacher's questions and/or worksheets) to examine textual choices for their motivation (i.e., the views, values, or ideologies the writer might be promoting). Instructors may draw from the tools of critical literacy and CDA to help learners unveil these (hidden) values.

Applying

This component entails the "creation of new texts on the basis of existing ones, or reshaping texts to make them appropriate for contexts of communication"

(Kern, 2000, pp. 133–134). *Writing* tasks, for example, can be designed that ask students to create their own version of a genre modeled in class; this type of activity demands that students activate their knowledge of the generic conventions (learned in the previous "phases" of the pedagogy), but goes beyond the mere repetition of the resources, and "parroting" of discourses encountered earlier. It is an opportunity for learners to appropriate the words and other meaning-making resources that they were only imitating previously. Other tasks can be formulated that allow students to "play" (design) with the resources to create more freely.

The Way Forward

World language/cultural studies programs in the US collegiate context have been, of late, heavily scrutinized, from the inside as well as the outside. The number of publications that have occupied themselves with questions regarding the mission, the goals, the curriculum, and the structure of these departments speaks of the interest in the topic. This work (as a whole) also suggests that these departments are deeply involved in a process of reimagining themselves—"mapping" their territory—and undergoing what could be seismic changes—"transforming"—as the titles of the work of Swaffar and Arens (2005) and Swaffar and Urlaub (2014) attest to.

In this chapter we have argued, following the lead of other world language scholars and educators such as Kern, Kramsch, Byrnes, Maxim, and many others, that the key to redrawing the space of these departments is *multiliteracies*. The framework, the underpinnings of which we explored in some detail, can resolve many of the issues these departments endure. First, it can redress the excessive emphasis on oral language and reintroduce, in the lower levels, writing and reading as processes of design—rather than of encoding and decoding—through which learners are apprenticed into "*languacultures*" (Agar, 1994) other than their own (i.e., the "target" languacultures). Second, multiliteracies can reunite the lower and higher levels of the curriculum (thus bringing cohesion to the programs), through their understanding of language as a social semiotic system (i.e., a system that links language to contexts, and specifically to social practices). Third, the framework can provide a clear "map" of the curriculum—charting when to teach what kind of meaning-making resources—by engaging the construct of genre. Fourth, it helps reconnect world language/cultural studies departments with their humanistic origins, and to disassociate them from the image of acritical and skill-obtaining spaces; and, relatedly, it re-establishes them as legitimate spaces in higher education, contributing to the development of critical thinking. Fifth, it prepares students to participate fully in our globalized, digitally mediated society, by creating learning opportunities that engage them as (critical/aware) consumers and able producers of those discourses. And, finally, but perhaps most importantly, multiliteracies pedagogies prepare learners to be agents of change, and to create "paths to improvement in our human futures."

A world language/cultural studies department that is envisioned and articulated according to the principles and pedagogy described in this chapter is one that ultimately prepares the learners to be empowered translingual and transcultural citizens under the conditions of superdiversity. We hope that this book inspires world language educators to, to use Thorne's words, "develop curricular innovations and pedagogically supported environments that are adaptive to emergent communicative needs, open to a diversity of genres and potentially mixed language communicative dynamics, and that offer experientially and linguistically rich opportunities for engagement" (2013, p. 3). It is our hope that this book contributes to creating classrooms and entire programs as those kinds of spaces, and contributes to expanding the boundaries of the profession.

Notes

1 Throughout this volume we refer to world and foreign language education interchangeably.
2 For more information about the project, see http://newlearningonline.com/.
3 Some are calling this phenomenon "superdiversity" (e.g., Blommaert & Rampton, 2011; Thorne, 2013).
4 See Mills (2010) for a comprehensive review of the "digital turn" in new literacy studies/multiliteracies projects.
5 One example is a Canadian national project initiated by Early and Cummins in 2002. The project, "From literacy to multiliteracies: Designing learning environments for knowledge generation within the new economy," implemented in the school curriculum various pedagogical innovations (e.g., "Dual language authoring activity") that promoted developing multilingual literacies practices among ethno-racial and language minority students in Toronto.
6 See http://newlearningonline.com/new-learning/chapter-8/learning-by-design-knowledge-processes.
7 As originally conceived, the framework did encompass "the use of spoken and written texts, and the interaction of speakers, and listeners, texts and their readers" (Kramsch, 2006, p. 249), but this agenda fell short of its realization, possibly broadening the gap between instruction at the upper and lower levels.
8 Prior to Kern, a number of scholars (Berman, 1996; Kramsch & Nolden, 1994, among others) had enlisted "literacy" as a goal for foreign language education, but they had not put forward a fully developed framework to implement it.
9 For details of the curriculum, its five levels, and the focus of the different levels, see the GUGD web page, "Developing multiple literacies: A curriculum renewal project of the German department at Georgetown University, 1997–2000" (http://german. georgetown.edu/scholarship/curriculumproject; see also Byrnes et al., 2006, 2010).
10 The tasks the GUGD envisioned are not primarily based on the "traditional, interactive, oral communicative exchanges of daily life, [but] oriented towards textuality and literacy" (Byrnes et al., 2006, p. 86). They are tied to the particular genres and texts explored at each level; this linkage between task and text affords the construction of a multiyear trajectory that has internal consistency, creating assessment measures that are integrated with the curriculum (Byrnes et al., 2010).
11 The genre theory invoked by most FL practitioners was originally formulated within the Australian educational context, by scholars seeking to create ways to redress the effects of the hidden curriculum derived from a progressivist approach that privileged students with access to (school) literacies in their homes (Kalantzis & Cope, 2005).

References

Agar, M.H. (1994). *Language shock: Understanding the culture of conversation.* New York, NY: Harper.

Allen, H.E., & Paesani, K. (2010). Exploring the feasibility of a pedagogy of multiliteracies in introductory foreign language courses. *L2 Journal, 2*(1), 119–142.

Bakhtin, M.M. (1986). The problem of speech genres. In C. Emerson, & M. Holoquist (Eds.), *M.M. Bakhtin: Speech genres and other late essays* (pp. 60–102). Austin: University of Texas Press.

Barton, D., & Hamilton, M. (2000). Literacy practice. In D. Barton, M. Hamilton, & R. Ivanic (Eds.), *Situated literacies: Reading and writing in context* (pp. 7–15). New York, NY: Routledge.

Baynham, M. (1995). *Literacy practices: Investigating literacy in social contexts.* Singapore: Longman Singapore.

Bazalgette, C., & Buckingham, D. (2013). Literacy, media and multimodality: A critical response. *Literacy, 47*(2), 95–102.

Bazerman, C., & Prior, P. (Eds.) (2004). *Digital literacies in foreign and second language education.* Mahwah, NJ: Erlbaum.

Belz, J. (2002). Social dimensions of telecollaborative foreign language study. *Language Learning & Technology, 6*(1), 60–81.

Berman, R.A. (1996). Reform and continuity: Graduate education toward a foreign cultural literacy. *ADFL Bulletin, 27*(3), 40–46.

Bernhardt, E.B. (1991). Development in second language literacy research: Retrospective and prospective views for the classroom. In B.F. Freed (Ed.), *Foreign language acquisition research and the classroom* (pp. 221–251). Lexington, MA: D.C. Heath.

Blommaert, J., & Rampton, B. (2011). Language and superdiversity. *Diversities, 13*(2), 1–21.

Blyth, C.S. (2014). Exploring the affordances of digital social reading or L2 literacy: The case of eComma. In J.P. Guikema, & L. Williams (Eds.), *Digital literacies in foreign and second language education* (pp. 201–226). San Marcos, TX: CALICO Monograph Series, 12.

Bourdieu, P. (1991). *Language and symbolic power.* Cambridge, MA: Harvard University Press.

Byrnes, H. (2006). Perspectives. *Modern Language Journal, 90*(2), 244–266.

Byrnes, H., Crane, C., & Maxim, H.H. (2006). Taking texts to task: Issues and choices in curriculum construction. *International Journal of Applied Linguistics, 152,* 85–110.

Byrnes, H., & Maxim, H.H. (Eds.) (2004). *Advanced foreign language learning: A challenge to college programs.* Boston, MA: Heinle & Heinle.

Byrnes, H., Maxim, H.H., & Norris, J.M. (2010). Realizing advanced foreign language writing development in collegiate education: Curricular design, pedagogy, assessment. *Modern Language Journal, 94* (Monograph Series, Issue Supplement s1), 1–235.

Byrnes, H., & Sprang, K.A. (2004). Fostering advanced L2 literacy: A genre-based, cognitive approach. In H. Byrnes, & H.H. Maxim (Eds.), *Advanced foreign language learning: A challenge to college programs* (pp. 47–85). Boston, MA: Heinle Thomson.

Christie, F. (2002). The development of abstraction in adolescence in subject English. In M.J. Schleppegrell, & M.C. Colombi (Eds.), *Developing advanced literacy in first and second languages: Meaning with power* (pp. 45–66). Mahwah, NJ: Erlbaum.

Cloonan, A., Kalantzis, M., & Cope, B. (2010). Schemas for meaning-making and multimodal texts. In T. Locke (Ed.), *Beyond the grammar wars: A resource for teachers and students on developing language knowledge in the English/literacy classroom* (pp. 254–275). New York, NY: Routledge.

Cope, B., & Kalantzis, M. (1993). Introduction: How a genre approach to literacy can transform the way writing is taught. In B. Cope, & M. Kalantzis (Eds.), *The powers of literacy: A genre approach to teaching writing* (pp. 1–21). London: The Falmer Press.

Cope, B., & Kalantzis, M. (Eds.) (2000). *Multiliteracies: Literacy learning and the design of social futures.* New York, NY: Routledge.

Cope, B., & Kalantzis, M. (2009). "Multiliteracies": New literacies, new learning. *Pedagogies: An International Journal, 4*(3), 164–195.

Crane, C., Liamkina, O., & Ryshina-Pankova. (2004). Fostering advanced level language abilities in foreign language graduate programs: Applications of genre theory. In H. Byrnes, & H.H. Maxim (Eds.), *Advanced foreign language learning: A challenge to college programs* (pp. 150–177). Boston, MA: Heinle-Thomson.

Developing Multiple Literacies (1997–2000). Developing Multiple Literacies: A curriculum renewal project of the German department at Georgetown University. Retrieved from http://german.georgetown.edu/scholarship/curriculumproject.

Early, M., & Cummins, J. (2002). From literacy to multiliteracies: Designing learning environments for knowledge generation within the new economy. Proposal funded by the Social Sciences and Humanities Research Council of Canada.

Fairclough, N. (1992). *Discourse and social change.* Malden, MA: Blackwell.

Gee, J.P. (1990). *Social linguistics and literacies: Ideology in discourses.* London: The Falmer Press.

Gee, J.P. (1998). What is literacy? In V. Zamel, & R. Spack (Eds.), *Negotiating academic literacies: Teaching and learning across languages and cultures* (pp. 51–59). London: Routledge.

Gee, J.P. (2002). Literacies, identities and discourses. In M.J. Schleppegrell, & M.C. Colombi (Eds.), *Developing advanced literacy in first and second languages: Meaning with power* (pp. 45–66). Mahwah, NJ: Erlbaum.

Gee, J.P. (2007). *Good video games + good learning: Collected essays on video games, learning and literacy.* New York, NY: Peter Lang.

Gee, J.P. (2010). A situated-sociocultural approach to literacy and technology. In E.A. Baker (Ed.), *The new literacies: Multiple perspectives on research and practice* (pp. 165–193). New York, NY: Guilford Press.

Guikema, J.P., & Williams, L. (Eds.) (2014). *Digital literacies in foreign and second language education.* San Marcos, TX: CALICO Monograph Series, 12.

Halliday, M.A.K. (1978). *Language as social semiotic: The social interpretation of language and meaning.* London: Edward Arnold.

Hampel, R., & Hauck, M. (2006). Computer-mediated language learning: Making meaning in multimodal virtual learning spaces, *The JALT CALL Journal, 2*(2), 3–18.

Heath, S.B. (1983). *Ways with words: Language, life, and work in communities and classrooms.* New York, NY: Cambridge University Press.

Homstad, T., & Thorson, H. (2000). Writing and foreign language pedagogy: Theories and implications. In G. Bräuer (Ed.), *Writing across languages* (pp. 3–14). Stamford, CT: Ablex.

Iwasaki, N., & Kumagai, Y. (2008). Towards critical approaches in an advanced level Japanese course: Theory and practice through reflection and dialogues. *Japanese Language and Literature, 42,* 123–156.

Janks, H. (2000). Domination, access, diversity and design: A synthesis for critical literacy education. *Educational Review, 52*(2), 175–186.

Janks, H. (2010). *Literacy and power.* New York, NY: Routledge.

Jewitt, C., & Kress, G.R. (2003). *Multimodal literacy.* New York, NY: Peter Lang.

Jimenez-Caicedo, J.P., Lozano, M.E., & Gomez, R.L. (2014). Agency and Web 2.0 in language learning: A systematic analysis of elementary Spanish learners' attitudes, beliefs, and motivations about the use of blogs for the development of L2 literacy and language ability. In J.P. Guikema, & L. Williams (Eds.), *Digital literacies in foreign and second language education* (pp. 87–117). San Marcos, TX: CALICO Monograph Series, 12.

Johns, A.M. (1997). *Text, role, and context: Developing academic literacies.* Cambridge, UK: Cambridge University Press.

Kalantzis, M., & Cope, B. (Eds.) (2005). *Learning by design.* Melbourne, VIC: Victorian Schools Innovation Commission and Common Ground.

Kalantzis, M., & Cope, B. (2008). Language education and multiliteracies. In S. May, & N.H. Hornberger (Eds.), *Encyclopedia of language and education, 2nd edition, Vol. 1: Language policy and political issues in education* (pp. 195–211). New York, NY: Springer.

Kern, R. (2000). *Literacy and language teaching.* New York, NY: Oxford University Press.

Kern, R., & Schulz, J.M. (2005). Beyond orality: Investigating literacy and the literacy in second and foreign language instruction. *The Modern Language Journal, 89*(3), 381–392.

Kramsch, C. (2006). From communicative competence to symbolic competence. *The Modern Language Journal, 90*(2), 249–252.

Kramsch, C., & Nolden, T. (1994). Redefining literacy in a foreign language. *Die Unterrichtspraxis, 27*, 28–35.

Kress, G.R. (2000). Multimodality. In B. Cope, & M. Kalantzis (Eds.), *Multiliteracies: Literacy learning and the design of social futures* (pp. 182–202). New York, NY: Routledge.

Kress, G.R. (2003). *Literacy in the new media age.* New York, NY: Routledge.

Kress, G.R., & van Leeuwen, T. (2006). *Reading images: The grammar of visual design* (2nd ed.). New York, NY: Routledge.

Kumagai, Y., & Iwasaki, N. (2011). What it means to read "critically" in a Japanese language classroom: Students' perspective. *Critical Inquiry in Language Studies, 8*(2), 125–152.

Kurek, M., & Hauck, M. (2014). Closing the digital divide: A framework for multiliteracy training. In J.P. Guikema, & L. Williams (Eds.), *Digital literacies in foreign and second language education* (pp. 119–140). San Marcos, TX: CALICO Monograph Series, 12.

Lankshear, C., & Knobel, M. (2008). Introduction. In C. Lankshear, & M. Knobel (Eds.), *Digital literacies: Concepts, policies and practices* (pp. 1–16). New York, NY: Peter Lang.

Lo Bianco, J. (2000). Multiliteracies and multilingualism. In B. Cope, & M. Kalantzis (Eds.), *Multiliteracies: Literacy learning and the design of social futures* (pp. 92–105). New York, NY: Routledge.

Luke, A., Cadzen, C., Lin, A., & Freebody, P (2004). *The Singapore classroom coding scheme* (Tech. Rep.). Singapore: National Institute of Education, Center for Research on Pedagogy and Practice.

Malinowski, D. (2014). Drawing bodies and spaces in telecollaboration: A view of research potential in synaesthesia and multimodality, from the outside. *Pedagogies: An International Journal, 9*(1), 63–85.

Martin, J.R. (1985). Process and text: Two aspects of human semiosis. In J.D. Benson, & W.S. Greaves (Eds.), *Systemic perspectives on discourse* (pp. 243–274). Norwood, NJ: Ablex.

Matsuda, P.K. (2001). Reexamining audiolingualism: On the genesis of reading and writing in L2 studies. In D. Belcher, & A. Hirvela (Eds.), *Linking literacies: Perspectives on L2 reading–writing connections* (pp. 84–105). Ann Arbor: University of Michigan Press.

Maxim, H.H. (2009). Developing advanced formal language abilities along a genre-based continuum. In S. Katz Bourns, & J. Watzinger-Tharp (Eds.), *Conceptions of L2 grammar: Theoretical approaches and their application in the L2 classroom* (pp. 173–188). AAUSC's Issues in Language Program Direction, Annual Series. Boston, MA: Heinle and Heinle.

Maxim, H.H. (2014). Curricular integration and faculty development: Teaching language-based content across the foreign language curriculum. In J. Swaffar, & P. Urlaub (Eds.), *Transforming postsecondary foreign language teaching in the United States* (pp. 79–101). New York: Springer.

Michelson, K., & Dupuy, B. (2014). Multi-storied lives: Global simulation as an approach to developing multiliteracies in an intermediate French course. *L2 Journal, 6*(1), 21–49.

Mills, K.A. (2010). A review of the "digital turn" in the new literacy studies. *Review of Educational Research, 80*(2), 246–271.

Modern Language Association (MLA) Ad Hoc Committee on Foreign Languages. (2007). Foreign languages and higher education: New structures for a changed world. *Profession 2007*, 234–245.

New London Group (NLG). (1996). A pedagogy of multiliteracies: Designing social futures. *Harvard Educational Review, 66*(1), 60–92.

New London Group (NLG). (2000). A pedagogy of multiliteracies: Designing social futures. In B. Cope, & M. Kalantzis (Eds.), *Multiliteracies: Literacy learning and the design of social futures* (pp. 9–37). New York, NY: Routledge.

Nelson, M.E., & Kern, K. (2012). Language teaching and learning in the postlinguistic condition? In L. Alsagoff, S.L. McKay, G. Hu, & W.A. Rendandya (Eds.), *Principles and practices for teaching English as an international language* (pp. 47–66). New York: Routledge.

O'Dowd, R., & Waire, P. (2009). Critical issues in telecollaborative task design. *Computer Assisted Language Learning, 22*(2), 173–188.

Oskoz , A., & Elola, I. (2014). Integrating digital stories in the writing class: Toward a 21st century literacy. In J.P. Guikema, & L. Williams (Eds.), *Digital literacies in foreign and second language education* (pp. 179–200). San Marcos, TX: CALICO Monograph Series, 12.

Pennycook, A. (1996). TESOL and critical literacies: Modern, post, or neo? *TESOL Quarterly, 30*(1), 163–171.

Pennycook, A. (2001). *Critical applied linguistics: A critical introduction.* New York, NY: Routledge.

Peters, M., & Frankoff, M. (2014). New literacy practices and plagiarism: A study of strategies for digital scrapbooking. In J.P. Guikema, & L. Williams (Eds.), *Digital literacies in foreign and second language education* (pp. 245–264). San Marcos, TX: CALICO Monograph Series, 12.

Reinhardt, J., Warner, C., & Lange, K. (2014). Digital games as practices and texts: New literacies and genres in an L2 German classroom. In J.P. Guikema, & L. Williams (Eds.), *Digital literacies in foreign and second language education* (pp. 159–177). San Marcos, TX: CALICO Monograph Series, 12.

Rothery, J. (1996). Making changes: Developing an educational linguistics. In R. Hasan, & G. Williams (Eds.), *Literacy in society* (pp. 86–123). London: Longman.

Ryshina-Pankova, M.V. (2006). Creating textual worlds in advanced learner writing: The role of complex theme. In H. Byrnes (Ed.), *Advanced language learning: The contribution of Halliday and Vygotsky* (pp. 164–183). New York, NY: Continuum.

Scribner, S., & Cole, M. (1981). *The psychology of literacy.* Cambridge, MA: Harvard University Press

Street, B. (1995). *Social literacies: Critical approaches to literacy in development, ethnography and education.* New York, NY: Longman.

Swaffar, J.K., & Arens, K. (2005). *Remapping the foreign language curriculum: An approach through multiple literacies.* New York, NY: MLA.

Swaffar, J.K., & Urlaub, P. (2014). *Transforming postsecondary foreign language teaching in the United States.* New York, NY: Springer.

Thorne, S.L. (2013). Language learning, ecological validity and innovation under conditions of superdiversity. *Bellaterra Journal of Teaching & Learning Language & Literature, 6*(2), 1–27.

Thorne, S.L., & Reinhardt, J. (2008). "Bridging activities," new media literacies, and advanced foreign language proficiency. *CALOCO Journal, 25*(3), 558–572.

Unsworth, L. (2010). Resourcing multimodal literacy pedagogy: Toward a description of the meaning-making resources of language–image interaction. In T. Locke (Ed.), *Beyond the grammar wars: A resource for teachers and students on developing language knowledge in the English/literacy classroom* (pp. 276–293). New York, NY: Routlege.

Unsworth, L., & Bush, B. (2010). Introducing multimodal literacy to young children learning English as a second language. In D.R. Cole, & D.L. Pullen (Eds.), *Multiliteracies in motion: Current theory and practice* (pp. 59–83.). New York, NY: Routledge.

Wallace, C. (2003). *Critical reading in language education.* New York, NY: Palgrave Macmillan.

Yang, Y-F. (2012). Multimodal composing in digital storytelling. *Computers and Composition, 29*, 221–238.

Designing Multiliteracies Curricula

2

DEVELOPING MULTILITERACIES THROUGH GENRE IN THE BEGINNER GERMAN CLASSROOM

Mackenzie Warren and Claudia Winkler

The "Why" and "How" of a Multiliteracies Curriculum in College-Level Foreign Languages

Over two decades ago, in 1996, the New London Group (NLG) compellingly answered the question of "why" a need existed to implement curricula aimed at achieving multiliteracies: In a world that is growing increasingly more "multi," both in the sense of a media landscape that incorporates evermore modes of meaning-making and in the sense of a society that is increasingly culturally, socially, and linguistically diverse, a certain level of fluency in multiple modes of meaning (textual, visual, audio, etc.) and a variety of social and linguistic settings is a prerequisite for future economic success and social advancement (NLG, 1996, pp. 63–67). Yet, while the NLG (1996) also addressed "the 'how' of a pedagogy of multiliteracies" (p. 82), the development and implementation of a curriculum aimed at achieving multiliteracies still presents a challenge for educators across all disciplines and at all levels of education. The trouble for many foreign language departments is that they lack a curriculum that is underpinned by a theory of language. At the lower levels, "language" is taught as a series of grammar rules and vocabulary. "Content" courses are reserved for upper-level students who have achieved a high degree of familiarity with the rules and vocabulary. Language is seen as the vehicle for communicating content, not as the content itself. Emphasis in upper-level courses shifts to the "what" of communication, rather than focusing on how language itself—the mode, the linguistic choices as they relate to the social setting, etc.—*is* meaning. In such curricula, students fail to achieve fluency in multiple modes of meaning and a variety of social settings because these aspects of language are treated as secondary to the content itself. The unfortunate side effect of this language–content split in foreign language courses is that, in addition to failing to produce multiliterate students, foreign language programs have sent the message to universities that the content they are teaching can be learned apart from language—in an English course, a cultural studies course, and so on (see Byrnes, 2001, p. 514).

Recognizing that serious problems existed in foreign language programs that were detracting from their academic relevance and thus threatening their viability, the Georgetown University German Department (GUGD) overhauled its curriculum in the years 1997 to 2000. The GUGD wanted to work against trends in the foreign languages that fostered the artificial split between "language" and "content" courses and that put the primary emphasis on oral production in transactional and informational contexts (Byrnes, 2001, p. 515), as both of these departmental tendencies prevented students from achieving high levels of second language abilities. The GUGD recognized that being a part of an institution of post-secondary education meant producing language users who could function in German academic and professional environments (i.e., as multiliterate users of German, that is, language users literate in a variety of modes, particularly reading, writing, listening, and speaking, and literate in a variety of contexts ranging from the personal to the public). It is the aim of this chapter to describe how the GUGD, which has made developing multiliteracies the goal and literally the title ("Developing Multiple Literacies") of its curriculum, realizes its objectives in practice. Specifically, this chapter will illustrate the foundations of a multiliteracies-based curriculum by discussing how, within the context of an action research project, one entire unit at the German beginner level was developed and taught, and what the outcomes of this pedagogical sequence were. The findings of this action research project were first presented at the 2013 AAAL Annual Conference (Warren & Winkler, 2013).

To develop a curriculum that achieves the goal of producing multiliterate users of German, the GUGD opted for systemic functional linguistics (SFL) as a theoretical framework. SFL posits that language developed out of a need to fulfill specific functions, namely, making meanings in social and cultural contexts. There can be no language–content divide in an SFL-based curriculum because language *is* content. As a result, students learn to focus on the structure and mode of texts as they relate to meaning. For example, rather than discussing what the introduction to a paper literally says, they might focus on what beginning an essay with an introduction does for conveying meaning to a reader. How does it allow the reader to process subsequent information? What would happen to the essay if the introduction were not there? They also focus on linguistic choices as they relate to the social and cultural context. How might asking, "How are you?" in English prompt a friendly exchange of small talk, whereas the German equivalent of "*Wie geht's?*" might come across as nosy and rude? SFL works well for a multiliteracies curriculum because it posits that meaning only exists through embedded language choices: Without an understanding of the cultural and societal context and the different meaning-making potential of written versus spoken versus visual modes, one cannot communicate effectively.

Within SFL, the construct of genre became particularly important to guiding the development of the GUGD curriculum. Genre is "a staged, goal-oriented, purposeful activity in which speakers engage as members of our culture" (Martin in Eggins, 2004, p. 55). Virtually every meaningful interaction we have with one another is guided by generic conventions. The reason the construct of genre is particularly useful for a curriculum aimed at multiliteracies is manifold. First, each genre can be identified by certain schematic structures and recognizable patterns of lexicogrammatical realizations that recur in similar communicative contexts. Thus, students can quickly learn the structure of a genre—say, a short story—and can follow that pattern over and over again each time they are tasked with writing a short story. Second, each genre is tied to a series of social and cultural factors, as well as to the mode of communication. For example, asking a friend for the time will require many of the same steps as asking a stranger, but the setting with a stranger may require additional steps, such as a polite interruption ("Excuse me"), or certain linguistic choices, such as indirect questions ("Would you mind telling me . . ."). Third, genres are affected by the mode. Telling you a recipe as the host of a TV show will involve all of the same steps as communicating a recipe to you through a cookbook, but my linguistic choices will vary between the two modes. Genre not only provides students with repeatable patterns appropriate for communicating meaning across a series of similar situations, but also demonstrates that certain additional steps or certain linguistic realizations are more appropriate depending on the social context and the mode. Finally, in spite of being highly formulaic, genres retain a degree of flexibility and choice. For the GUGD, approaching texts through the lens of the genre allows instructors to discuss with students which organizational sequences and lexicogrammatical realizations are necessary or typical when trying to accomplish certain communicative goals, while still allowing students to make their own choices within a frame (Byrnes, Crane, Maxim, & Sprang, 2006, p. 89).

In practice, the construct of genre proves very useful in the curriculum because it allows instructors to develop clear tasks and allows students to successfully complete them. Each unit in the GUGD is thematically oriented and culminates in a speaking and/or writing task that represents a certain genre—a speech, a fairytale, a recipe, etc. We will discuss task and text selection in more detail below, but it is important to note here that the choices of texts and tasks are mutually influential: An instructor may begin with a certain task in mind that is representative of a given theme. For example, if the unit is on food and cooking, a logical choice for a final task would be a recipe in written or oral form. That choice will influence the choice of model texts. Other times texts may inform the task. In a unit on East Germany, for instance, there may not be a particularly obvious choice of task, but an instructor may have found several speeches on the topic that address relevant issues, and may then choose to have students write and deliver a speech at the end of that unit. In either case, genre is the guiding construct—the task and model text(s) are always generically similar. Sometimes the mode is changed from model text to task (e.g., from a written recipe to a cooking show), thus requiring the students to employ different lexicogrammatical structures. But, in all cases, students know how to organize their tasks and which lexicogrammatical choices are appropriate to achieve their communicative objectives, because they have discussed the model text(s) in a given unit within the framework of genre. Additionally, by opting for genre as a foundational construct, the GUGD is able to sequence texts (including songs, films, and images) over the four-year course of study not only thematically, but also according to a progression from private to public language use, which is reflected in increasingly more lexically dense (i.e., greater use of nominalizations) and covertly dialogic texts (Byrnes et al., 2006, pp. 90–91).

Given the long-term trajectory of the GUGD curriculum and its ultimate goal to "allow learners to become competent and literate non-native users of German who can employ the language in a range of intellectual and professional contexts and who can also draw from it personal enrichment and enjoyment" (Department of German, 2011c), it is essential to establish a foundation that provides students with a meta-awareness of the construct of genre, develops socially situated language use, and encourages a "willingness to communicate" (MacIntyre, Dörnyei, Clément, & Noels, 1998) in the L2. In order to demonstrate how the GUGD develops this foundation, we provide a detailed look into the pedagogical sequence of the beginner-level unit *Reisen und Erholung* [Travel and Relaxation]. In what follows, we situate the unit within the broader GUGD curriculum and give a brief description of our choice of model texts based on the generic conventions of the speaking and writing tasks in which this unit culminates. We then discuss the instructional sequence of the unit to illustrate how theory is translated into classroom practices. Finally, we discuss the outcomes of this unit as measured in an action research project and their relationship to the curricular goal of achieving multiliteracies.

Toward Multiliteracies at the Beginner Level: Writing and Speaking Tasks

In order to support the development of multiliteracies from the very beginning, the GUGD exposes students in its introductory courses to "a variety of genres and themes in a variety of media" ranging from "personal and interactional to routine public" (Department of German, 2011a). During the first year of instruction, students advance through 12 instructional units, which focus on content in private areas of language use such as leisure activities; talents, plans, and obligations; eating and drinking; and school and work. Genres typical of these private contexts are used in each unit's final speaking and writing task, and thus form the basis for selecting the model texts students are exposed to throughout the unit. The model texts not only contain relevant topical vocabulary, but also epitomize the linguistic features associated with the genres targeted by the speaking (e.g., fashion show, cooking show) and writing tasks (e.g., postcard, recipe, personal letter).

The pedagogical sequence under focus in this chapter is the tenth instructional unit at the beginner level and appears midway through the second-semester Introductory German course. This unit, *Reisen und Erholung* [T&R], culminates in both a writing task and a speaking task in which students are asked to imagine a vacation they have taken to a German-speaking city. This unit was chosen for discussion in this chapter, because it was recently redesigned within the context of an action research project aimed at developing a pedagogical sequence that better prepared students for the final tasks at the end of the unit. By contrasting the redesigned unit with the previous materials and instructional sequence, we hope to highlight not only the new sequence, but also the choices and benefits involved in ongoing curricular revision.

In the T&R writing task, students recount experiences from their imaginary trip in a first-person monologic narrative. In the speaking task, they have a conversation with one or two of their peers about their activities and experiences during the trip. To prepare for these tasks, students must conduct online research in German about their chosen city and, using the models provided to them in the instructional sequence, reorganize this information to conform to the modeled genres. Both tasks offer students the opportunity to take ownership of the newly learned material through repeated practice and transformation in socially situated contexts. Each task targets a specific genre in a different mode with a distinct communicative purpose and linguistic features.

More specifically, the writing task asks students to produce a narrative report for the university website recounting the details of their imaginary trip, including evaluations of their experiences. This requires discourse markers of time and chronology and the use of the simple past (typical of written language in German), as well as words and phrases that express thoughts, feelings, and evaluations, especially adjectives and their endings (see Appendix A, Writing Task). The speaking task is framed as a conversation between two or three peers, who have independently traveled to the same city and, like the writing task, requires recounting and evaluating personal experiences on the trip. The task sheet stresses the speaking task's interactive component as the "most important element" (see Appendix B). To fulfill this communicative function, students need to use some of the features of the written narrative such as markers of chronology and past tense (in this case, past perfect, a feature of spoken language in German), but also questions, responses, and reactions associated with verbal interaction. The ability of the students to identify and perform the array of generic features in the model texts and tasks is scaffolded by the pedagogical sequence described below. First, however, we discuss the motivation for choosing these particular genres and the focus on the salient feature of evaluation.

Selecting Appropriate Genres

The selection of target genres for all tasks in the GUGD curriculum, including those in the T&R unit, is based on multiple factors. The most important selection criteria are oriented toward enhancing multiliteracies via the reinforcement and expansion of the students' linguistic, generic, and cultural repertoire. When selecting target genres, instructors focus on two questions: (1) Does the genre draw on linguistic resources familiar to students to provide them a foundation for language production?, and (2) Does the genre push students to use new linguistic and generic features that allow them to expand their repertoire of literacies?

The narrative writing task of the T&R unit very clearly fulfills the first criterion. It falls well within the private sphere of personal experience typical of the beginner level. Features encountered in previous units (e.g., markers of time and the past tense) provide the building blocks for narrative cohesion in this task. The monologic nature of the first-person narrative is also familiar to students from previous tasks. These features form the foundation of language necessary to completing the task. To push students into new literacies, and fulfill the second criterion, this task also offers the unfamiliar context of L2 travel within which students can expand their repertoire of interactions, experiences, and associated linguistic resources.

The writing task serves, in turn, as a basis for the speaking task. The speaking task—a conversation about an imaginary travel experience—is a spoken, dialogic, narrative genre within the realm of private discourse. Like the writing task, the speaking task also fulfills both criteria for selecting appropriate genres: To complete this task, students draw on all of the linguistic features of personal narrative and experiential knowledge of travel used in the writing task, and move beyond them to develop the spoken, dialogic elements of conversation.

In addition to needing to meet the two above criteria, genre selection in the GUGD is determined by several other factors. The GUGD curriculum, like many foreign language curricula, strives for a balance between written, spoken, and even visual modes, as well as for authenticity in textual models and assignments. Thus, this unit incorporates both a writing task and a speaking task that reflect real situations. Additionally, by presenting students with the building blocks for participation in secondary discourses, the genres in this unit support the curricular goal of advanced multiliteracies. Narratives, such as those in the T&R unit, are "a useful way for highlighting central characteristics of cohesive and coherent texts and for making learners aware of the shift in semiotic practices that accompanies the shift from telling private stories to presenting public (hi)stories" (Department of German, 2011b). Moreover, the informal personal conversation in the T&R unit will give way to increasingly formal interpersonal interactions as students progress through the curriculum. Thus, through the instructional sequence and culminating tasks for the T&R unit, the learning that happens at the beginner level prepares students for the kind of language use expected of them at later stages in their L2 development within the curriculum and beyond.

Identifying Salient Linguistic Features

It is important to select genres that align with curricular goals and a long-term learning trajectory. It is equally important to didacticize the genres through model texts in such a way that clearly highlights key features, so that targeted instruction can take place. For the genres of narrative and conversation, that key feature is evaluation, and for this reason we chose to place the instructional focus on evaluation when redesigning the unit for our action research project.

In narrative, evaluation establishes significance, creates personal interest (Labov & Waletzky, 1967), and answers the question "What is the point?" (Labov, 1972). It also creates coherence by providing commentary that makes the text meaningful. In focusing on evaluation in the T&R unit, we provide students with tools for building coherence in the task at hand and in subsequent, more complicated narratives. Through instruction, students also gain the additional metaliteracy for recognizing how evaluative resources create coherence in texts.

In addition to being a central feature of narratives, evaluation is a cornerstone of conversation. Eggins (2004, p. 74) explains that casual conversation is a type of "interpersonal interaction" motivated by "the exploring and establishing of interpersonal relations" rather than by the motivation of achieving a clear, tangible goal. Evaluative vocabulary, among other linguistic features, helps to realize this interpersonal aspect of conversation.

The centrality of evaluation to narrative and conversation hinges on its personal and interpersonal value. Through evaluation, the narrative of the writing task and the conversation of the speaking task provide affordances for communication that is personally meaningful to the language users and their interlocutors. The instructional sequence described here aims to capitalize on this interpersonal value to support long-term curricular goals. Meaningful interaction has been linked to an increased willingness to communicate—a phenomenon described by MacIntyre et al. (1998) as "the ultimate goal of the learning process." It can lead to the increased amount of language production ideal for developing multiliteracies from the very beginning of an L2 curriculum. Additionally, several past studies found a correlation between the ability to detect and/or produce evaluative language and advancedness (see Coffin, 2002; Liskin-Gasparro, 1996; Rintell, 1990; Swain, 2010). For these reasons, we chose to focus on evaluation in this pedagogical sequence and selected models to fit this focus.

Selecting Appropriate Model Texts

After establishing appropriate genres and identifying their salient linguistic features, we selected model texts to serve as the basis for the instructional sequence and to guide students in fulfilling the requirements of the writing and speaking tasks. Prior to the T&R unit redesign for our action research project, materials had been developed around a model text from the website of the Schönbrunn Palace in Vienna, Austria. While this text contained ample amounts of evaluative language, because it came from a tourist website, the evaluation was overwhelmingly positive. The pedagogical sequence described in this chapter employs a new model text that better represents the genre and interpersonal context of the unit's tasks and contains a broader range of evaluative features. It thus provides students with a more diverse set of resources to draw on.

The new model text was written by German high school students about their class trip to Berlin. It was posted on their school's website to be read by their peers and parents. In the text, the students discuss both the positive and negative aspects of their experience, while chronologically recounting the events of the trip. This text effectively models the type of text students are expected to produce in the writing task. As a model for the speaking task, students observe a teacher-produced conversation based on the model text and performed by the instructor and a colleague. Many of the same vocabulary items and phrases that are found in the written task are reused in the speaking task, including evaluative vocabulary, but the speaking task differs from the writing task in its dialogic quality. This dialogic aspect is highlighted in the model through questions (including follow-up questions) and engaged responses (i.e., "That's so interesting" or "Me too"), as well as through body language, tone of voice, and other non-linguistic modes of expression.

The next section describes in detail the pedagogical sequence developed around these models. It is important to note that, while we teach mainly for the task, more broadly we aim to create multiliterate language users. This means that throughout the instructional sequence we frequently emphasize literacy in multiple modalities and in multiple situations as it relates to the task *and* beyond. This strategy underlies all instructional sequences in the GUGD and in our view is the key to any multiliteracies-oriented curriculum. In subsequent sections, we discuss the outcomes of the action research project and the implications of a focus on evaluation for developing multiliteracies.

Pedagogical Sequence: Theoretical Framework

As is the case with all units in the GUGD and any sequences designed using this methodology, in the T&R unit, we began developing the daily lesson plans after selecting target genres and model texts. As a framework for the pedagogical sequence, we primarily used the teaching cycle proposed by Rothery (1996; see Figure 2.1). This genre-based teaching cycle has four distinct stages, namely *Negotiating Field*, *Deconstruction*, *Joint Construction*, and *Independent Construction*. These stages have some parallels, but not a one-to-one correspondence, to the NLG's (1996) pedagogical constructs of *Situated Practice*, *Overt Instruction*, *Critical*

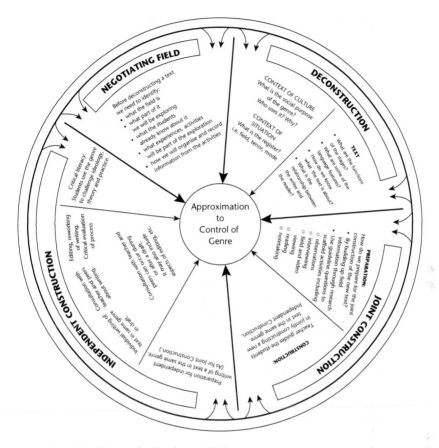

FIGURE 2.1 Teaching cycle (Rothery, 1996).

Framing, and *Transformed Practice*, which inform many pedagogies of multiliteracies. In our sequence, Situated Practice and Overt Instruction occur in the Negotiating Field and Deconstruction phases, while Critical Framing appears primarily during Joint Construction, and Transformed Practice constitutes the final phase of completing the unit's tasks during Independent Construction.

In the Rothery model, the initial step when working with a new genre is Negotiating Field, which involves exploring students' prior knowledge of the topic at hand. Through the process of Negotiating Field, students are being introduced to the language of that field, as "the two are inseparable: we cannot know the field unless we know the language of the field" (Rothery, 1996, p. 103). Following Negotiating Field is the process of Deconstruction, which involves direct engagement with the model text(s). Here the students and instructor engage with the text on a meta-level by trying to discover its communicative goal and the stages and linguistic features that allow the text to fulfill this purpose.

Deconstruction is followed by Joint Construction, which involves students and instructors jointly creating texts following the model of the target genre discussed in the prior phase. With the help of the metalanguage developed in the Deconstruction phase and scaffolded through guiding questions and reformulations by the instructor, students produce semi-autonomous texts. After going through these three stages, perhaps even multiple times with a number of texts of the same genre, students are ready to enter the final stage of the pedagogical cycle, namely Independent Construction. Here students apply what they have learned during the instructional sequence and produce their own texts without direct teacher input (Rothery, 1996, pp. 102–107). The following describes our seven-day instructional sequence for the T&R unit using the stages mapped out above.

Pedagogical Sequence: The Seven-Day Teaching Cycle

Day 1: Negotiating Field

The first day of the teaching cycle focuses on Negotiating Field. In the T&R unit, this involves a warm-up conversation that introduces the new topic, followed by the organizational tool of the *Wortfeld* [mind map]. This opening sequence of activities consists of three distinct parts and pedagogical goals.

In part one, the instructor asks opening questions to the topic e.g., "Do you like to travel?" "Have you ever been to Germany?" "If so, which cities/places did you visit?", with the aim of having students draw on their own experiences that relate to the topic of travel, on foundational vocabulary from the prior units *Durch Stadt und Land* [Through Cities and the Countryside] and *Essen und Trinken* [Food and Drink], and on familiar structures, especially the past tense. In part two, the instructor seeks to elicit new words and phrases related to the topic by posing additional questions that place students in an imaginary frame e.g., "If you could travel to Germany, which cities/places would you like to visit?" "What would you do there?". The instructor also scaffolds the activity with sample answers e.g., "*Ich **würde** die Berliner Mauer besuchen*" [I **would** visit the Berlin Wall], "*Es **wäre** schön, Berlin zu besuchen*" [It **would be** nice to visit Berlin]. This imaginary frame is necessary for the final task of the unit, in which students begin to develop advanced narrative abilities (see Rothery, 1996, p. 112), by learning to decontextualize their personal travel experiences and recontextualize them in an imaginary setting. The imaginary frame also provides a context for introducing new verb modes and forms, such as the Subjunctive II for new verbs *haben* [to have], *sein* [to be], and *werden* ([to become]; the auxiliary verb used to express futurity). By the end of this two-part warm-up activity, students have begun to develop a lexicogrammar around the topic of travel and relaxation.

In the third part of the opening sequence, students begin to organize the lexicogrammar they are developing around this topic in a *Wortfeld*. The instructor elicits words and phrases in several categories related to travel and relaxation:

Menschen / Teilnehmer [people/participants], *Unterkunft* [accommodations], *Essen* [food], *Sehenswürdigkeiten* [attractions], *Wetter* [weather], *Transport* [transportation]. These categories are selected based on the model text, which, in this unit, primarily describes and evaluates experiences related to these six topics. In focusing students' attention on words and phrases in these specific areas, instructors are priming them specifically for working with the model text the following day. The instructor provides scaffolding by translating or expanding on words and phrases (e.g., a student suggests *"die Führung"* [tour], and the instructor adds *"der Reiseführer"* [tour guide/guidebook] or *"eine Führung machen"* [to take a tour]). Thus, students' lexicogrammar begins to grow in a contextualized, semantically organized way.

It is important to note that any grammar instruction that takes place in the sequence should be highly contextualized. For example, in this opening sequence, students are not simply asked to read an explanation of the Subjunctive II and complete verb conjugation exercises, as would occur in an additive instructional sequence that moves from one grammar topic to the next. Instead students are exposed to new structures as they become necessary for achieving certain communicative goals—in this case, expressing hypothetical wishes. This serves to emphasize that language structures and vocabulary are always linked to specific contexts—an understanding that is fundamental to developing multiliteracies.

Day 2: Deconstruction

During the second day of instruction, the class works with the model text—a recount of a middle school *Klassenfahrt* [class trip] to Berlin—and enters into the Deconstruction phase of the pedagogical cycle (a phase that will be re-entered on Day 4 with the speaking task model; see below). First, students are asked to identify the genre of the model. Typically, rather than naming the specific genre, student responses are descriptive, focusing on the text's communicative goals and its target audience. However, because they are familiar with the genre of narrative from past units, they may at this point recognize the text as some kind of a story and, upon prompting, are usually able to identify two key linguistic features of the narrative genre, namely past tense and chronology. The instructor usually aids in the process of labeling the text specifically as a written recount.

Once the communicative purpose and the basic linguistic features of the text are established, students are asked to mark up their copies of the recount, adding dividing lines wherever they perceive a break or new stage. This exercise pushes students to identify larger moves in the text, which in turn affords them a meta-awareness of its overall structure. In the case of the *Klassenfahrt* text, breaks generally correspond with the chronology of the trip—each new day constitutes a new stage of the recount. Once students have identified the macro structure, they are asked to look more closely at each section and explain which specific linguistic realizations made them divide the text as they did. Instructors ask questions (in German) such as "Why did you put a break here?", "Which words or phrases influenced your decision?" And, indeed, students tend to find that the stages they have identified are marked by temporal phrases such as *am nächsten Morgen* [the following morning] and *nach dem Frühstück* [after breakfast]. In addition to ensuring that students notice markers of time, instructors also ask that students underline the past tense. Upon closer inspection, students notice that the text is written using the simple past tense—another key feature of written recounts. Emphasis on the tense is particularly important for developing multiliteracies, as German practices the convention of using two different forms of the past tense in different modes of communication: Written German in general and particularly in formal situations calls for the use of the simple past, whereas spoken German favors the past perfect form. This will be a very important distinction later in the unit, as students must move from the written to the oral mode for the unit's writing and speaking tasks.

Finally, students' attention is guided to a new feature of recounts (and, more broadly, narratives), namely evaluation. Initially the instructor asks the students to explain the function of phrases such as *sehr lustig* [very fun], *sehr lang* [very long], or *sehr anstrengend* [very exhausting/difficult], which they are usually able to identify as the writer's opinion regarding his/her various travel experiences. After providing students with the metalinguistic category of "evaluation" or *Berwertungen* and pointing to some manifestations of evaluation in the text, instructors have students find all instances of evaluation in the model with the help of a special worksheet (see excerpt in Table 2.1).

In the left-hand column of the worksheet, partially reproduced in Table 2.1, all of the things/experiences being evaluated in the *Klassenfahrt* text are listed under the six categories identified for the *Wortfeld* on Day 1. The right-hand column of the worksheet asks students to find the specific evaluative words and phrases used in the text to describe the items listed under these categories, and to label them as either positive or negative evaluations. Aside from a few instances of evaluation listed to scaffold the exercise, this column remains empty for students to fill in. Although evaluation is a new concept to students, at this point

TABLE 2.1 Excerpt: Klassenfahrt Evaluation Worksheet

Was/Wer wird bewertet? [What/who is being evaluated?]	*Bewertung* (+/−) [Evaluation]
Essen [food]	
Welches (das Abendessen) [which (the dinner)]	
Frühstück [breakfast]	
Mamas Küche [Mom's kitchen]	
das Essen [the food]	
Unterkunft [accommodations]	+ *ein klein wenig weiblicher*
das Zimmer [the room]	[a little more feminine]
die Gestaltung des Zimmers [the room's setup]	

they have enough vocabulary to identify most phrases involving evaluation or an emotional response on the part of the writer. By asking students to mine the text for instances of evaluation, and to further identify them as positive or negative, this exercise guides students toward an awareness of evaluation's interpersonal role and communicative purpose (e.g., to paint a picture of the experience and create interest for the reader) through Deconstruction.

Day 2 of instruction ends by:

- giving students the writing and speaking task sheets (Appendices A and B) and informing them that the *Klassenfahrt* text should serve as a model for their own tasks;
- assigning students a city and partner/s with whom to complete the speaking task;
- instructing students to begin conducting research on tourist sites and activities in their assigned cities.

Days 3/4: Joint Construction and Continued Deconstruction

Collecting the Building Blocks

The third day of the T&R unit commences with the Joint Construction phase of the pedagogy cycle. At this point, students have received and read a handout for homework that highlights four tourist sites in Berlin—the Reichstag, the Alexanderplatz TV tower, the Jewish Museum, and the Berlin Cathedral. In bullet-point format, this handout lists historical and architectural facts pulled off of websites about each of the sites. Information about the TV tower, for example, relays its height, how far one can see from its viewing platform on a clear day, and the history of its construction. Precisely these kinds of materials are what students will be working with when they research information about the cities and sites they have selected for their final tasks. In order to further help students imagine trips to these four attractions in Berlin, the instructor also incorporates visual materials into the instructional sequence. S/he shows a PowerPoint presentation featuring various images of the four sites, so that students can see the architecture and location of and (in some cases) even the view from the four buildings. Combining the visual and factual information they have received, students are now prepared to move forward in the Joint Construction phase by transforming this information into a recount that retells the chronology of an imaginary visit to these sites and evaluates the experience.

Students collect the building blocks for their jointly constructed text by completing a table about the four attractions (see Table 2.2). This exercise requires students to form and articulate their own evaluations of the sites in short lexico-grammatical chunks that will be assembled into a longer text in the next activity. This scaffolds the process of interpreting the information gathered through research and recontextualizing it in the form of a written recount.

TABLE 2.2 Berlin Attractions Worksheet

Bewertungen [Evaluations]

Sehenswürdigkeit [Tourist attraction]	*Interessen; Fakten über die Sehenswürdigkeiten in Verbindung zu Ihrer persönlischen Interessen* [Interests; facts about the attractions in relation to your personal interests]	*Reaktion und Beurteilung (Nennen Sie genaue Aspekte, worauf Sie diese Reaktion haben oder worüber Sie beurteilen)* [Reactions and evaluation (Name specific aspects of the attraction to which you are having this reaction or which you are evaluating)]
der Reichstag	*Ich interessiere mich für Politik: das Reichstagsgebäude ist Sitz des Bundestages.* [I'm interested in politics: the Reichstag building is the seat of the German legislative body.]	
der Fernsehturm [the TV tower]		*wunderschöner Blick von oben: man kann ganz Berlin sehen* [beautiful view from above: one can see all of Berlin]
der Dom [the Cologne Cathedral]		
das jüdische Museum [the Jewish Museum]		

The first empty column asks students to connect factual information about a given site (e.g., the Reichstag) to their personal interests (e.g., I am *interested* in politics). The second column requires that students list reactions and evaluations in response to specific aspects of, or experiences at, the respective sites. In response to the TV tower, for instance, one may write, "beautiful view from above: one can see all of Berlin." Here again students are asked to reinterpret the factual and visual materials gathered through research to fit the imaginary context of a trip. In the above response, the information about the height of the TV tower together with pictures taken from the viewing platform elicit the evaluation that one has a "*beautiful* view from above." For additional scaffolding, students are encouraged to use the table with evaluative words and phrases mined from the *Klassenfahrt* text during the previous class (see Table 2.1).

Assembling the Pieces

The final phase of Joint Construction involves the production of an actual cohesive recount of one day in Berlin. Again this step is scaffolded, this time with a teacher-produced model text, which includes information about transportation, accommodations, attractions, people/participants, food, and the weather; it also recycles phrases from the *Klassenfahrt* text and from the table about the four attractions in Berlin.

The instructor presents the teacher-produced recount and highlights the phrases that have been reused from previous activities to illustrate how students can piece together the language they have already produced to create a longer text. Developing an awareness of this process of recontextualization is key to the Joint Construction phase. As a brief review before students write their own paragraphs in groups, the teacher leads the class through a mini-Deconstruction activity, in which they mine the model paragraph for the salient linguistic features of recounts, namely chronology, simple past tense, and evaluation.

Finally, students work in groups to write a paragraph recounting their imaginary experience at one of the four Berlin attractions on the above handout. Like the model, they are required to include information concerning the travel-related topics of transportation, accommodations, attractions, people/participants, food, and weather, and to organize their recounts chronologically and evaluate their virtual experiences.

Peer-Reviewing

During the next class period (Day 4), students meet again with their groups, and each group is given another's mini-recount for analysis. The following text is an example of a group-produced recount that is given to peers for analysis.

Text 2—Group-produced recount: One day in Berlin

> *Zuerst sind wir mit dem Zug nach Berlin gefahren. Wir kamen in der Nacht in Berlin an. Während der Fahrt sahen wir die Landschaften, weil das Wetter wunderbar war. Am nächsten Morgen sind wir zum Fernsehturm gegangen. Der Fernsehturm war das größte Gebäude, das wir gesehen haben. Dann besuchten wir den Dom, weil wir uns für die Geschichte von dem Berliner Dom interessieren. Der Berliner Dom wurde unter Kaiser Wilhelm II in den Jahren 1894 bis 1905 neu gebaut. Wir waren völlig von den Socken gehauen, als wir den Berliner Dom gesehen haben! Wir haben uns für die Architektur vom Reichstag interessiert. Der Reichstag mischt Elemente aus der Renaissance, dem Barock und dem Klassizismus zusammen. Wir fanden die Architektur sehr interessant. Wir mochten die gläserne Kuppel. Endlich gingen wir in die Jugendherberge, um uns zu erholen.*

[First we rode to Berlin with the train. We arrived in Berlin at night. During the drive we saw the landscape, because the weather was excellent. The next morning we went to the TV tower. The TV tower was the tallest building that we saw. Then we visited the cathedral, because we are interested in the history of the Berlin Cathedral. The Berlin Cathedral was renovated under Kaiser Wilhelm II from 1894 to 1905. We were totally swept off our feet when we saw the Berlin Cathedral! We were very interested in the architecture of the Reichstag. The Reichstag mixes elements of Renaissance, Baroque, and Classical architecture together. We thought the architecture was really interesting. We liked the glass dome. Finally we went back to the youth hostel to rest.]

When analyzing their peers' texts, groups are asked to do the following:

- identify and underline all of the evaluation in the recount;
- point out what, aside from the attraction, the text describes (e.g., food, transportation, accommodations);
- offer criticisms (this allows better writers and students more aware of generic conventions to scaffold this activity for their less-advanced peers).

After student input, the instructor gives final comments, which focus on pointing out additional opportunities to elaborate on or evaluate experiences and on creating cohesion. For the above text, for instance, one might point out the overuse of the evaluative word *interessant* [interesting] and the related phrase *sich für etwas interessieren* [to be interested in] as well as the repeated emphasis on architecture. Moreover, while the authors used many temporal phrases to structure the text, the recount is not entirely cohesive, because transitions between temporally and spatially separate elements are often missing.

Outcomes of Joint Construction—Examining Genre and Shifts in Mode

This round of peer review completes the Joint Construction phase of the instructional sequence, a step that is crucial both for preparing students for the upcoming Independent Construction phase and for helping to develop multiliteracies. In the early part of Joint Construction, students work with visual materials and informational, factual texts (i.e., an online encyclopedia) in order to gather necessary information for their mini-recounts and familiarize themselves with research tools. In working with photographs, students practice "reading" images, in a sense, by learning to translate what they see into the context of a travel story. These different modes complement each other to create a full picture and a more detailed narrative. They also help students learn to work in multimodal environments and to transition from one mode (the visual) to another (the written/textual). Moreover, in working with encyclopedic texts and then learning to recontextualize that information into a narrative, students are again being exposed to the importance of genre—that is, social context and communicative goals—when producing different texts. An encyclopedia entry primarily serves to *inform* readers, not to tell a story or to (overtly) judge the value of something. Hence, certain lexicogrammatical features (temporal phrases, evaluation) are largely absent from the encyclopedic texts and must be added to construct a narrative. This shift from one genre to another again draws students' attention to the crucial link between language and meaning.

Revisiting Deconstruction

Another shift highlighted on Day 4 of the instructional sequence is the shift from the written to the spoken mode. Day 4 ends with another phase of Deconstruction, when the instructor and a colleague model the speaking task, which, in terms of its content and evaluative phrases, borrows heavily from the *Klassenfahrt* text. Modeling the speaking task is, however, more than simply reading an appropriate text that meets all of the task requirements. The model presenters must be well practiced so that they only require notes and can concentrate on *performing* the task, since spoken genres are as much about voice quality, tone, and body language as they are about language and content. After modeling the speaking task, the instructor asks students to concentrate on the text-external qualities of the model: the tone of voice—namely, the enthusiasm and lack of monotony that is characteristic of a conversation between friends—and on body language. In highlighting these two aspects, instructors focus on aspects of oral communication often overlooked in L2 instruction despite their importance in all social environments, and particularly in professional settings, where oral communication frequently constitutes a cornerstone of success.

After working with non-textual aspects of the model presentation, students receive the conversation scripts for further analysis. First, the instructor projects an image of a marked-up version of the *Klassenfahrt* text, in which all of the phrases that have been reused in the speaking task are highlighted. Through this process, students can see the close links between content in the written and spoken texts. After that, the class re-enters the phase of Deconstruction by recalling the main features of the written recount (i.e., chronology, simple past tense, and evaluation) and subsequently looking for similarities and differences in the oral recount. One easily discernable shift in the oral text is from the simple past (written) to the past perfect tense (spoken), which, as mentioned above, is typical of German language texts. Students also quickly notice that a strict chronology is no longer the primary element structuring the text. Instead, a series of questions, responses, reactions, and follow-up questions structure the conversation. To highlight this important aspect of conversation, the instructor emphasizes the following features of the model:

- the length of the responses;
- the recount-like character of responses (including evaluative phrases);
- reactions in the form of direct replies and follow-up questions.

At the end of this phase of Deconstruction, students receive a list of suggested questions and reactions (see Appendix C) to help guide them in the final phase of Independent Construction.

Days 5 and 6: Additional Practice and Preparation

By days 5 and 6 of the instructional sequence, students have already begun working on their writing and speaking tasks, thus entering the final phase of the teaching cycle: Independent Construction. Before they complete their tasks, though, some activities remain that help them gather information for their tasks and focus on developing multiliteracies. Day 5 is spent deconstructing a text from a Berlin hotel's website. The primary purpose of this exercise is to help students learn how to glean from hotel web pages relevant information such as cost and location of accommodations. Central to developing multiliteracies is a discussion of the linguistic features of hotel websites and their relationship to communicative purpose. These types of web pages tend to contain a great deal of evaluative language (as opposed to the encyclopedic websites from Day 3) and the evaluations are exclusively positive. When asked about this prominence of evaluation, students are usually able to explain that the hotel websites have the communicative purpose of selling their accommodations to potential guests. A recount, however, does not aim to sell anything, and thus, in this genre, both positive and negative evaluations are commonly used to generate interest. By highlighting these generic differences with regard to the salient feature of evaluation, the instructor again reinforces the link between communicative goals and linguistic realizations.

The sixth day of instruction focuses on reading maps and asking for directions. The activities and their pedagogical goals are outlined below:

- Part I (Negotiating Field): The instructor opens with the rhetorical questions "What happens if you're in a German city and cannot find your hotel?" "How do you ask someone the way?" and introduces students to the new structure of indirect questions; instructor and textbook offer scaffolding via directional and command phrases.

  o Goal: to identify the connection between grammatical structures (indirect questions) and social conventions (politeness) → situated language use.

- Part II (Joint Construction): Instructor initiates role play activity by projecting a map of the National Mall in Washington, DC, on to the wall and posing as a German tourist needing directions; role play activity is continued in small groups, this time with a Georgetown campus map.

  o Goals:

    □ to practice newly acquired structures (indirect questions) and vocabulary (directional phrases);

- to practice familiar structures (commands, imperative);
- to navigate between formal ("tourist"–student) and informal (student–student) situations and select appropriate grammatical forms (*Sie, du*)
- to translate what they see (a map) into oral communication (giving directions) → operating between different modalities.

Day 7: Independent Construction

The last day of the unit is devoted to student presentations of the conversation that they have independently prepared in their groups. The presentations are audio-recorded and graded by the instructor according to a grading rubric. (Each student also completes the writing task independently, which is graded with a similar rubric.) All GUGD grading rubrics assess three equally weighted categories: task, content, and language focus. Task elements grade the students' performances on broad issues. In the case of the T&R speaking task, the task portion of the rubric focuses on students' adhering to the task length requirements, engaging in conversation, and speaking clearly. The content category focuses on whether or not students addressed all of the topics laid out in the task. For this speaking task, students are required to discuss and evaluate their experiences in each of the six travel-related fields under focus in this unit (transportation, accommodations, attractions, people/participants, food, and weather) and to discuss what they would do differently if they could make the trip again. Finally, the language focus category for the T&R speaking task focuses on the interaction with speaking partners through questions and responses, the use of temporal and spatial markers to structure one's speech and any corresponding verb forms, the use of topical vocabulary, and grammatical elements such as adjective endings, cases, and verb placement. While the grading rubric divides the task into three separate grading categories, the reality is that the categories are very closely related. A student who fails to evaluate his/her experiences, for example, does not just fall short in the content category, but inevitably fails to effectively engage in conversation and use relevant vocabulary and structures. Nevertheless, the grading rubric helps to isolate students' successes and shortcomings when completing a task. In the following section, we discuss the outcomes of the Independent Construction phase as they relate to the goals of this unit and the overall trajectory of the program.

Developing Multiliteracies: An Ongoing Process

The pedagogical sequence just presented shows how to target a variety of modes, situations, and related linguistic resources within the contextual frame of traveling in the German-speaking world. It also exemplifies the foundational learning occurring at the introductory level of the curriculum that lays the groundwork for advanced multiliterate abilities at later stages of development. In order to ensure that this instructional sequence was not only grounded in theory, but also informed by practice, we conducted an action research project that investigated the outcomes of this new, evaluation-focused sequence in comparison to the previously used materials and activities. The results of this action research project illustrate more precisely the outcomes of employing an instructional approach focused on developing multiliteracies.

The data for the action research project were collected in parallel sections of the second-semester Introductory German course in spring 2012. One section (nine participants, Group 1) used the previous model text and materials (described in the section "Selecting Appropriate Model Texts") and did not focus explicitly on evaluation, while two other sections (13 participants, Group 2) used the new model text and materials presented in the detailed pedagogical sequence. We recorded the speaking tasks in class, transcribed them, coded them for features of evaluation, and conducted quantitative and qualitative analyses.

The analysis of the data showed that the language produced by the two groups differed quantitatively and qualitatively in important ways.

Students working with the old text and materials produced:

- fewer than three clauses per turn on average;
- brief answers to each other's questions.

The students working with the new text and materials produced:

- a greater amount of evaluative language related to their personal reactions and feelings;[1]
- a greater variety of evaluative lexical items;
- more than three clauses per turn on average;
- group discussions that were often twice as long as the question/answer sequences about those same topics in Group 1.

Measured in terms of both clauses per turn and sustained discussion, Group 2 produced longer stretches of discourse. Their increased language production suggests an increased willingness to communicate,[2] which in turn affords learners more opportunities to practice and refine their language use, to explore the genre in more depth, and, in general, to engage in meaningful communication in the L2, all of which supports the development of multiliteracies.

The qualitative analysis revealed the students' multiliterate development more precisely, specifically in the form of awareness of, and adherence to, new generic conventions in the speaking task. Qualitative differences between the groups suggest that the evaluation-focused pedagogical sequence affected students' strategic use of evaluation to structure their language output. Additionally, the extended discourse produced by Group 2 can be linked to successful compliance with the task's generic conventions.

Excerpt 1 illustrates how Group 1 incorporated evaluation into their task, but struggled to create narrative coherence and engage in conversational interaction.

Excerpt 1—Group 1 Speaking Task

1. Adam: *Haben Sie irgendwelche Tageausflüge?*
   [Have you taken any day trips?]
2. Rick: *Ja! Habe ich nach Luxemburg einen Tagesauflug gemacht.*
   [Yes! I took a day trip to Luxembourg.]
3. *Es war 2 Stunden von Trier mit dem Auto.*
   [It was 2 hours from Trier by car.]
4. Adam: *Als ich nach Köln ging,*
   [When I went to Cologne,]
5. *ich lernte eine Menge über ihre Geschichte und Kultur.*
   [I learned a whole lot about its history and culture.]
6. *Es war **beregend**.*
   [It was **exciting**.]
7. *In Köln traf ich viele **freundliche** Menschen.*
   [In Cologne I met many **friendly** people.]
8. *Ich hatte viel **Spaß** gemacht.*
   [I had a lot of **fun**.]
9. Susan: *Ja meine Reise nach Frankfurt war sehr **interessant** auch.*
   [Yes, my trip to Frankfurt was also very **interesting**.]
10. Rick: *Ja, als ich in Luxemburg war,*
    [Yes, when I was in Luxembourg,]
11. *habe ich die Nationale Geschichte Museum besicht.*
    [I visited the National History Museum.]
12. *Es war interessante und schön.*
    [It was interesting and nice.]
13. *Aber wenn nächstes Mal mag ich das Wetter warmer und sonniger sein.*
    [But the next time I want the weather to be warmer and sunnier.]

In terms of cohesion, the utterances by any one student in Excerpt 1 lack the elements of chronology and evaluative clauses typical of narrative. Isolated evaluative lexical items do appear (Lines 6–9, 12), but lack both the chronological, logical, or interpersonal connection to other events, evaluations, and speakers that enhance overall narrative and conversational coherence.

In Excerpt 2, by contrast, students from Group 2 who used the new pedagogical sequence employ evaluation as an opportunity to elaborate on their experiences—with significant results.

Excerpt 2—Group 2 Speaking Task

1. Chris: *Ben, was noch hast du gesehen?*
   [Ben, what else did you see?]

2.   *Etwas **interessant**?*
   [Anything **interesting**?]

3. Ben: *Ja ich bin auch zum Andechskloster gegangen.*
   [Yes, I also went to Andechs Abbey.]

4.   *Ich wurde sehr **überrascht***
   [I was very **surprised**]

5.   *als ich gelernt habe,*
   [when I learned,]

6.   *dass das Kloster auch eine Brauerei ist!*
   [that the monastery is also a brewery!]

7. Liz: *Auf keinen Fall!*
   [No way!]

8.   *Machen die Mönchen Bier?*
   [Do the monks make beer?]

9. Ben: *Ja, sie machen verschiedenen Bier.*
   [Yes, they make different beers.]

10.   *Etwas Bier sind leicht*
   [Some beers are light]

11.   *und einige sind dunkel*
   [and some are dark]

12.   *und sie war ausgezeichnet!*
   [and they were excellent!]

13.   *Was sonst machtest du, Liz?*
   [What else did you do, Liz?]

14. Liz: *Ich habe paar Souveniers auf dem Markt bei Schwabing gefunden.*
   [I found a few souvenirs at the market near Schwabing.]

15.   *Die Flohmarkt waren **wunderschön**.*
   [The fleamarket was **wonderful**.]

16.   *Alle Arten von Lebensmittel, Kunsthandwerk und andere Dinge.*
   [All kinds of foods, crafts, and other things.]

17.   *Man kann eine Bierstein oder Postkarten zum Beispiel kaufen.*
   [You can buy a beer stein or postcards, for example.]

18.   *Ich habe Souveniers für meine Eltern und meine Bruder gekaufen.*
   [I bought souvenirs for my parents and my brother.]

19.   *Ich wollte nicht bezahlen viel und war ganz **toll**.*
   [I didn't want to pay a lot and it was so **great**.]

20. Chris: *Ich habe noch nicht auf die Flöh-Flohmarkt uh in Schwabing gegangen,*
   [I haven't been to the fleamarket in Schwabing yet,]

21.   *aber jetzt bin ich **interessant**.*
   [but now I'm **interested**.]

22.   *Was ist ein Bierstein?*
          [What is a beer stein?]

23. Liz: *Ein Bierstein ist ein traditionelle deutsche Krug,*
          [A beer stein is a traditional German jug,]

24.   *der man mit Stein machen.*
          [made out of stone.]

25.   *Normalerweise ist ein Bierstein färbgemalt.*
          [Normally a beer stein is handpainted.]

26. Ben: *Chris, kennst dir-du die Frauenkirche?*
          [Chris, do you know the Frauenkirche (a church in the city)?]

The evaluative elaborations by these students contributed to narrative coherence, developed both within and across turns. Furthermore, the evaluation generated interest that led to interjections (Line 7), responses (Lines 20–21) and follow-up questions by peers (Lines 8, 22). These too extended the discourse and supported the overall coherence and flow of the conversation. For Group 2, evaluation became a reason to speak more, functioned to tie together a speaker's own narrative, and served to connect speakers with each other throughout the conversation. These results suggest that the instructional focus on evaluation was indeed a factor in the students' willingness to communicate and in their ability to fulfill the generic requirements of the speaking task.

The possible causes of these outcomes are complex and interrelated. On the one hand, the new pedagogical sequence explicitly provides students with linguistic resources for producing the narrative recount and conversation genres. This explicitness eliminates the unknowns of performing the task and reduces guesswork and uncertainty on the part of the students, boosting students' confidence and willingness to communicate. On the other hand, the instructional focus on evaluative language allows students to reflect on their personal connection to the topic and enables them to say something personally meaningful about the foreign language culture they are being introduced to. As empowered foreign language meaning makers, students can more fully engage with the topic at hand, master the target genres, and develop a linguistic meta-awareness that helps them achieve their communicative goals. This awareness is fundamental to any multiliteracies curriculum, where understanding and navigating connections between form and meaning is paramount.

Conclusion

By enabling students to speak at length and by guiding them toward a meta-awareness of the strategic use of evaluation, the instructional sequence outlined here pushes students toward mastery of the unit's target genres of narrative recount and informal conversation. Through multimodal, multi-situational activities, even beginner students become multiliterate language users.

The approach here and throughout the GUGD curriculum enables students to demonstrate their awareness of a genre, to successfully negotiate its conventions, and, by implication, to master the additional, embedded literacies necessary to perform it. And the development of multiliteracies does not stop there. Across the curriculum, genres accumulate, so that students build up their repertoire of literacies one genre at a time over a semester and throughout their course of study.

This ongoing process of literacy development makes the selection and sequencing of genres of utmost importance. The inclusion of genres of personal narrative and conversation at the beginner level provides contexts in which features of advanced language use can be introduced and scaffolded. Contextualized practice in using these resources aids students in the transition from private to public discourse when similar linguistic resources and interpersonal strategies resurface in new contexts later in the curriculum.

Finally, through an instructional approach such as this one, students begin to develop a metaliteracy for approaching texts and language learning. In this approach, Rothery's pedagogical cycle represents the key phases of scaffolded language learning. Learners build familiarity with the topic of travel and relaxation (Negotiating Field) and with the genres of narrative and conversation (Deconstruction). They are then guided to create their own texts with their instructor and peers (Joint Construction), and finally to produce autonomous texts in the target genres (Independent Construction).

The learning that happens for students through this type of instruction is not limited to new vocabulary, grammatical features, or cultural knowledge. The development of multiliteracies, in fact, cultivates awareness of metalinguistic aspects of language use and learning, of language's communicative function, and its situatedness. This in turn heightens students' awareness of their strategies for language learning and their own ability to structure discourse through language. Ultimately, this metaliteracy is empowering, because it enables students to "design their social futures" and "participate fully in public, community, and economic life" (NLG, 1996, p. 60). As students learn to apply it in new contexts, from other foreign language learning environments to academic and professional pursuits in their native language, their literacies and chances for success continue to multiply.

Please direct any questions regarding the pedagogical sequence and associated teaching materials to the authors.

Notes

1 Overall, there was a negligible difference in the amount of evaluative language produced by students. However, in the category of Affect (see Martin & White, (2005), students in Group 2 produced more evaluative language, likely as a result of being exposed to it in the model texts.
2 Willingness to communicate is difficult to measure because, like many aspects of motivation, there are many contributing factors. However, an important aspect is perceived

competence, or the feeling that one is capable of communicating effectively at a particular moment that arises when in a familiar situation for which one has language knowledge and skill (MacIntyre et al., 1998, p. 549). The instructional sequence and student performance in our action research project suggest that this is at play in the speaking task.

3 All task sheets and models are given to students in German. If you are interested in seeing the German original, please contact the authors of this chapter.

References

Byrnes, H. (2001). Reconsidering graduate students' education as teachers: "It takes a department!" *The Modern Language Journal, 85*(4), 512–530.

Byrnes, H., Crane, C., Maxim, H.H., & Sprang, K.A. (2006). Taking text to task: Issues and choices in curriculum construction. *ITL, 152*, 85.

Coffin, C. (2002). The voices of history: Theorising the interpersonal semantics of historical discourses. *Text, 22*, 503–538.

Department of German. (2011a). Curriculum Overview. Georgetown University. Retrieved from www1.georgetown.edu/departments/german/programs/undergraduate/curriculum/curriculumoverview/#Level I: Contemporary Germany.

Department of German. (2011b). Genre and Narrativity. Georgetown University. Retrieved from www1.georgetown.edu/departments/german/programs/undergraduate/curriculum/genreandnarrativity/.

Department of German. (2011c). Goals. Georgetown University. Retrieved from www1.georgetown.edu/departments/german/programs/undergraduate/curriulum/goals/.

Eggins, S. (2004). *Introduction to systemic functional linguistics.* New York, NY: Continuum.

Labov, W. (1972). The transformation of experience in narrative syntax. In W. Labov, *Language in the inner city: Studies in the black English vernacular* (pp. 354–396). Philadelphia: University of Pennsylvania Press.

Labov, W., & Waletzky, J. (1967). Narrative analysis: Oral versions of personal experience. In J. Helms (Ed.), *Essays on the verbal and visual arts: Proceedings of the 1996 Annual Spring Meeting of the American Ethnological Society* (pp. 12–44). Seattle: University of Washington Press.

Liskin-Gasparro, J.E. (1996). Narrative strategies: A case study of developing storytelling skills by a learner of Spanish. *Modern Language Journal, 80*, 271–286.

MacIntyre, P.D., Dörnyei, Z., Clément, R., & Noels, K.A. (1998). Conceptualizing willingness to communicate in an L2: A situational model of L2 confidence and affiliation. *The Modern Language Journal, 82*(4), 545–562.

Martin, J.R., & White, P.R.R. (2005). *The language of evaluation: Appraisal in English.* New York, NY: Palgrave Macmillan.

New London Group (NLG). (1996). A pedagogy of multiliteracies: Designing social futures. *Harvard Educational Review, 66*(1), 60–92.

Rintell, E. (1990). That's incredible: Stories of emotion told by second language learners and native speakers. In R. Scarcella, E. Anderson, & S. Krashen (Eds.), *Developing communicative competence in a second language* (pp. 75–94). Boston, MA: Heinle & Heinle.

Rothery, J. (1996). Making changes: Developing an educational linguistics. In R. Hasan and G. Williams (Eds.), *Literacy in society* (pp. 86–123). New York, NY: Longman.

Swain, E. (2010). Getting engaged: Dialogistic positioning in novice academic discussion writing. In E. Swain (Ed.), *Thresholds and potentialities of systemic functional linguistics:*

Multilingual, multimodal and other specialised discourses (pp. 291–317). Trieste: EUT Edizioni Universita di Trieste.

Warren, M., & Winkler, C. (2013). A systemic-functional approach to teaching and learning evaluative language in the L2 classroom. American Association for Applied Linguistics Presentation, Dallas, Texas, March 16–19.

Appendix A: Unit 10 Writing Task—English Translation[3]

Level I: Contemporary Germany
Chapter 10 Writing Task
A three-day virtual trip in a German-speaking city

Task:

You have traveled to a city in Germany, Austria, or Switzerland for a three-day trip with a group of university students. You are now writing a **report** of this trip for the university website, in which you retell what you and your group did during this trip and evaluate your experiences. Your report should be structured as a **narrative/recount** (i.e., with temporal phrases) and should be thorough in the sense that it gives many details from each day/experience and expresses your evaluations, thoughts, and feelings concerning these experiences.

Content:

In your report, you should address and evaluate the following points:

- the weather
- transportation and accommodations
- food
- people you met
- activities (ex. tours)
- at least three attractions that are historically or culturally interesting. Why did you choose these attractions/what did(n't) you find interesting?
- What would you change about the trip, if you could do it again? Why?

Language Focus:

Concentrate on the following:

Level of discourse:

- Markers of time and place, ex. two-way prepositions—dative und accusative (*in der Stadt vs. in die Stadt fahren; neben dem/das Rathaus, auf dem/den Fernsehturm, am nächsten Tag, am Nachmittag, am Abend*)

Lexis:

- Vocabulary of travel/vacation

Syntax/Grammar:

- relative clauses und subordination: *wenn, als, nachdem, weil*
- simple past
- adjective endings
- subjunctive.

Length: at least one full, double-spaced page, 12 pt font (Times New Roman) The first draft is due on _____ .

Assessment: Task 33%, Content 33%, Language focus 33%

Appendix B: Unit 10 Speaking Task—English Translation

Level I: Contemporary Germany
Chapter 10 Speaking Task
A three-day virtual trip in a German-speaking city

Task:
Two or three Georgetown students have (independently of one another) gone on a three-day trip to the same city in Germany, Austria, or Switzerland. There they meet each other in a café to have a **conversation** about what they did on their trip and to evaluate their experiences. You will have three main tasks in this conversation: You must ask your partner/s questions, you must react to the answers your partner/s give/s, and you must answer questions that your partner/s ask/s. Your answers should be formulated as a **narrative** (i.e., with markers of time) and should be thorough in the sense that you give details on what you did every day and give your evaluations, thoughts, and feelings about these experiences.

Content:
In your conversation you should address and evaluate the following points in question-and-answer format:

- the weather
- transportation and place of lodging
- food
- people that you met
- activities (ex. tours)
- at least three landmarks/tourist attractions that are of historical or cultural interest—Why did you choose these attractions? What did you think was (un)interesting?
- What would you change about your plans, if you would take this trip again? Why?

Language Focus:

Concentrate on the following:

Level of discourse:

- Interactive speaking with your partner using questions and answers, reactions, comparisons. This is the most important element of the conversation.
- Markers of time and place, ex. two-way prepositions—dative und accusative (*in der Stadt vs. in die Stadt fahren; neben dem/das Rathaus, auf dem/den Fernsehturm, am nächsten Tag, am Nachmittag, am Abend*)

Lexis:

- Vocabulary of travel/vacation.

Syntax/Grammar:

- relative clauses und subordination: *wenn, als, nachdem, weil*
- simple past
- adjective endings
- subjunctive.

Preparation: You and your partner(s) should meet at least once to practice the entire conversation. Use the models and suggested questions to structure your task.

Process of Communication:

- You should speak freely, using only notes (which should not consist of complete sentences on note cards, but perhaps of the names of important attractions).
- The conversation must be comprehensible! You may use vocabulary and phrases from websites, so long as they are not too complicated—for you to say or for the class to understand.
- New vocabulary can briefly be explained in German.
- Prepare a PowerPoint slide for your background.

Length: The whole conversation should take roughly 10 minutes.

Assessment: Task 33%, Content 33%, Language focus 33%

Appendix C: Questions and Reactions Handout

Fragen	*Reaktionen*
Wie war die Reise?	Meine Reise war/Mein Hotel/Die
Mit wem reist du?	Jugendherberge ist genauso gut.
Wo liegt dein Hotel/die Jugendherberge?	...genauso schlimm.
Wie findest du das Hotel/die	...nicht viel besser.
Jugendherberge?	Das Gericht habe ich [auch/nie] gegessen!
Wie findest du dein Zimmer?	Ich kenne das Hotel/das Restaurant!
Wie findest du das Essen im Hotel/die	Das Hotel/das Restaurant kenne ich
Jugendherberge?	nicht!
Warst du schon in einem Restaurant?	Es klingt [sehr gut/super/etc.]!
Wie gefällt dir das Essen?/Wie hat dir das	Ich habe die gleiche Erfahrung gemacht!
Essen gefallen?	Ich habe eine andere Erfahrung gemacht!
Was hast du am ersten/zweiten/dritten	Mir gefällt [Sehenswürdigkeit] [auch/
Tag gemacht?	nicht], weil ...
Hast du eine Stadtrundfahrt gemacht?	Also ...
Wie hat dir der Führer gefallen?	Ehrlich gesagt ...
Was für Sehenswürdigkeiten hast du	Meiner Meinung nach ...
besichtigt?	Du hast Recht!
Hast du dort eine Führung gemacht?	Wie schön!
Wie hast du die Führung gefunden?	Wirklich?
Welche Sehenswürdigkeit hat dir am	
besten gefallen?	
Was hältst du von [Sehenswürdigkeit]?	
Warst du schon in/bei	
[Sehenswürdigkeit]?	

3

REDESIGNING THE INTERMEDIATE LEVEL OF THE SPANISH CURRICULUM THROUGH A MULTILITERACIES LENS

Ana López-Sánchez

The 2007 MLA Report, or How to "Rewrite" Foreign Language Programs

In its, by now much discussed, 2007 report, "Foreign languages and higher education: New structures for a changed world," the Modern Language Association (MLA) Ad Hoc Committee on Foreign Languages called for the transformation of language departments, claiming that the actual "two-tiered configuration" of these programs—in which a two- or three-year language sequence feeds into a set of core courses primarily focused on canonical literature—"[had] outlived its usefulness" (2007, p. 2). In its call for reform, the committee also identified a sole *unified goal* for the language major: to produce "educated speakers who have *deep translingual and transcultural competence*" (p. 2; my emphasis).

A newly coined term, *translingual and transcultural competence*, served the committee to signal a departure from the traditional view of foreign language (FL) education, and to redefine language, language learning, and language use (Kramsch, 2010). The committee defined this competence as the "ability to operate between languages" (2007, pp. 3–4), understood as a "shuttling" from one language to another, in which values are circulated, identities negotiated, and meanings inverted or even invented (Kramsch, 2010; Zarate, Lévy, & Kramsch, 2008). To make such shuttling possible, language teachers "of course must continue to teach the structures of the symbolic system, and ensure that their students master those structures" (Kramsch, 2010, p. 18), but they also must go beyond structure. "[C]ritical language awareness, interpretation and translation, historical and political consciousness, social sensibility, and aesthetic perception" (MLA, 2007, p. 4) will also have to have a place in the curriculum. The foreign language education the committee is advocating is, in short, an education that "through the use of literature, film, and other media . . . challenge[s] students' imaginations and help[s] them consider alternative ways of seeing, feeling, and understanding things" (p. 4). To achieve this kind of education, the committee argues, departments need to put into place a unified curriculum where "a series of complementary or linked courses . . . holistically incorporate content and cross-cultural reflection at every level" (p. 5).

A discussion of what such curricula would look like was, however, not included in the report. On the one hand, this omission, justifiably, cost the committee much criticism (see, for example, Byrnes, Maxim & Norris, 2010; Levine, Melin, Crane, & Chavez, 2008), and remains a problem. Calls for a holistic curriculum, on the other hand, have existed for some time that also identify specific frameworks to create such curricula, and that provide specific proposals for the overhaul of departments. Many scholars, in fact, had addressed the *problem* of language departments and had come forth with specific proposals to overhaul the curriculum and create more cohesive programs. In particular, Byrnes, Weger-Guntharp, and Sprang (2006a), Kern (2000), and Swaffar and Arens (2005), in their book-length treatments of the topic, had quite explicitly stated that new constructs beyond those provided by communicative language teaching needed to be used to reimagine foreign language departments. They invoked one particular such construct, *literacy* (a qualified literacy): Swaffar and Arens (2005) and Byrnes et al. (2006a) talk about *multiple literacies*, while Kern (2000), following the New London Group (NLG), talks about *multiliteracies*. While these authors constructed their proposals around slightly different notions and frameworks, their proposals share a common premise and goal: the articulation of FL curricula through texts, reading, writing, and (critically) discussing these texts.

This chapter engages with the ongoing discussion in language departments, identifies a pedagogical framework to design the curriculum, and proposes curricula for a particular level of the language program. More specifically, the chapter first discusses the scenario typically found in Spanish courses at the intermediate level (courses that correspond to the third, fourth, or even fifth semester in the curricular program),[1] and the extent to which these courses are typically not aligned with the more critical and humanistic objectives identified by the MLA, as described above. It then proposes an alternative curriculum and pedagogy that can better prepare students to meet the objectives delineated by the MLA. The pedagogy proposed adheres to the notions advanced by (new) literacy advocates, and in particular to the multiliteracies framework of the NLG, as presented in the introductory chapter of the book and briefly reviewed in this chapter. The *model curriculum* presented identifies textual and multimodal genres, specific texts, and specific pedagogical practices that were used in a fourth-semester course, and are appropriate for all intermediate level students. Many (if not all) of the practices discussed, while particularly suited for students with this level of competence, can be implemented at other levels of the curriculum, and are appropriate to teach Spanish, as well as other languages.

Instruction at the Intermediate Level

The Current State of Affairs

Courses offered in Spanish departments and labeled "intermediate" are usually heavily enrolled courses,[2] mostly populated by first-year students who have prior experience learning the language. (A much lower percentage of students taking this language level have learnt their Spanish in an introductory college class.)

It is often the case that departments and instructors at this level choose to limit their role to the selection of a textbook. That means that course content and syllabus design are to a large extent determined by existing textbooks (that may or may not articulate well with other courses/levels). An examination of these textbooks, thus, offers us a good idea of both the content covered and the pedagogy used in the lower levels of Spanish language collegiate education.

Predictably, most textbooks marketed in the US for third- and fourth-semester Spanish courses subscribe to a communicative language approach, and as such favor activities for conversation.[3] Most books also market themselves as emphasizing all four skills and culture, and, accordingly, include sections devoted to listening, reading, writing, and to highlighting some cultural information.[4] These sections are, for the most part, made of texts composed in a simplified language for the book audience; put differently, authentic texts, with the exception of some literary pieces, are rarely found in these textbooks. Also, there is little expectation that the students engage with those *fabricated texts* language or content—the ideas, beliefs, or worldviews—critically. Overall, the range of exercises offered in relation to the texts is rather limited and, in most cases, the exercises fail to make students aware of the connections between grammar, discourse, and meaning, and to confront them with cultural patterns different from their own.

This tendency is exacerbated by content that emphasizes the students' immediate world, including family, university life, hobbies, relationships, travel, and food. The activities proposed in relation to these topics rarely encourage the students to question the transferability of their views on, and experiences of, a particular topic to the other culture(s), thus leading them "not to see the [other] culture as different but instead to see it as essentially the same as their own" (Schultz, 2004, p. 262). Swaffar and Arens (2005) sum it up well: "[W]hen presenting language that describes homes, eating practices, or shopping, virtually all textbooks offer language in isolated forms; excluded are all but minimal opportunities to access text" (p. 21) and, thus, context. Language, in other words, is not connected to sites and identities; it is not connected to Discourses, to use Gee's notion (2008 [1990])—that is, it is not seen as a practice that is embedded in other practices and specific contexts, and the opportunity to raise awareness about a country's stories and narratives is lost.

The Way Forward

It seems obvious from the above, that existing textbooks for the intermediate levels of the curriculum may not be creating the right foundations to prepare students to "shuttle" from one language to another. Neither the type of content nor the pedagogies just described are adequate to teach "differences in meaning, mentality and worldview,"[5] or to foster the critical language awareness, interpretation, and historical and political consciousness the MLA hopes will characterize FL programs. Important changes, both in the content and pedagogies currently used at these levels, are thus called for. As said in the introduction, this author argues that the framework that can bring about such changes is one that emphasizes texts, and reading and writing (in addition to talking) about those texts: a *multiliteracies-based framework*. This framework's most notable departure from the traditional (communicative-based) approach (which, as said, makes scarce use of texts, and especially of authentic ones) lies in the centrality it confers on texts: They are used throughout the entire curriculum—from the beginner to the advanced level, without exception. This decision is not without controversy.

Many have argued that learners with limited competence do not yet have sufficient knowledge of the language to have access to the more complex narratives and concepts, and that a focus on structure and the rudiments of the language should precede a focus on stories and texts. The decision to postpone engaging with texts to the more advanced levels is, however, erroneous and unjustified. As Swaffar, Arens, and Byrnes (1991), among others, have pointed out, the cognitive abilities of adult learners can take care of or help resolve the (linguistic) difficulties they experience: "[B]ecause of the cognitive maturity and the extra linguistic capabilities that adult learners bring with them from the first language (L1) to the foreign language classroom, thinking textually in the L2 language is not necessarily a cognitive challenge" (Maxim, 2006a, p. 21). Some have, indeed, reported success in implementing the kind of textual thinking and reading practiced at upper levels at the beginner level (see, for example, Maxim, 2006a). L2 literacy development, thus, can begin as early as the study of the language begins, and should certainly be the organizing principal at the intermediate level and beyond.

This is not to suggest, however, that a *text-centered curriculum* can be deployed full force without making some concessions: it is important to scaffold the students' transition from communicative language classes to this *new* pedagogy, by including discussions about the goals and expectations of their college language classes, and connecting them to their own. Also, to avoid too big a disconnect between secondary and post-secondary curricula that could "potentially [jar] students' expectations and motivation" (Levine et al., 2008, p. 248), the materials selected should at first be related to topics and genres the students will have found earlier.

That being said, waiting for the coupling of content, form, and critical thinking until a/the proverbial *bridge course* (where, as Byrnes et al. say, "FL language educators attempt to right what is wrong" (2010, p. 76)) is unnecessary.

Language departments can make (and should make) such coupling happen earlier: at the elementary level and, certainly, at the intermediate level, when most students enter the curriculum.

Additionally, articulating the entire curriculum around texts will help departments find the programmatic and structural coherence they are missing today, as well as a continuous focus on critical thinking that will position them squarely within the humanities, all the while attending to the truer goals of communicative language teaching (i.e., those that ring closer to the original understanding of the method), and to the students' perceptions and desires (e.g., to communicate with others).

In the next section, an outline of the theoretical framework that backs this and other text-based proposals currently being implemented across different languages (and of which there are several examples in this book) is presented, followed by a curriculum appropriate for these levels; the chapter ends with suggestions of pedagogical practices that work across languages.

Literacy, Multiliteracies, Genre-Based Pedagogies and the Foreign Language Curriculum

Literacy and its "sister" constructs (multiple literacies, multiliteracies, and advanced literacies), as used here and throughout this book, comprise more than the ability to read and write, in the sense of encoding and decoding words. The terms suggest that "reading" and "writing" may involve semiotic signs other than words, and that multiple abilities are involved in reading different types of texts and doing so in specific ways (Gee, 2008 [1990], p. 44). "Texts are instances of linguistically construed cultural situations that themselves are reflective of the entire cultural system" (Byrnes et al., 2010, p. 55). Reading texts "correctly" hinges on having access to the larger social practices in which the texts are immersed. A multiliteracies-based education aims to familiarize learners with meaning resources (the *Available Resources*, to use the NLG terminology (1996)) that they may not otherwise have access to; upon appropriating those resources, learners can participate in social practices that would otherwise be inaccessible to them.[6]

For L2 learners, who are learning a language in an instructional situation, access to those resources will come through the study of texts. "Becoming a competent FL user is about acquiring a rich set of resources best expressed in terms of facility with diverse textual repertoires in all modalities" (Byrnes et al., 2010, p. 55). To achieve that goal, I am advocating here the use of a pedagogy based on the proposals of the NLG (a pedagogy of multiliteracies), in conjunction with (the more foreign language-specific) genre-based approaches, and particularly the approach put forward by the Georgetown University German Department (GUGD).

The NLG proposed, in 1996, a pedagogy with four major dimensions that were originally called *Situated Practice, Overt Instruction, Critical Framing*, and *Transformed Practice*. The group later renamed and somewhat reframed these categories into the more recognizable knowledge processes identified in theories such as Bloom's and Kolb's (Cope & Kalantzis, 2009; Kalantzis & Cope 2005). The pedagogy, then, can be thought of as an integration of four types of knowing: *Experiencing, Conceptualizing, Analyzing*, and *Applying*. I explore these processes and how they may translate in the curricula of language departments in detail, in the pedagogical section of the chapter. It is important to note at this point, however, that there is no particular order to the integration of the processes, and that not all learning activities need to integrate all four processes (Kalantzis & Cope, 2005, p. 72). FL curriculum developers should be careful to emphasize all four processes or forms of knowledge throughout the entire program: learners in the lower levels (beginner and certainly at the intermediate levels on which we are focusing), need to be involved in Analyzing and Applying activities, and not only in Experiencing and Conceptualizing ones; and the reverse is true of learners at the advanced level.

The multiliteracies pedagogy was primarily conceived for first language education, and while it provides an adequate framework for any teaching/learning endeavors, it needs to be further delineated for the foreign languages. As described in our introduction, an increasing number of FL practitioners have attempted to do just that (Kern, 2000, in particular, but also others following him—Allen, 2009; Allen & Paesani, 2010). One group of FL scholars, who did not adopt the NLG model, but who share its understanding of language, sought to develop a pedagogical model that would address programmatic considerations. These scholars adopted a *genre-based* pedagogy, a pedagogy that has focused on relating the linguistic choices made by writers to the social role of the text. The most salient and publicized case of this model in the FL is that of the GUGD, which has reformulated its entire curriculum in accordance with the framework. (But see also other examples, such as Kumagai and Iwasaki, Chapter 5, this volume.) Adoption of the model hinges on the fact that genres "as socially and culturally embedded text types are ideally suited for modeling and exploring how language functions in a specific situation to convey meaning" (Byrnes et al., 2010, p. 83). Genres, members of the GUGD argue, "exemplify in clear and identifiable ways the connections among social context, language, and content" that FL educators strive to make, and are thus "'particularly efficacious' as a sequencing and unifying principle" (p. 83).

The literature produced by the GUGD (e.g., Byrnes, Crane, Maxim, & Sprang, 2006b; Byrnes et al., 2010; Crane, 2006) was critical to the design of the course described in this chapter, in particular in what concerned the identification of some of the genres appropriate for the intermediate level. While not strictly following a genre-based pedagogy that structures learning around the phases of modeling, joint negotiation, and context of production (Maxim, 2009, p. 177), the teaching/learning model proposed here (based on the NLG pedagogical components) does not differ much from that of the GUGD. In what is left of the chapter, I flesh out the details of the course design.

A Pedagogical Proposal for an Enriched, Transformative Classroom

This chapter, as said earlier, identifies texts appropriate for use in a fourth-semester[7] Spanish course, and pedagogical practices to work with those texts or similar ones. These materials and practices were designed for, and are used in, a course taught in a selective college in the mid-Atlantic area. The materials and activities selected aim to further develop students' knowledge about the social, historical, and political realities of the Spanish-speaking world.[8] More precisely, they seek to educate learners about the regional, national, and transnational narratives that are found in Spain and Latin America, through, among other genres, short stories, poems, advertisements, songs, and movies.

The Content of the Course

Making decisions about the contents to include in a course with the above described goals is no easy task. Needless to say, the sheer number of territories and sociocultural realities a Spanish department aims to explore poses an enormous challenge in any selection process. One key criterion that can help shape the selection and sequencing of materials is the degree of (un)familiarity of the students with topics and places/spaces. Because (un)familiarity affects comprehensibility and motivation, countries and regions that are geographically close to the US, or that have clear historical and present connections to the US, can be presented earlier,[9] as are more familiar topics such as relationships, school, migration, and music; narratives related to country-specific events can come after. In other words, rather than confronting first what is most new to them, students initially work with what they relate to more easily; gradually, however, they are introduced to more challenging (unfamiliar) material, and asked to question their ideas and stereotypes of the territories/spaces they are learning about.

The specific sequence adopted in the course is as follows: The course first focuses on Spain, to then focus on Mexico, before it moves to Central America and Cuba (and more broadly the Caribbean), conforming four units. All four units lend themselves to the exploration of different types of relationships (such as romantic, friendship, family, and communal identities). On the one hand, the familiar ring of the (relationship) topic ensures learners do not feel alienated by the material; the exploration of the unfamiliar contexts within which those relationships unfold, on the other hand, move learners beyond the realm of their personal lives and engage them in the narratives of the target cultures. The newer or less familiar country/region-specific (social, political and/or economic) issues presented include the drug cartels and related culture in Mexico, the art scene (and especially the music scene) in Cuba, migration, and national conflicts—civil war in Spain and Guatemala, revolutions in Mexico, Cuba, and Nicaragua—that have contributed to shaping those countries' or regions' histories greatly, and whose impact is still strongly felt today.

Once the general content areas have been identified, one needs to find level-appropriate genres, and good representative texts of those genres. To develop in the students (a competency in) different literacies, it is also critical to include a wide variety of genres and texts (written ("alphabetical") as well as visual and multimodal texts).

The selection and sequencing of the different texts was done in accordance with their genre, and, as said earlier, are generally inspired by the proposals of the GUGD model. Given the students' abilities at this level, attention to *primary discourses* (Gee, 2008 [1990]—characterized by more personal and informal communication and including casual conversations and personal narratives—is still critical. Students, however, are ready to work with discourses that stand in the middle of the continuum of primary to secondary discourses, or *"blurred" discourses* (Byrnes et al., 2006b), including literary works and songs, as well as with certain *secondary discourses* (Gee, 2008 [1990])—the discourses of public life—such as newspaper articles, brochures, and movie reviews. In each unit, genres are sequenced from the more personal and intimate, to the more artistic, to end with the more public discourses.

The inclusion of literary texts (which, as said above, are considered blurred discourses) is critical to the course make-up for several reasons. A major consideration at this level is to challenge learners' schemas, which in turn play a role in the stereotypes they hold. Literary texts are texts that, as Cook (1994, cited in Wallace, 2003, p. 22) points out, have a "schema breaking function" and should therefore be emphasized.

Poetry in particular features in the program to highlight the playful and creative side of language. As Maxim says "students need to see the foreign language as an object of play rather than as some monolithic entity that they are fated to never master" (2006b, p. 252). Activities that involve writing creatively (such as writing poems) should be emphasized often, to impress upon the students the notion that they can express themselves without feeling that their use of the language is deficient. These activities also help learners to see themselves as not just consumers of (literary) products, but as designers, capable of creating their own meaning in the L2.

The emphasis on literary texts, however, should not be read as a preference for literary discourses over other types of text; other discourses also feature prominently in the program. Secondary discourses are, as mentioned earlier, included: Specifically, the learners get exposed to and work with newspaper articles, film reviews, and expository texts (this will be discussed in more detail below).

Additionally, multimodal and visual materials are well represented in this intermediate curriculum. As argued by Cope and Kalantzis, the growing presence of visual and mixed modes in our society, and the "mix of parallelism and incommensurability" (i.e., "one mode cannot be directly and completely translated into another") between these modalities make addressing multimodality integral to the pedagogy of multiliteracies (2009, p. 180). The use of the visual and mixed modes in the course speaks to this concern. But the use of visual texts serves other purposes as well: (1) Movies and a TV series (a *telenovela*) are a source for the primary discourses[10] utilized in the class—dialogues extracted from them serve to study the (socially situated) oral language as occurring between known participants; (2) the movies and the *telenovela* facilitate the reading process: Some of the narratives in the courses (short stories and excerpts from novels) were explicitly selected because there was a film adaptation of them, and because the visual representation could serve, on occasion, to navigate the written text or compensate for some of the difficulties in interpretation.[11]

Table 3.1 shows the sequence followed in the course, a sequence that captures and responds to the criteria identified earlier. The program presented here is, of course, one of many possible iterations for this level, and one which, indeed, leaves out extensive areas of Spanish America, and leaves many possible critical topics unexplored. The course following this in the intermediate sequence could focus on South American nations/regions (Southern Cone, Andean region) and include some of the same genres, but also more secondary discourses such as argumentative essays. A well-articulated curriculum will build on expanding the focus of the intermediate level courses, with a growing emphasis on more secondary discourses and blurred discourse.

The Pedagogical Practices

As I have been saying, a text-based curriculum, taught with a multiliteracies-oriented pedagogy, aims to expose learners to a larger number of Available Resources with the goal of preparing them to eventually use those resources in the production of new texts; through their ability to (re)produce the language resources, in turn, learners gain agency in the target language community. Pedagogies that integrate all four of the NLG's components in their approach to study texts can deliver those goals.

As said earlier, the pedagogical components identified by the NLG in 1996, and called Situated Practice, Overt Instruction, Critical Framing, and Transformed Practice, were later reframed as the "knowledge processes" of Experiencing, Conceptualizing, Analyzing, and Applying (Cope & Kalantzis, 2009, p. 184). The group also characterized the process of "moving backwards and forwards across and between these different pedagogical moves as *weaving*" (p. 184). The processes do not have to follow any particular order; they are, to use Kalantzis and Cope's metaphor, like "movements" in a musical composition: active and explicit moves,

TABLE 3.1 Content/Genre Model for a Fourth-Semester Spanish Course

	Genres / Text types	Sample Material
Weeks 1–3	Focus on Spain PD: Casual conversation BD: Short story (excerpts) SD: Newspaper articles, movie review MM: Tourist campaigns, posters	Selections from short story "La lengua de las mariposas" (M. Rivas); movie *La lengua de las mariposas*; movie reviews (several movies); advertisements: Catalunya promotional campaign; Barcelona; civil war posters; songs
Weeks 4–6	Focus on Mexico PD: Casual conversation, interviews, oral narratives BD: Songs, excerpts from novels SD: Newspaper articles, reviews TV drama MM (visual): Murals	TV drama (telenovela) *La reina del Sur*; selections from novel *La reina del Sur* (Pérez Reverte) Songs: "La reina del Sur", "México insurgente" (I. Serrano), "Justicia, tierra y libertad" (Maná); murals: "Tarde de domingo en la Alameda"
Weeks 6–8	Focus on Central America PD: Interview BD: Poems, songs SD: Testimonio MM: Maps, paintings	Poems: "Tamalitos de Chambray" (C. Alegría) Paintings: "Las castas". Songs: "Los desaparecidos" Testimonio: "Me llamo Rigoberta Menchú y así me nació la conciencia"
Weeks 9–13	Focus on Cuba (& Caribbean region) PD: Casual conversation BD: Poems, excerpts from short stories SD: Newspaper articles; movie review MM (visual): Movies	Movies: *Habana blues* Selections from readings: "Viaje a la Habana" (R. Arenas), "El bosque, el lobo y el hombre bueno" News articles: "Amor sin papeles" Movie reviews of *Habana blues* and *Fresa y chocolate*

Note: PD = primary discourses, BD = blurred discourses, SD = secondary discourses, and MM = multimodal text.

leading into one another, each with an internal dynamic, and each begging the other's perspective (Kalantzis & Cope, 2005, p. 74). The movements (processes) can be short or long, and "a particular pedagogical cycle may go through any number of knowledge processes or movements, and any number and varieties of transition from one movement to another whilst nevertheless sticking to the same theme" (p. 74). That being said, it is generally the case that Applying comes after one or more of the other three processes have taken place.

Below, I discuss in detail the four knowledge systems as they apply to the language classroom, and the specific focus they should have at the intermediate

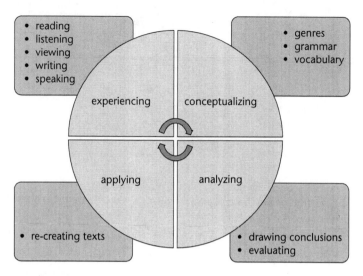

FIGURE 3.1 The pedagogical cycle.

level of the curriculum. I also discuss sample activities that trigger these processes. Figure 3.1 captures the cyclical characteristics of the pedagogy, and introduces the activities that are discussed below.

Experiencing, or Gaining Access to and Using the Resources

Experiencing refers to the kind of knowing that occurs "through immersion in the real, everyday stuff of the world" (Kalantzis & Cope, 2005, p. 75). In the typical intermediate language classroom, Experiencing most often involves communicating in the language and, to a much lesser extent, reading, viewing, or listening to texts, and reacting to them. By contrast, in the multiliteracies-based class, while there are ample opportunities for speaking, learners *experience the language* much more by reading, viewing, listening to, and writing texts. This immersion[12] in a multitude of designs is key to developing *transcultural* and *translingual* competence, and overcoming the limitations of old curricula. As discussed earlier, the materials chosen for the course include both oral-written and multimodal genres, ranging from casual conversations to the movie review, and include different types of narratives. Some of the texts used (narratives and the movie review) are deconstructed and used as models that the learners are expected to replicate, while others (such as news articles and songs) are included mostly for their content, but they are not expected to be re-created.

When experiencing, one draws from "the known"—prior knowledge and familiar experiences—while confronting unfamiliar and new information and situations ("the new") (Kalantzis & Cope, 2005, p. 76). When immersed in the texts, learners experience both known linguistic (e.g., vocabulary, grammar) and structural resources (e.g., the genres, the stories) and known experiences, and new ones. Incidentally,[13] through the weaving of the two, they begin to access "new domains of action and meaning" (Cope & Kalantzis, 2009, p. 185).

Below, I look at how this process unfolds in two different types of activities.

Reading/Viewing/Listening Activities

As said above, a multiliteracies-based approach differs from a more traditional approach not only in the weight it assigns to the reading, viewing, and listening to of texts, but also in the pedagogical practices deployed around these processes, and their sequencing (Kern, 2000; López-Sánchez, 2014). One stark difference lies in the fact that, in a multiliteracies approach, rather than assigning a new text as homework (i.e., as reading/viewing to be done individually, outside of the classroom), some part of that reading/viewing is done *in* the classroom and in a collaborative manner, with the instructor guiding the learners through the meaning-making process. This ordering is justified by the difficulty that students with limited resources have to access meaning and to recognize certain textual phenomena; as Kerns rightly suggests, "simply handing [them] a text will not be enough" (2000, p. 131). (Pre-reading activities, such as a group discussion, or a writing task—see, for example, the free-form writing task discussed in the following section—that activate the pertinent schemas and orient students to the topics, themes, and even genres they are about to confront, should, of course, also be provided.)

The reading/viewing can be conducted as a *directed reading-thinking activity* (DRTA), where the instructor selects stopping points in the text and ask students to predict what will happen next, and to justify their prediction, engaging them in a cyclical process of predicting, reading, and thinking (Kern, 2000, p. 135). For example, before assigning students the short story "La lengua de las mariposas" ("Butterfly" in English)—the story explores the relationship between a teacher and his young student in the times leading to the Spanish Civil War—the instructor reads the opening lines (or has students watch the corresponding scenes in the movie):

> *Cuando yo era un niñito, la escuela era una amenaza terrible. Una palabra que se blandía en el aire como una vara de mimbre . . . [S]oñaba con ir a América sólo por no ir a la escuela . . . [H]abía historias de niños que huían al monte para evitar aquel suplicio . . . La noche de la víspera no dormí.*

> [When I was a little kid, school was a huge threat . . . A word that was brandished in the air just like a wicker cane. There were stories of kids who escaped to the mountains to avoid such torture . . . The night before I didn't sleep.]

He/she then stops to ask learners to predict what happens in the following paragraphs/scenes and to explain what their answers are based on.

The activity trains learners to activate their schemas ("the known") to predict what may be taking place in the story. The schemas can help them fill in the gaps in instances where they do not have access to the vocabulary or other meaning resources ("the new") in the text. More importantly, DRTA (which could perhaps more appropriately be called *directed experiencing-thinking activity*) makes learners more aware of those schemas, their beliefs systems, and the structuring of knowledge around them, and, eventually, of the fact that those schemas do not translate over into other languages and cultures. With further reflecting and analysis (*analyzing*, as explained below), the *new* meanings will be appropriated and will create new horizons of expression for the learner.

Free-Form Writing Activities

Writing, just like reading and viewing, is strongly emphasized in the multiliteracies approach; it is not only expected at the end of a unit, but throughout, including, as mentioned above, before any reading/viewing or discussing has taken place. The increased presence of writing in the curriculum is justified, because, as proponents of the foreign language literacy model posit, writing, as the recursive task that it is, "might be better able to raise learners' awareness ... of the link between meaning and form that has been possible in orally focused communicative language teaching" (Byrnes et al., 2010, p. 55).

In the initial stages of a unit, learners are asked to write short paragraphs, responding to or reflecting about a theme or experience that appears in the text. (Unlike later in the unit, they are not provided with a *model text* to follow in these tasks—and it is in that sense that they are *free-form* writing.) One of these tasks' goals is to get learners to reflect on "the known"—"[their] own experiences, interests, perspectives, familiar forms of expression and ways of representing the world in [their] own understanding" (Cope & Kalantzis, 2009, p. 185), before they confront the unfamiliar experiences and resources (the "new"); that is, the learners' previous knowledge—including knowledge about the genres that the tasks elicit (descriptions, recounts, reactions)—is activated to prepare them to incorporate new knowledge. For example, before reading the story "La lengua de las mariposas," or viewing the movie based on it, students were asked to reflect (in writing) on their relationship with one of their teachers or mentors, and with learning and school. Immediately after reading a short excerpt of the story (or seeing the corresponding scene in the movie) where the main character remembers his first school day, they were asked to write about their own school memories.

The tasks, then, are opportunities for the learners to communicate in the language (i.e., to be immersed in it), without reflecting on the language or the resources they need. This reflection, however, can take place later thanks to the materiality of writing. As Byrnes et al. (2010) point out: "[T]he materiality of the finished product readily allows for repeatedly and differentially focused forms of reflection and analysis after the composing process has been concluded" (p. 55). The texts produced by the students (and their thinking about the topic at this stage) become traceable, observable objects, themselves subjected to analysis, and tools for further learning. Indeed, the primary reason to assign these short, *free-form texts* is that they can serve, among other possibilities, as the basis for: (1) learners and instructors to observe the forms (linguistics resources) used by the learners, and how appropriately (or not) these forms convey the meanings the learners were aiming for; (2) learners to critically analyze their worldviews and compare them with those presented in the texts; and (3) learners to produce new texts *applying* new knowledge (for example, by rewriting the texts or in a short oral presentation— see more below). In short, the short writing activities lend themselves to weaving the different types of knowledge processes and to powerful learning.

Conceptualizing, or Understanding the Design

Conceptualizing is the kind of process that leads to conscious control and aware-ness of what is being learnt through the development of abstract, generalizing concepts[14] via theory or a metalanguage ("by naming") (Cope & Kalantzis, 2009; Kalantzis & Cope, 2005; NLG, 2000). It is facilitated by the use of "ideal tools" (Vygotsky, 1987), such as graphic representations, mind maps, and sche-mas, and the interaction with the teacher and other experts. Drills, rote memorization, or direct transmission, however, have no effect on the process (NLG, 2000, p. 33).

Unlike in the more traditional classroom, where grammatical and other lin-guistic resources are the focus (and organizing principle) of instruction,[15] in the approach advocated here, genres are the primary focus of the Conceptualizing processes that take place in the class. A set of *core genres* is selected, in turn, defines which grammatical and lexigrammatical resources will be targeted. That is, in developing conscious control of the core genres, learners also develop control of the linguistic resources associated with those genres.

Below, I describe the practices (and the theory behind those practices) that, I argue, lead to the control of targeted resources, and that are commensurate with the principles of the NLG. At the intermediate level, because control of the resources is still rather limited, these practices occupy a large chunk of classroom time.

Conceptualizing Genres

As said earlier, *genres* are how things get done through language, and where the cultural system and the lexicogrammatical resources intersect, and thus need to be the focus of explicit instruction. To conceptualize any given genre, learners need to understand its goal (i.e., its connection to a situation) and its components (i.e., the moves and resources that define it). This is achieved through what in genre-based curricular models (such as the one based on Rothery's cycle (1996) and used by the GUGD) is called "*modeling*": In its first phase, modeling "is characterized by the presentation of the textual genre, and a discussion of its purpose, social function and context of production" (Maxim, 2009, p. 177). In a second phase of modeling, learners analyze "how the genre is structured into stages and how the genre's purpose is realized linguistically at each stage" (p. 177).[16] Instructors scaffold the analysis through questions such as: "What kind of text is this?" and "What leads you to believe so? (i.e., what specific features have you identified that have led you to believe this is a (the-type-of-text-identified))?," and "How is the (multimodal/visual/written) text structured?" The types of processes and activities involved here clearly straddle Conceptualizing and Analyzing (as explained below), attesting to the usual interconnectedness and weaving of the multiliteracies framework pedagogical processes.

The genres modeled in the course (the *core* genres) include several types of stories (including the personal recount and narratives), historical genres (including the autobiography, in its form of *testimonio*, and the historical recount), and movie reviews. (Learners are exposed to other genres—for example, news— but those genres are not modeled and no independent production of those genres is expected.) The genres modeled first (narratives including *testimonios*) emphasize concrete and highly situated activities, which are conceptualized in terms of actors and actions and expressed through what Halliday (1985 [1994]) calls "congruent" semiosis. The course later begins to familiarize learners with the genres typical of the public sphere, including the historical recount and the movie review. These genres, which are often realized through nominalizations, construe "human experience as objectified knowledge" (Maxim, 2009, p. 174). All of the genres-in-focus rely to different extents on chronological ordering, accomplished through the temporal system, and include an evaluation move, accomplished through the mood system; the temporal and mood systems, thus, become the main focus of the "grammatical" conceptualization as described below. (Appendix A contains the worksheet students receive to analyze movie reviews.)

Conceptualizing Grammatical Resources

Grammar teaching has been one of the hottest topics in SLA/SLL (second language acquisition/learning) and a great source of controversy. A discussion of the controversy it has generated is beyond the scope of this article, but suffice to say, the question of "whether" grammar should be taught has been tentatively settled, but the "how to" of grammar teaching is still open to debate. (For a detailed discussion see, for example, Dekeyser, 2007; Norris & Ortega, 2000). The pedagogical options are, certainly, many; but not all are compatible with the principles of multiliteracies: A pedagogical approach to grammar teaching that makes sense for a multiliteracies approach must draw on concepts.

To be sure, this emphasis on concepts can be found in SLA among those working within the sociocultural paradigm (SCT-L2 to use Lantolf's term

(2011)). Following Vygotsky, SCT-L2 scholars purport that learners cannot gain full access to the representation of reality being constructed through the (second/foreign) language unless they have access to the categories or constructs (concepts) of that language (Lantolf & Poehner, 2014; Lantolf & Thorne, 2006). Furthermore, Negueruela (2003, 2008a, 2008b) most notably, but also Yáñez-Prieto (2008) and Lai (2012) among others, have adapted concept-based instruction (CBI), a pedagogical model for teaching/learning concepts developed by one of Vygosky's students, Gal'perin[17] (1989), for L2 instruction and specially for the instruction of grammatical concepts.[18] According to Negueruela (2008a), developing control over the concepts requires following a four-phase process. The first phase, *explanation* (or conceptualization), is the formulation of the concept. This involves identifying the "category of meaning that underlies the use of [the] specific grammatical feature" (p. 160). For example, the semantic basis of the preterite/imperfect distinction is "aspectual meaning" (p. 160). This phase is followed by a *materialization* phase, where tools such as graphic representations and schemas (or SCOBAs[19]) are presented to the learners to help them think *through* concepts (rather than *about* the concepts) (p. 160)—needless to say, the typical rules of thumb found in textbooks do not create such processes. The materialization process is then followed by *verbalization*, where learners are given tasks where they need to explain their use of the concept (using the tools or learning aids provided to them earlier). One final step is the *articulation* or "creation of webs of meanings," where different types of conceptualization are connected (pp. 165–166).

As is clear, CBI is in line with the NLG's notion of Conceptualizing and, thus, I argue for its adoption for conceptualizing the L2 grammar in multiliteracies-based frameworks. Undeniably, CBI's expectation that learners have access to sophisticated knowledge of the L2 from the start poses great challenges, the first of which might be providing learners with the right materialization (or tools or SCOBAs) for understanding the concepts. However, and while the development of these tools is in its infancy and much material-development needs to take place before the curriculum can be organized around concepts, SCOBAs for teaching/learning the central grammatical concepts of the intermediate level are readily available for use in the classroom. For reasons of space, these SCOBAs cannot be reproduced here; but the reader can refer to Negueruela and Lantolf (2006) and Yáñez-Prieto (2008)[20] for SCOBAs for teaching aspect, and to Negueruela (2008b) to teach mood.

Conceptualizing the Lexicon

Vocabulary, like grammar, has traditionally received a lot of attention, and much has been said about the best learning/teaching practices. Space precludes a discussion of the literature here. What is important to note, though, is that vocabulary learning has been typically associated with lists and the memorization of a definition, both of which suggest one-to-one correspondence between a word in the L1 and the L2. Vocabulary, instead, should be associated with networks of meaning and multidimensional knowledge. Learners need to learn basic word meanings, but as Kern (2000) suggests:

> they must also learn how those basic meanings are contingent on actual use. They must develop a sense of how words can be put together appropriately, how context may affect their connotational auras, how they may be used metaphorically, and so on. (p. 76)

To help learners conceptualize words in this way (i.e., as systems and relationships), learners in the course are asked to build semantic maps. Prior to reading and working in groups, learners draw their own maps for the topics associated with the readings (and that are provided by the instructor); for example, before they read the text from "La lengua de las mariposas" mentioned earlier, learners are asked to think about school (including personal experiences and the educational model) and create their maps. After the reading, learners check the maps they produced against the text; that is, learners go back to the text they had read to identify words that can be part of the school schema and that they had not included in their maps, and add those new words to the maps. At this point, one of the groups' map is shared with the rest of the class,[21] built upon with everyone's collaboration, and supplemented by the instructor if necessary. This activity helps learners focus on words and expressions they may not know and on their association with specific contexts and genres. Additionally, by weaving it in with a critical thinking activity (analyzing), the task creates awareness of the fact that semantic fields might not coincide cross-culturally, and ultimately helps to generate culturally appropriate schemas.[22]

Analyzing, or Framing Critically

This type of process is about engaging and developing the learners' critical capacity (Cope & Kalantzis, 2009, p. 185). This takes place when *analyzing functionally* (p. 186), that is, when learners are asked to reason and draw conclusions about, for example, specific lexicogrammatical elements and their meaning and use in context, as described above, in the conceptualization of genres; or about the cultural specificity of schemas as made evident in a discussion about the differences and coincidences between what the learners predict in their semantic maps and what they actually find in the texts. It also occurs when *analyzing critically*, that is, when evaluating "one's own and other people perspectives, interests and motives" (p. 186). This may involve the instructor leading the class in an examination of the writers' choices in the text, to move the learners beyond the text and into an understanding of the values or ideologies the writer might be promoting, and ultimately into examining their own experiences and views. For example, issues about representation (e.g., "Which social actors are included in the text?" "Which are excluded?" "What kind of actions are these actors doing?") can be brought up, as can specific words or structures chosen by the author and critical to the text's meaning (e.g., "What are the effects of the writer using ___?" "Why is the text structured the way it is?"). The answers to some of these questions may elude learners at this level. Posing such questions is, nonetheless, necessary for students to learn how to interrogate texts, and to begin to develop critical language awareness. The integration of this type of process from the beginning of the curriculum is what will render the ultimate goal of *transcultural and translingual competence* more likely.

Applying, or Re-Creating the Designs

Applying involves learning through the application of experiential, conceptual, or critical knowledge, and making an intervention in the world (Kalantzis & Cope 2005, p. 78), in a predictable way (applying appropriately) or in an innovative and creative way (applying creatively). In the L2 classroom, applying takes place when, in a writing or speaking task, learners construct or "design" something new and unique to them, using the *Available Designs* on which they have been focusing. Here, we will explore only the writing tasks assigned to students, as they are the major way of evaluating them.

(Re-)Creating the Model Texts

One main (longer) task was assigned at the end of each unit, with other several (shorter) writing tasks also completed throughout the semester (this, in addition to the "free-form writing tasks" described earlier). The longer tasks focused on the (re)production of the core genres that were chosen to be modeled throughout the semester. As mentioned earlier (see the "Conceptualizing genres" subsection, above), the genres modeled in the course were personal narratives, the movie review, and the historical recount. These tasks—which served as the main assessment measures in the course—required control of narrativity, as well as evaluative statements, linguistic features that are appropriate for this level of the curriculum. The tasks are, in a way, rewriting tasks, where students show their awareness and knowledge of the generic conventions and the lexicogrammar that were the focus of the Experiencing, Conceptualizing, and Analyzing activities described above. Learners, however, are not being asked to merely regurgitate the resources encountered earlier and learnt. They have experienced how other voices have constructed certain events, but they now need to decide where they stand vis-à-vis those voices, and create their own unique meaning, picking from the Available Resources they now know.

The same is true of the shorter tasks designed for the course. These tasks— some assigned to be done collaboratively—typically involved re-creating the model text by, for example, modifying the starting point of the narration, or changing its point of view; a few tasks involved redesigning the text as a different (multimodal) genre. Students, for example, transformed the oral narratives of migrant children in Mexico into blogs (where they used images and written text).

Both types of Applying activities used in class, thus, seek to create awareness from the inside and to get the learners to think with new eyes. It is in these writing tasks that they have a chance to appropriate the words, and other meaning-making resources that previously they were only imitating. The tasks, in other words, allow the learners to become the "authors of their own words" (Kramsch, 1993, p. 27), and to find a voice that is "predictable enough to be generally comprehended, but unique enough to be listened to and understood" (p. 24).

Conclusion

The course presented here seeks to provide opportunities to develop critical language awareness, historical and political consciousness, social sensibility, and aesthetic perception—the desirable outcomes identified by the MLA, and well-suited goals for higher education. Through a curriculum that is text-based, and a pedagogy inspired in genre-based approaches, the course provides a window into the regional, national, and transnational narratives of the countries/regions in which the texts are situated, and invites learners to become participants in these narratives, by engaging them in a variety of meaning-making tasks.

Designing a multiliteracies-based course for any level involves the following steps: (1) identifying a few *core genres* on which the class will focus; at the intermediate level, the core genres should emphasize narrativity, and should be primarily personal narratives, but other texts that involve secondary discourses should also be presented; (2) identifying appropriate texts in the core genres that can serve as *model texts*; (3) identifying a few additional texts (beyond the core genres texts): written, visual, and multimodal texts that are appropriate for the learners' level and that help to explore the topics selected further; these texts (e.g., songs, advertising campaigns, movies) are the basis of additional *Experiencing* and *Analyzing* activities; (4) creating appropriate teaching materials that ensure adequate conceptualization of the core meaning-making resources (genres, grammar, and lexicogrammar); (5) creating learning opportunities that activate the critical thinking of the learners; and (6) designing learning units that ensure an overall balance of the four knowledge processes (i.e., there should be an emphasis on all components of the multiliteracies pedagogy, regardless of the level of the curriculum). Adopting a similarly inspired multiliteracies pedagogy—that combines experiential, conceptual, and critical analytical learning—across the curriculum of an entire departmental program will prepare learners to "operate between languages."

Notes

1 The level in these courses can range from the intermediate-high through the mid-advanced level in the ACTFL scale.

2 Existing statistical analysis (MLA, 2009; NCAS, 2012) distinguishes only between course enrollments at the "introductory" (first two years, which comprise beginning and intermediate courses) and "advanced" (last two years) levels. My comments here are based on discussions with colleagues from various institutions.

3 These, however, coexist with rote activities (substitution and fill in the blanks exercises) that are not true to the communicative model.

4 As Dorwick and Glass (2003) discuss, most textbooks are made up of an almost identical (relatively) small set of sections.

5 While certain textbooks have specific strengths, one would be hard-pressed to find one that fully addresses and works toward the goals identified by the MLA.

6 Enabling and empowering students to be full participants in these new social practices is a distinctive objective of the multiliteracies agenda in order to be emancipatory and contribute to "paths of improvement" (Cope & Kalantzis, 2009, p. 184)

7 This may vary somewhat across different institutions. It could work as a fifth-semester course at some places.

8 It is expected, as said earlier, that most students entering college have some basic knowledge about the realities of Spanish-speaking countries. The assumption here, made based on many years of experience, however, is that their knowledge is mostly limited to certain colorful, folkloric, traditional cultural practices—such as Día de los Muertos, and popular fiestas, tango, and flamenco—and that prior experience with the language most likely does not include reading and discussing texts.

9 There is one exception to this, and that is Spain, which, while not geographically close to the US, comes at the beginning of the course. The decision to present Spain first is based on the fact that Latin-American countries cannot be understood without understanding their history of colonialism and relationship to Spain.

10 As Byrnes et al. (2010) point out with regard to a TV drama, movies are not primary discourses, yet the "depicted context is ... construed through the primary discourse" (p. 87).

11 Needless to say, this is not always the case, as films often depart from their written source. Yet, there are instances where the film is faithful to the written story.

12 Learning happening through immersion here is somewhat akin to what mainstream SLA would describe in terms of access to input and more unconscious learning.

13 The learning occurring through immersion is more incidental and of a more unconscious nature than the types of learning occurring in the other processes (Kalantzis & Cope, 2005, p. 76).

14 Concepts here are to be understood in the Vygotskian sense, that is, as culturally organized artifacts that play a central role in regulating mental activity (Lantolf & Thorne, 2006, p. 108).

15 Some textbooks have begun to discuss genres. Typically, as a preface to the writing tasks that they propose, the textbook presents some information on a few generic conventions (e.g., of narratives), also highlighting some of the lexicogrammar associated with those genres (e.g., sequencing vocabulary). Although this is a step in the right direction—these sections do point out the connections between text, context, and grammar—genres need to define what gets conceptualized in terms of the lexicogrammar, and not the other way around; and they also need to be better conceptualized than they presently are (i.e., more information about their situatedness and stagedness should be provided).

16 Specifically, what is being described here corresponds to the *Negotiating Field* and *Deconstruction* phases of the Rothery model (1996). For a detailed discussion of these phases, and examples of this part of the GUGD teaching cycle, see Warren and Winkler (Chapter 2, this book) and Byrnes et al. (2010).

17 Gal'perin's model, also known as systemic theoretical instruction (STI), develops Vygotsky's ideas for a theory of developmental psychology, and expands upon them.
18 A simpler concept-based pedagogy than Gal'perin's, derived from Davydov's MAC (or movement from the abstract to the concrete), has also been developed by Ferreira (2005) to study L2 genres (Ferreira & Lantolf, 2008).
19 Gal'perin called the visualization of a concept a "scheme for a complete orienting basis of an action" (or SCOBA).
20 Yáñez-Prieto's SCOBA for aspect relies on images (rather than on the verbal flowchart developed by Negueruela), and draws on the work of cognitive linguists (Lantolf & Poehner, 2014, p. 121).
21 The groups can work on computers or iPads and, once they are done, their maps can be shared on the classroom's screen. The final map, collaboratively constructed by the class with the instructor, is later saved to the class's course management system for study purposes.
22 Learners also work with new vocabulary individually, outside of class. They each create a glossary on the course site, to which other students have access.

References

Allen, H.W. (2009). A literacy-based approach to the advanced French writing course. *The French Review, 83*, 368–385.

Allen, H.W., & Paesani, K. (2010). Exploring the feasibility of a pedagogy of multiliteracies in introductory foreign language courses. *L2 Journal, 2*, 119–142.

Byrnes, H., Crane, C., Maxim, H.H., & Sprang, K.A. (2006b). Taking text to task: Issues and choices in curriculum construction. *International Journal of Applied Linguistics, 15*, 85–110.

Byrnes, H., Maxim, H.H., & Norris, J. (Eds.). (2010). Realizing advanced foreign language writing development in collegiate education: Curricular design, pedagogy, assessment. *Modern Language Journal, 94* (Monograph series, Issue Supplement s1), 1–225.

Byrnes, H., Weger-Guntharp, H., & Sprang, K.A. (Eds.). (2006a). *Educating for advanced foreign language capacities: Constructs, curriculum, instruction, assessment.* Washington, DC: Georgetown University Press.

Cope, B., & Kalantzis, M. (2009). "Multiliteracies": New literacies, new learning. *Pedagogies: An International Journal, 4*(3), 164–195.

Crane, C. (2006). Modelling a genre-based foreign language curriculum: Staging advanced L2 learning. In H. Byrnes (Ed.), *Advanced language learning: The contributions of Halliday and Vygotsky* (pp. 227–245). New York, NY: Continuum.

Dekeyser, R. (2007). *Practice in a second language: Perspectives from applied linguistics and cognitive psychology.* Cambridge, UK: Cambridge University Press.

Dorwick, T., & Glass, W.R. (2003). Language education policies: One publisher's perspective. *Modern Language Journal, 87*, 592–594.

Ferreira, M. (2005). An application of the concept-based approach to academic writing instruction. Unpublished doctoral dissertation, The Pennsylvania State University, University Park, PA.

Ferreira, M., & Lantolf, J.P. (2008). A concept-based approach to teaching: Writing through genre analysis. In J.P. Lantolf, & M. Poehner (Eds.), *Sociocultural theory and the teaching of second languages* (pp. 285–320). London: Equinox.

Gal'perin, P.I. (1989). Organization of mental activity and the effectiveness of learning. *Soviet Psychology, 27*, 65–82.

Gee, J.P. (2008 [1990]). *Social linguistics and literacies* (3rd ed.). New York: Routledge.

Halliday, M.A.K. (1985 [1994]). *An introduction to functional grammar.* London: Edward Arnold.

Kalantzis, M., & Cope, B. (2005). *Learning by design.* Melbourne, VIC: Common Ground.

Kern, R. (2000). *Literacy and language teaching.* Oxford, UK: Oxford University Press.

Kramsch, C. (1993). *Context and culture in language teaching.* Oxford, UK: Oxford University Press.

Kramsch, C. (2010). Theorizing translingual/transcultural competence. In G.S. Levine & A. Phipps (Eds.), *Critical and intercultural theory and language pedagogy. AAUSC's issues in language program direction. Annual Series* (pp. 15–31). Boston, MA: Heinle and Heinle.

Lai, W. (2012). Concept-based foreign language pedagogy: Teaching the Chinese temporal system. Unpublished doctoral dissertation, The Pennsylvania State University, University Park, PA.

Lantolf, J. (2011). The sociocultural approach to second language acquisition. In D. Atkinson (Ed.), *Alternative approaches to second language acquisition* (pp. 24–47). New York: Routledge.

Lantolf, J., & Poehner, M. (2014). *Sociocultural theory and the pedagogical imperative in L2 education: Vygotskian praxis and the research/practice divide.* New York, NY: Routledge.

Lantolf, J., & Thorne, S. (2006). *Sociocultural theory and the genesis of second language development.* Oxford, UK: Oxford University Press.

Levine, G.S., Melin, C., Crane, C., Chavez, M., & Lovik, T.A. (2008). The language program director in curricular and departmental reform: A response to the MLA ad hoc report. *Profession 2008,* 240–254.

López-Sánchez, A. (2014). Hacia una pedagogía para la multialfabetización: El diseño de una unidad didáctica inspirada en las propuestas del New London Group. *Hispania, 97*(2), 281–297.

Maxim, H.H. (2006a). Integrating textual thinking into the introductory college-level foreign language classroom. *MLA, 90*(1), 19–32.

Maxim, H.H. (2006b). Giving beginning adult language learners a voice: A case for poetry in the foreign language classroom. In J. Retallack, & J. Spahr (Eds.), *Poetry and pedagogy: The challenge of the contemporary* (pp. 251–259). New York, NY: Palgrave Macmillan.

Maxim, H.H. (2009). Developing advanced formal language abilities along a genre-based continuum. In S.L. Katz, & J. Watzinger-Tharp (Eds.), *Conceptions of L2 grammar: Theoretical approaches and their application in the L2 classroom. AAUSC's issues in language program direction. Annual Series* (pp. 173–188). Boston, MA: Heinle and Heinle.

Modern Language Association (MLA). (2009). *Enrollments in languages other than English in United States institutions of higher education.* Retrieved from www.mla.org/2009_enrollmentsurvey.

Modern Language Association (MLA) Ad Hoc Committee on Foreign Languages. (2007). Foreign languages and higher education: New structures for a changed world. *Profession 2007,* 234–245.

National Center for Education Statistics (NCAS). (2012). *Enrollment in postsecondary institutions.* Retrieved from https://nces.ed.gov/pubsearch/pubsinfo.asp?pubid=2013183.

Negueruela, E. (2003). Systemic theoretical instruction and L2 development: A sociocultural approach to the teaching, learning and researching of L2 languages. Unpublished doctoral dissertation, The Pennsylvania State University, University Park.

Negueruela, E. (2008a). A conceptual approach to promoting L2 grammatical developments: Implications for language program directors. In S.L. Katz, & J. Watzinger-Tharp (Eds.), *Conceptions of L2 grammar: Theoretical approaches and their application in the L2 classroom.*

AAUSC's issues in language program direction. Annual Series (pp. 151–171). Boston, MA: Heinle and Heinle.

Negueruela, E. (2008b). Revolutionary pedagogies: Learning that leads (to) second language development. In J.P. Lantolf, & M. Poehner (Eds.), *Sociocultural theory and second language teaching* (pp. 189–227). London: Equinox.

Negueruela, E., & Lantolf, J.P. (2006). Concept-based instruction and the acquisition of L2 Spanish. In B. Lafford, & R. Salaberry (Eds.), *The art of teaching Spanish: Second language acquisition from research to praxis* (pp. 79–102). Washington, DC: Georgetown University Press.

New London Group (NLG). (1996). A pedagogy of multiliteracies: Designing social futures. *Harvard Educational Review, 66*(1), 60–92.

New London Group (NLG). (2000). A pedagogy of multiliteracies: Designing social futures. In B. Cope, & M. Kalantzis (Eds.), *Multiliteracies: Literacy learning and the design of social futures* (pp. 9–37). New York, NY: Routledge.

Norris, J.M., & Ortega, L. (2000). Effectiveness of L2 instruction: A research synthesis and quantitative meta-analysis. *Language Learning, 50*, 417–528.

Rothery, J. (1996). Making changes: Developing an educational linguistics. In R. Hasan, & G. Williams (Eds.), *Literacy in society* (pp. 86–123). London: Longman.

Schultz, J.M. (2004). Towards a pedagogy of the Francophone text in intermediate language courses. *The French Review, 78*(2), 260–275.

Swaffar, J.K., & Arens, K. (2005). *Remapping the foreign language curriculum: An approach through multiple literacies.* New York, NY: MLA.

Swaffar, J.K., Arens, K.M., & Byrnes, H. (1991). *Reading for meaning: An integrated approach to language learning.* Englewood Cliffs, NJ: Prentice Hall.

Vygotsky, L.S. (1987). *The collected works of L.S. Vygotsky, Volume 1. Thinking and speaking.* New York, NY: Plenum Press.

Wallace, C. (2003). *Critical reading in language education.* New York: Palgrave Macmillan.

Yáñez-Prieto, M.C. (2008). On literature and the secret art of invisible words: Teaching literature through language. Unpublished doctoral dissertation, The Pennsylvania State University, University Park, PA.

Zarate, G., Lévy, D., & Kramsch, C. (Eds.). (2008). *Précis du plurilinguisme et du pluriculturalism.* Paris: Edition des Archives Contemporaines.

Appendix A: *Movie Review* Worksheet (Translated)

1. What purpose does this text have? (i.e., Why is it written?) For whom is it written?

2. Does the text have different parts? If so, draw a line to separate each part, identify it by labeling it (i.e., name it), and briefly explain what happens in each of those parts.

3. Look now at the lexicon (= vocabulary) and grammar of the text. Answer the following questions:

   - Identify the words in the review that refer to different elements of the film (e.g., that refer to the actors, plot, theme, etc)?

   - In the first paragraph of the review, what verb tense is used to summarize the movie? Write down some examples of the verb forms you found.

   - What words are used to review the film (e.g., is it a good/OK movie) and its various elements? Write all the examples you find below.

4

MULTILITERACIES AND MULTIMODAL DISCOURSES IN THE FOREIGN LANGUAGE CLASSROOM

Christine Sagnier

Introduction

Curricular reform presents many challenges. In the United States, many Foreign Language (FL) departments have been searching for ways to offer coherent undergraduate curricula that allow smooth transitions between introductory, intermediate, and advanced levels. As yet, however, not many have succeeded. In most institutions, the structural dichotomy in FL departments is still associated with divergent pedagogical approaches, making articulation of learning goals almost impossible to accomplish (see Chapter 1, this volume).

In "language" courses at the lower levels, communicative language teaching (CLT) is still largely dominant. Unfortunately, CLT, as it has been implemented in FL departments, with its focus on oral proficiency, has marginalized reading and writing and has had "limited success in developing students' abilities to interpret and create written texts" (Allen & Paesani, 2010, p. 122). The lack of metacognitive and metalinguistic activities around textual material and writing practices in CLT has led to an impoverished curriculum that does not help foster the kind of intellectually driven approach that should define higher education programs.

For Allen and Paesani (2010), the pedagogical goals of the upper and lower divisions, literary-cultural interpretation on the one hand and functional, interactive language use on the other, are "typically seen as incompatible" (p. 120). The lower levels have a "skill-based orientation, where texts function as a vehicle for language practice and cultural content is explored superficially" (p. 120), whereas, in the upper division, students are expected to engage with complex literary texts, to read them closely and write literary essays without having really addressed textual thinking in previous levels.

What is lacking in FL curricula are opportunities for students to analyze and appropriate various types of discourses in the foreign language, to reflect on "meaning-making," and to have the possibility of gradually gaining an understanding of discourse practices, even though their linguistic skills are not fully developed. The profession is recognizing these curricular issues and seeking ways to respond, but change is slow to come.

In 2007, the Modern Language Association (MLA) Ad Hoc Committee's report called for a large-scale reform in university FL departments, recommending the elimination of the language-content structure and advocating "a broader, more coherent curriculum, in which language, culture and literature are taught as a continuous whole" (p. 3). The report foregrounds the role of cultural narratives as core elements of instruction, proposing that translingual and transcultural competence become the primary goal of FL academic programs. Translingual competence, on the one hand, is defined as "the ability to operate between languages" (p. 2), whereby "students are trained to reflect on the world and themselves through the lens of another language and culture" (p. 2). Transcultural competence, on the other hand, is defined as "the ability to comprehend and analyze the cultural narratives that appear in every kind of expressive form—from essays, fiction, poetry, drama, journalism, humor, advertising, political rhetoric and legal documents to performance, visual forms and music" (p. 3).

As Allen and Paesani (2010) rightly pointed out, these recommendations are laudable, yet "the report failed to address how foreign language departments might bring about the large-scale changes necessary to develop integrated, text-based curricula or which pedagogical approaches might facilitate implementing such curricula" (p. 120). This chapter will argue that, in light of the outlined challenges, what is now needed is not just superficial reform, but a true shift in paradigm. It will posit that a paradigm which understands language as a sociocul-turally situated semiotic system (Bronckart, 1985; Halliday, 1978) can help reconceptualize teaching and learning in FL departments and bring about innovative pedagogical practices.

A New Paradigm

The multiliteracies framework, as many scholars (Allen & Paesani, 2010; Byrnes & Maxim, 2004; Kern, 2000; Swaffar & Arens, 2005; Swaffar, Arens, & Byrnes, 1991) in the field have advocated, emphasizes connections between "language," "literature," and "culture" and offers great potential for innovation toward more coherent programs. Several of these scholars have offered roadmaps for reform, with varied proposals in which the main emphasis is on the understanding of meaning-making through texts. Many refer to the notions originally put forward by the New London Group (NLG, 1996), as well as Gee (1990), whose work extended the notion of literacy well beyond the traditional definition of reading and writing. Literacy is now understood as a complex social practice involving "critical awareness of the relationships between texts, discourse conventions and social and cultural contexts" (Kern, 2000, p. 6).

The term "multiliteracies" was coined "as a way to focus on the realities of increasing local diversity and global connectedness" (NLG, 1996, p. 61) and to stress the importance of preparing learners to negotiate discourse differences, given the plurality of representational forms and the variety of text forms that circulate and interrelate in contemporary communication.

It is important to note that adopting a multiliteracies framework does not mean going back to the old traditional grammar-translation method, or rejecting everything that CLT has brought to the classroom. In fact, it is not so much the fundamental notions that form the basis of CLT that are challenged, but the narrow functional interpretation that has been implemented in the FL classroom. Textual engagement in CLT is often limited in lower-level courses; texts are generally used to convey cultural information or perform interpersonal communicative activities, rarely leading to analytical and metacognitive activities. On the contrary, in a *pedagogy of multiliteracies*, "learners are encouraged to interpret, transform and think critically about discourse through a variety of contexts and textual genres" (Allen & Paesani, 2010, p. 122). At the core of this type of new curriculum are activities involving structured guidance and explicit teaching in the reading and writing of many types of discourses. As Maxim (2006) reminds us, because literacy and textual engagement are a long-term process, it is essential to start offering new pedagogical practices as early as possible in the curriculum.

Adopting this new paradigm might seem like a difficult enterprise. Lack of department buy-in, of understanding of the socio-discursive foundations on which the proposals are based, and lack of professional training, along with the quasi-absence of pedagogical material, can make the best-intentioned reformers feel overwhelmed by the enormity of the task. In the French Program at Princeton University, the pedagogy of multiliteracies provided the theoretical foundations for our reform. However, because this author, who is the Language Program Director, was also familiar with Socio-Discursive Interactionism (henceforth SDI), developed by scholars at the University of Geneva (Bronckart, 1985, 1996; Dolz & Schneuwly, 1996, 1998, 2010), the department's reform was shaped by the notion of "didactic sequence" (*séquence didactique*), one of the group's important contributions to the field. This chapter discusses how the notion of didactic sequence can help language educators rethink the way they approach texts in the classroom and briefly sketches some of the theoretical connections between the multiliteracies framework and SDI, highlighting their complementarity for curricular reform.

SDI and the Notion of Didactic Sequence

SDI postulates that human actions should be treated in their social and discursive dimensions. The framework is based on a Bakhtinian[1] theory of discourse.

It understands speech genres as a social phenomenon, as products of goal-oriented social-verbal interactions between members of discourse communities, shaped by social and historical forces (Bakhtin, 1986; Bakhtine & Volochinov, 1977):

> A particular function (scientific, technical, commentarial, business, everyday) and the particular conditions of speech communication specific for each sphere [of human activity] give rise to particular genres, that is, certain relatively stable, thematic, compositional and stylistic types of utterances. (Bakhtin, 1986, p. 64)

These typified utterances that circulate in a given discourse community, although dynamic and heterogeneous, present some level of recurring features that can be identified and examined. Genres establish a certain level of norms of interaction that the native speakers learn to master to different extents. For Bakhtin, genres are utterances that are "filled with echoes and reverberations of other utterances" (1986, p. 91). Language learners do not learn isolated words; they do not assimilate just vocabulary and syntax, but rather, to enter a community of practice, they must be able to assimilate creatively complex patterns of language use. They learn genres and discourses "through a process of assimilation—more or less creative— of others' words (and not the words of the language)" (Bakhtin, 1986, p. 89). Genre familiarization and assimilation in a native language often occur implicitly, through immersion in a discourse community. Native speakers, however, can benefit from explicit instruction of certain types of complex secondary genres and sub-genres (i.e., academic writing or presentations, journalistic writing, etc.). Yet, genre-based methodology is still seldom used in foreign language academic programs.[2]

The researchers at the University of Geneva conceive genres as "mega-tools" for language acquisition and literacy (Schneuwly, 1998). For these scholars, the understanding and mastery of a genre is the necessary basis for the analysis and critique of texts and for textual production. Drawing on Vygotskian theories of learning and human activity, they devised a pedagogical proposal called "didactic sequence," which is designed around the Bakhtinian construct of genre.

A didactic sequence is a series of instructional sessions around a given genre that seeks to provide students with mental categories and procedures for analyzing how texts work, through explicit and scaffolded instruction. The aim of a didactic sequence is not to teach and imitate a standard, but to have students reflect critically and actively transform or create discourses, gaining linguistic, discursive, and cultural knowledge in the process. Although the sequences were originally designed for French as a native language, they can easily be adapted to FL learning (including lower levels)[3] and provide clear guidance, grounded on solid theoretical and empirical research, for instructors interested in teaching through the notion of genre (Bronckart et al., 1985; Dolz & Schneuwly, 1998).

In a didactic sequence, the instructor is a mediator who raises students' awareness of genre through a series of guided activities involving reflection, analysis, shared metacognition (thinking about thinking collectively), and metalinguistic activities grounded in practice, to facilitate genre acquisition and admission into a discourse community. A sequence typically culminates with students' own productions and is generally conducted along a series of steps.

At the start of the sequence, students read a selection of authentic texts and are asked to work collectively in order to respond to a set of questions presented by the instructor. The first part of the didactic sequence aims at raising awareness of the social dimension of communication, before having students gradually discover the relationships between the "features of discourse" (the lexicogrammatical structures) and the "practice of discourse" (the types of utterances that circulate in a given discourse community).

Questions will therefore target the following aspects:

- *the situation of communication* (i.e., Who is writing? For whom? On what topic? Where? When? With what purpose?);
- *the architecture of the text* (i.e., introduction, body of text, conclusion); and
- *the linguistic means* to achieve the goals.

The instructional strategies foster metacognitive strategies for reading. Collective analysis and discussion, under the guidance of the instructor, lead to the exploration of the main dimensions of a genre (content, communicative structure, and specific configurations of linguistic elements).

In order to be effective, the didactic sequence must be adapted to the abilities of the students. The instructor has to be aware of the initial abilities of the learners and design scaffolded activities that enable them to go well beyond these initial abilities, a process called working in the "zone of proximal development" (ZPD) in Vygotskian theory (1986). Teaching in the ZPD means designing activities that are within the learners' zone of intelligibility, yet present challenges to them. Social interactions and mediation are at the core of the process. Instructors offer mediation, scaffolding, and guidance until learners are able to accomplish tasks independently. This means that instructors assess learners' abilities and scaffold according to needs. They might choose to emphasize the understanding of the situation of communication, or they might decide to spend more time segmenting a text to look at the different elements, in order to recognize words, to explain new vocabulary, or look for examples of newly learnt grammatical rules. They might focus on syntactic structures at the sentence level, working at the micro level of the text, before moving on to the macro level (the architecture of the text). At the macro level, they might ask students to identify structural elements or markers, or to use inference to predict meaning, by reading closely and looking for linguistic clues, for example.

Through this active engagement with the texts, through social interaction and collaboration, students understand how linguistic features are used for particular goals; they gain understanding and metalinguistic awareness of discourses and learn to critically appropriate the conventions of that discourse. They read texts very closely and engage with their intellectual and cultural content while working on their discursive dimensions.

Once the selected texts have been discussed,[4] students engage in producing their own text in the genre they have been studying (usually with one or two peers). During the following class sessions, they have the opportunity to present their text (or part of their text) to their peers and the instructor and discuss its strengths and weaknesses. Class sessions are conducted as "collaborative writing workshops." This means that the role of the instructor is not to conduct a summative evaluation, but to guide the students through a process of evaluating their own productions, with his/her help and that of their peers. This type of "formative evaluation" (Allal, 1999), involving self-assessment, reciprocal peer-assessment, and comparison between the instructor's and students' assessments, allows learners to improve their self-monitoring and self-regulation, two metacognitive skills that are essential for effective learning and development. Through this process, students learn to improve their productions gradually and internalize some of the features of the discourses studied, which they transform for their own purpose.

Cognitively, this pedagogical approach allows instructors to alternate bottom-up activities with top-down ones and facilitate both processes. As previously stated, the model goes beyond helping students deal with linguistic and textual features, as it also connects *text* and *context*. Students have to identify linguistic forms, and link them to meaning and intention; they reflect on issues of audience, purpose, form, and social conventions. They learn to understand narratives as utterances emerging from a particular social, historical, and cultural sphere, to examine their characteristics—their thematic, compositional, and stylistic features, as they link them to the practices of a discourse community, before launching into their own productions. The focus is on the agency of learners and on *meaning* as it is constructed through *form* in a given cultural, historical, and social context.

Theoretically and pedagogically, this conception of learning based on scaffolded, collaborative activities, developed by the teams at the University of Geneva, is compatible with the vision put forward in the English-speaking world by researchers previously cited in this chapter, who broadly base their ideas on those of the New London Group (NLG, 1996). The latter reflect on ways to make students aware of *Available Designs* in the production of discourses, linking the notion of *text* to the social, historical, and cultural context, going from *text* to *discourse*, analyzing linguistic conventions, paying attention to social context, and teaching students to engage with texts and cultural narratives in a valid intellectual way. The NLG advocates an understanding of language as a socioculturally situated semiotic system (Halliday, 1978), and meaning-making as a form of design or active and dynamic transformation (Cope & Kalantzis, 2009; NLG, 1996). The main objective of a pedagogy of multiliteracies is to read for meaning and form, to learn to understand texts as social practices, and to become more familiar with the way meaning is constructed. It also means reading for the purpose of writing and benefiting from overt, explicit instruction and activities to become better readers and writers. This closeness between SDI and the multiliteracies framework is not surprising, as they both have many theoretical references in common. They are similar on two grounds: They share the same understanding of language and they both invoke Vygotskian theories of learning. But their focus and contributions are nevertheless different. Highlighting their similarities and differences can inform curricular planning and foster pedagogical innovation.

The NLG framework, first formulated in 1996 and revisited by Cope and Kalantzis in 2009, lists four major dimensions of a pedagogy of multiliteracies. Originally called *situated practice, overt instruction, critical framing,* and *transformed practice*, these dimensions have been translated into "more immediately recognizable pedagogical acts or 'knowledge processes': *experiencing, conceptualizing, analyzing* and *applying*" (Cope & Kalantzis, 2009, p. 184). The instructional principles of the NLG are broader than those found in SDI; they rely on slightly different aspects of Vygotskian theories, but a close examination reveals many commonalities.

As an example, the first dimension of the multiliteracies framework (Cope & Kalantzis, 2009) is *experiencing*: It includes both *experiencing the known*, which entails reflecting on one's experiences, interests, perspectives, familiar forms of expression, and ways of representing the world in one's own understanding, and *experiencing the new*, which entails observing and reading the unfamiliar, immersion in new situations and texts, reading new texts, and being exposed to new information. In the framework, weaving between the known and the new is an essential pedagogical act. These processes resonate with educators familiar with Vygotskian or neo-Vygotskian educational theories such as SDI or metacognitive research (Brown, 1987, 1992; Brown & Palincsar, 1982). Researchers working within these traditions emphasize the fundamental role of metacognition (thinking about thinking, using specific meta-strategies to guide learning) (Flavell, 1979) for effective learning and students' agency. One of the most important metacognitive strategies, *elaboration*, entails connecting what is already known, experienced, and familiar ("experiencing the known" in the NLG framework) with new knowledge ("experiencing the new"). The connection with the notion of "weaving the familiar with the new knowledge" found in the multiliteracies framework is obvious.

Moreover, the process of helping learners to reflect and connect the *known* with the *new*, of exposing them to new information, experiences, and texts, has to take place within a "zone of intelligibility and safety" (Cope & Kalantzis, 2009, p. 185), in order to take the learners into new domains of action and meaning. This notion invoked by the NLG—that of the "zone of intelligibility and safety," an ideal "learning zone" that educators must find for students—closely parallels the aforementioned Vygotskian ZPD, but the NLG notion is a simpler one, since it does not refer explicitly to the essential role of mediation and scaffolding to facilitate and accelerate learning processes and drive learners' development. What is stressed, however, in the framework, is the transformative potential of a pedagogy of multiliteracies, which envisions learning as a process of self-recreation. Just as in Vygotskian theory, pedagogical intervention is clearly viewed here as leading to developmental change in learners.

The second dimension presented by the NLG, *conceptualizing*, is a "knowledge process in which learners become active conceptualizers, making the tacit explicit and generalizing from the particular" (Cope & Kalantzis, 2009, p. 185). This dimension involves two sub-categories: *conceptualizing by naming*, which involves drawing distinctions of similarity and differences, categorizing by naming, and *conceptualizing by theory*, which includes making generalizations, putting key terms into interpretative frameworks, and building mental models. Such cognitive processes are central to the neo-Vygotskian literature on metacognition. They involve "thinking about thinking," elaborating on previous knowledge, making connections, conceptualizing, and engaging with shared metacognitive activity and in collective critical thinking (Paris & Winograd, 1990).

The third dimension in the multiliteracies framework, *analyzing*, also involves two subcategories: *analyzing functionally*, which includes processes of reasoning, drawing inference, deducting, and establishing causal and functional relations between elements, and *analyzing critically*, which involves evaluation of one's and other people's perspectives and interests. Such activities are labeled in neo-Vygotskian research as cognitive and metacognitive; they imply having students use a wide range of strategies while engaging in texts (Boyer, Dionne, & Raymond, 1995; Brown, 1987, 1992; Brown & Palincsar, 1982; Flower, 1994; Kern, 2000; Swaffar & Arens, 2005; Swaffar et al., 1991).

The fourth dimension, *applying*, also has two dimensions: *applying appropriately*, which "entails the application of knowledge and understanding the complex diversity of real world and real life situations and testing their validity" (Cope & Kalantzis, 2009, p. 186), and *applying creatively*, which refers to the ability to make an intervention in the world which is truly innovative and creative and brings to bear the learner's interests, experiences, and expectations. Such processes are usually referred as "strategic or conditional knowledge," knowing how and when to use knowledge appropriately and creatively for a particular task, in a specific social context (Paris, Lipson, & Wixson, 1983).

As pointed out, the dimensions invoked by the NLG refer to recent neo-Vygotskian research (even though direct connections are not explicitly made), while SDI, with the construct of didactic sequence, focuses more directly and explicitly on the key Vygotskian notion of the ZPD and the crucial role of mediation, social interactions, and scaffolding in the learning process. Both SDI and the NLG framework stress the importance of conceptual and analytical activities, which have sometimes been lost in experiential learning models.

Both frameworks are transformative pedagogical orientations that take into account the importance of learners' agency, while still engaging students in the use of discourses. They both provide a roadmap for the extension of existing pedagogical repertoires and open the door for the implementation of a multiliteracies-based curriculum.

One of the great advantages of the format of didactic sequences is that the researchers have provided detailed, step-by-step accounts of classroom-based experiments. The availability of models for a wide range of written and oral genres makes it possible to design instructional sessions and greatly facilitates the training of novice instructors.[5] As recommended by the researchers, didactic sequences can be short or long; they can be integrated into the curriculum at different levels, depending on needs, students' abilities, and course objectives. The robust models, the solid theoretical research, and the abundance of publications make the concept of "didactic sequence" a great, yet flexible tool for rethinking the approach to texts through genres in the FL classroom.

The French Department at Princeton has found the guidelines provided by SDI extremely helpful for its curricular reform. Didactic sequences on different genres (newscasts, fairy tales, academic oral presentations, editorials, journalistic interviews, travel journals, fantastic short stories, biographies, etc.) have been integrated into the curriculum, enabling students to identify similarities and differences between various types of discourses and helping them develop their metalinguistic, pragmatic, and discursive knowledge.

However, thus far, SDI has concerned itself primarily with verbal language. Since the French Program wanted to expand beyond the study of verbal communication, the Language Program Director turned to some important notions developed by the NLG to push reforms further, as will be presented in the next part of this chapter.

Multiliteracies and Multimodality

The ambition of the multiliteracies framework is to go beyond verbal communication and encompass other types of semiotic resources. In line with Halliday's thinking, the NLG considers language "as the prototypical form of human semiotic" (Halliday, 1993, p. 93). Although this central role of language is recognized, a pedagogy of multiliteracies also "focuses on modes of representation much broader than language alone" (NLG, 1996, p. 63). Through the key concept of *Design*, the NLG proposes a dynamic conception of representation which sees human beings as "both inheritors of patterns and conventions and at the same time active designers of meaning" (p. 5). Resources for meaning-making are not limited to verbal language; there are different "modes," that is to say, socially shaped and culturally given resources for meaning-making that are available as "design elements." The various modes available for meaning-making identified by the researchers are:

- written language
- spoken language
- visual representation
- audio representation
- tactile representation
- spatial representation.[6]

"Multimodality" thus refers to "the use of several semiotic modes in the design of a semiotic product or event" (Kress & van Leeuwen, 2001, p. 20). The notion "draws the attention ... to the fact that language rarely stands alone in written and spoken discourses" (Ventola & Guijarro, 2009, p. 1). In the context of the dramatically changing landscape of contemporary communication, which generates new forms of discourses and designs for meaning-making, the ideas of the NLG around the notion of "mode" and "multimodality" offer the possibility of further reflections and pedagogical innovations. In Cope and Kalantzis' words, "old logics of literacy and teaching are profoundly challenged by the new media environment" (2009, p. 173) and educators have to take this into account. As "new media mix modes of communication more powerfully than was culturally the norm and even technically possible in the earlier modernity that was dominated by the book and the printed page" (Cope & Kalantzis, 2009, p. 178), language instructors need to rethink the way they approach discourses.

The NLG is interested in the representational potentials of different modes, in the "inherently different or incommensurate affordances as well as the parallel or translatable aspects of the representational jobs they do" (Cope & Kalantzis, 2009, p. 179). For these authors, today more than ever, "much of our everyday experience is intrinsically multimodal" (p. 179). Since different modes of meaning and communication are not simply parallel, it is important to address multimodality and raise students' awareness of the affordances of each mode, of the similarities and differences between the various modalities.

Pedagogically, it is possible to create experimental didactic sequences that focus on multimodal discourses. Just as key features of texts identified by researchers in order to develop "a metalanguage of linguistic design" (NLG, 1996, p. 78) serve as a basis for critical language awareness, key features and elements describing and explaining other modes of communication can serve as a basis for critical multimodal awareness.

The concept of Design provides an entry for new pedagogical proposals. As a reminder, Design for the NLG (1996) involves three elements: *Available Designs*, *Designing*, and *the Redesigned*, which together "emphasize the fact that meaning-making is an active and dynamic process" (p. 72). Semiotic activity is seen "as a creative application and combination of conventions (resources–Available Designs) that, in the process of Design, transforms at the same time it reproduces these conventions (Fairclough, 1992, 1995)" (p. 72). The outcome of Designing is the Redesigned, a new meaning, "founded on historically and culturally received patterns of meaning," yet at the same time "a unique product of human agency: a transformed meaning" (p. 75), which "becomes a new Available Design, a new meaning-making resource" (p. 75).

The French Program at Princeton University is experimenting with didactic sequences that integrate the notions developed by the NLG, to help students reflect, conceptualize, and analyze meaning-making in its multiple and multi-modal forms. A wide range of multimodal discourses is being used, blending canonical cultural productions with those from popular culture, providing students with ways to compare meaning-making processes and features. The notion of "Available Designs" as the "found or discernible patterns and conventions of representation" that are culture-, context- and purpose-specific (Cope & Kalantzis, 2009, p. 116) serves to highlight shifts across modes and times, allowing students to make connections between what they know (contemporary Available Designs, specifically those found in new media) with what they do not know (culturally or historically different Available Designs), while approaching semiotic activity from a critical perspective.

This pedagogical experimentation at different levels of the curriculum is an ongoing project. Students have so far engaged actively and enthusiastically in these collective explorations of multimodal texts and instructors are currently selecting material that can be integrated into different thematic units. It is, however, too early at this stage to report on these projects, but the French Program hopes to be able to do so in the near future. At the advanced level, a classroom-based research project on "bimodal discourses" (that is, discourses that include both the visual and the verbal mode) was launched by the Language Program Director in 2010 and has led to the creation of a permanent course. This chapter presents this pedagogical proposal, titled *Reading Images*, in the hope that it will serve as a springboard for other experimentations in the FL classroom.

Reading Images: An Experimental Project

As part of its efforts to innovate, the French Department at Princeton University supported the creation of a new advanced course, titled *Reading Images*, taught entirely in French.[7] The objective of the course is twofold: (1) to engage students in a reflection about the nature of communication and to sensitize them to the relationships between language, texts, images, and social and historical contexts; and (2) to hone students' linguistic skills while also developing their critical and interpretive abilities through the study of the production and reception of images in the target culture.

The course is one semester long (12 weeks, 36 contact hours). It is made up of a theoretical component (presented over a three-week period), followed by a series of five thematic units centered on the theme of persuasive communication. The thematic units focus on contemporary advertisements, 19th-century advertisements, visual propaganda, caricatures, and iconic media images.

The objective of the theoretical component is to give students an overview of some key issues in communication theory and to provide them with an opportunity to reflect on "meaning-making" through two modes: written language and visual representation. It also seeks to sensitize students to the limitations of linguistic theories for the purpose of analyzing images and to help them identify how the two modes of *writing* and *image* differ. The following account describes the latest implementation.

During the first three weeks of the course, students read excerpts of texts by French scholars that explored key notions such as signs, signifiers and signified, denotation and connotation, communicative purpose, functions of communication, discourse, genre, stylistic and rhetorical conventions, social representations and stereotypes, etc. The readings were selected to help students reflect on and discuss processes of communication and representation. Since many of the concepts they introduced were new for students, it was necessary to prepare lexical and conceptual cues, as well as pre-reading questions prior to each class meeting. The instructor also created PowerPoint presentations to illustrate key notions and synthesize important information for class discussion. Each presentation was then posted on the online course page for further reference.

At the end of the theoretical component unit, the class launched into the first thematic unit on advertisements on still printed images, a specific genre of persuasive communication. These "texts" combine the use of visual and verbal elements and are excellent starting points for analysis and discussion, because students have a certain level of familiarity with them, although they have rarely attempted to deconstruct these messages.

The format of the didactic sequence was used and adapted by introducing worksheets specifically designed for the study of bimodal texts. Because students are not familiar with the "reading" of images, specific steps are required. The focus at the start of the sequence is not on the situation of communication, as was the case for verbal language. Instead, students were first asked to work collaboratively on an activity worksheet (Activity worksheet 1; see Table 4.1) to describe an image displayed in class. Engaging students in a detailed description provides the

TABLE 4.1 Activity Worksheet 1. Describing an Advertisement (Translated Version)

Describing an advertisement (still image). *With your partner(s), describe in detail the image chosen for this activity*

---

1. First, give a detailed description of all *figurative (iconic) signs* in this image: people, place, objects shown (props), and product.
2. Now, describe in detail: all *plastic signs*, as identified in course materials: colors (hues, saturation, value), light, framing, spatial organization, forms, lines, texture, angle, point of view, etc.
3. Describe the *textual message(s)*; do not forget to note where it is/they are placed, which colors are used, which graphic means, etc.

---

scaffolding needed before launching into interpretation. This pedagogical technique has two advantages: First, it forces students to look closely at all the elements in the image before they attempt to interpret it. Second, in a foreign language setting, it enables the instructor to help students with lexical issues, since they rarely have the vocabulary, even at an advanced level, to describe an image in precise terms. Useful vocabulary was written on the board, providing lexical enrichment and a glossary of terms for reference.

At the conceptual level, spending time on detailed description also allowed the instructor to provide mediation and help students review and appropriate theoretical notions learnt during the first part of the course. As an example, they had to identify and describe all figurative (iconic) and plastic signs. For reference, figurative (iconic) signs are figurative elements, whereas plastic signs cover a wide range of visual elements, such as colors, light, framing, spatial organization, lines, textures, angle, point of view, etc. (Groupe μ, 1992).[8]

Once the description activity was completed, students collaborated in pairs on a second activity worksheet (Activity worksheet 2; see Table 4.2), to reflect on the communicative situation, on the "architecture" of the image, and on the multimodal means to achieve the communication goals. Having this second activity worksheet ensures that students learn to categorize important elements and proceed systematically before attempting to launch into interpretation. As is the case for textual material, questions focus on the *situation of communication* (Who is communicating? For whom? On what topic? Where? When? With what purpose?); on the "*architecture*" of the image (Which elements are present? How are they organized spatially? Which elements are salient? What is the overall composition?, etc.); and on the *multimodal* means to achieve the communicative goals (How are verbal and visual elements combined and what is the overall effect?).

The activity worksheets require students to identify the many components of the bimodal text (e.g., the figurative and plastic signs, as well as the verbal message), thereby helping them to create mental categories to analyze these messages. They also draw their attention to the nature and relationships of the many elements, to their organization and layout within the image. Through this activity, students are led to explore the three metafunctional aspects in a visual text (Kress & van Leeuwen, 2006), which are:

- the representational aspects of the image (the construction of events, the participants, the objects and circumstances in which they occur);
- the interactive aspects (the relationship between the viewer and what is viewed);
- the compositional aspects (the layout, the salience of some elements, used to draw the viewer's attention, etc.).

The overall aim of the instructional session is to sensitize students to the resources used for *meaning-making*, and to have them understand how different

TABLE 4.2 Activity Worksheet 2. Analyzing an Advertisement (Translated Version)

Analyzing an advertisement (still image). *With your partner(s), look at the information that you have in worksheet 1 and write comments on as many signs as possible. Once you have done this work, reflect on the overall message on the image and on the means to convey it.*

---

1. *Figurative (iconic) signs* in this image: people, place, objects shown, and product.
   Why, according to you, have these elements been chosen? What kind of secondary or symbolic meaning(s) do you think they might have? What is the intended effect? Think of how different the image would be if you replaced one element by another one in the same category (for example a baby by an old man, etc.).

2. *Plastic signs,* as identified in course materials: colors (hues, saturation, value, etc.), light, framing, spatial organization, forms, lines, texture, angle, point of view, etc.
   Why, according to you, have these elements been chosen? What kind of secondary or symbolic meaning(s) do you think they might have? What is the effect of the point of view? Of the colors? Of the lines and textures? Of the composition? What qualities might the viewer associate with the product? What is the intended effect? How would the image change if different choices had been made?

3. *Textual message(s)*
   How does the verbal message relate to the image? What can you say about its graphic realization? What is the primary function of the textual message? Does it add information (relay) or guide the reader (anchorage)? Can you identify the 'speaker'? What type of utterance can you identify? What is the intended effect and what visual means are used to convey a particular intent?

At the end of your discussion with your partner, you should try to answer the following questions:

- Who communicated (which company)?
- What was the product?
- Where was it published (medium: newspapers, magazine, etc.)?
- For whom? Who was the target audience, in your opinion? Justify your answer.
- When?
- What is the main purpose of the message, according to you?
- Which means were used to convey the message? You may now comment on whether you find the message effective and give your personal reaction to it.

---

categories of signs (figurative, plastic, and linguistic) contribute to the overall signification of the message. Students also reflect on how the visual and verbal modes are interrelated, how they interact to produce meaning. By identifying mode-specific elements and resources, they are led to think in terms of potential and affordances of each mode (Kress, 2010).

It is worth noting that, to ease the students into the process of analysis, for the introductory session, the instructor chose an advertisement that had been produced for an international audience by a global brand. These kinds of persuasive messages tend to avoid complex cultural allusions and are easier to decipher. Using this type of material provides adequate scaffolding before engaging with more complex multimodal texts.

Once the second worksheet was completed, the class regrouped for a discussion, in which students explained their findings, responded to others, and discussed their interpretation of the material. As is the case during didactic sequences on texts, the instructor's role is not to "uncover" some meaning, but to guide students through a critical reflection on meaning-making and Available Designs. At the end of the session on the "sample" image, students were presented with a series of advertisements of increasing visual complexity, in order to test their newly acquired skills. They were then asked to find an advertisement for a food product in their own culture and in the target culture and present their analysis and comparisons to the class during the following meetings. Because food advertisements rely more on cultural allusions than global luxury goods, they provide opportunities for students to identify differences in the use of conventions and allow them to explore cultural differences in meaning-making. During their presentations, students were, indeed, able to apply the linguistic and conceptual knowledge acquired to discuss and reflect on the situated dimension of communication and on the importance of understanding the context of production and reception of an image.

In sum, at the end of the first thematic unit, through the analysis of contemporary persuasive images such as advertisements, students grasped some key notions about multimodal communication. But since the images studied stemmed from French culture, the attempts at interpretations led not only to discussions on culture-, context-, and time-specific resources and conventions for making meaning, but also to the connotative and ideological dimensions of signs, to the polysemic nature of images and to notions such as "interpretative cooperation" (Eco, 1979 [1985]). The following thematic units allowed students to consolidate and deepen their knowledge and skills.

The Classroom as a Forum for Critical Viewing and Thinking

The remaining thematic units were conducted along the same lines as the unit presented above. As the semester progressed, it became no longer necessary to use the worksheets to describe and analyze images in each class, as students had understood the procedures and appropriated the tools to describe and analyze images. They were also able to make connections with the theoretical components studied in the first part of the course. The entries of the worksheets were only used as reference whenever students forgot important elements, to remind them to look closely. Readings, PowerPoint presentations created by the instructor, and educational internet sites were used to contextualize the images studied. Throughout each unit, the instructor first modeled the process with one sample image when necessary, before letting students discuss other selected images.

To emphasize the importance of thinking about ways in which meaning is created within a particular social, historical, and cultural context, after the first unit on contemporary advertisements, the class went on to study advertisements produced during the "Golden Age of the Poster" in 19th-century France, the second thematic unit in the course. Students first read articles about social and economic changes and about the social status of women in France at the time; they also referred to some of the literary readings they knew to "situate" the images to be studied and started to look into questions of social representations, stereotypes, stylistic conventions, horizons of expectations (Jauss, 1978), and context of production and reception.

The comparison between the contemporary advertisements studied in the first unit and late 19th–early 20th-century productions allowed students to understand how the means for making meaning and the means for communicating these meanings are shaped by social, cultural, political, technological, and economic factors (Kress, 2010). They asked themselves questions about the issue of the cultural technologies of representation, production, and dissemination that are available in a given time and cultural space. Additional readings about the importance of the invention of the lithography and the way it impacted the diffusion of images led to discussions on the current revolution brought about by new technologies and on the new "multimodalities" in contemporary digital communication.

The poster by Herzig shown in Figure 4.1 is one of the many images used in the second thematic unit. Digitized images can be found on the site of the Bibliothèque Nationale de France (gallica.bnf.fr) (henceforth BnF) and a lot of information is available on the site of the Musée des Arts Décoratifs in Paris (www.lesartsdecoratifs.fr/francais/publicite/).

To contextualize and offer additional iconographic material, the class also used the virtual exhibit created by the BnF, titled Zola (http://expositions.bnf.fr/Zola/), which includes a portfolio on "*Publicité*" and photographs of the streets of Paris at the turn of the century, when posters were omnipresent and artistic iconographic material "irrupted into the streets" (*L'Art dans la rue*), triggering the famous "*Affichomanie*"—the collectors' craze for posters. Lithographs by Toulouse-Lautrec, Cheret, and Steinlen were also examined and analyzed collaboratively during a field trip to a local museum, allowing students to engage with a wide range of material. To better understand the aesthetic revolution brought about by these artists, as well as the changes in Available Designs, students were able to compare their productions with earlier posters in a digitized version of *Les Affiches illustrées*, by Ernest Maindron (1896), one of the first books devoted to advertisements, available on the BnF/Gallica site.

The next thematic unit offered a look at propaganda posters and the use of "signs of collaboration and resistance" (Wlassikof, 2002) during the Vichy period. The pedagogical "portfolio" of the unit included scholarly texts in French on propaganda, which examined the formal features and devices of that type of communication, as well as archive material (newsreels and iconographic material from the Vichy period) and excerpts of scholarly texts by historians to help students

FIGURE 4.1   Poster by Edouard Herzig, *c*.1900–1908.

Source: Gallica.bnf.fr. This poster is an example of a travel advertisement from the turn of the 20th century. It was used in unit 2, "The Golden Age of the Poster." Students described and analyzed this bimodal text using Activity worksheets 1 and 2. For comparison, they then looked for contemporary travel advertisements, which they also analyzed and discussed. Comparing persuasive bimodal texts from different periods led to discussions on the social representations and stereotypes conveyed and to reflections on Available Designs in a given social, historical, and cultural context.

understand the historical, social, and political context before launching into the analysis of visual material and examining rhetorical features and devices used to convey messages. The site of the BnF also has a selection of propaganda posters, as does the Centre National de Documentation Pédagogique (www.cndp.fr/cnrd/), or the Musée de la Résistance (www.musee-resistance.com).

The following thematic unit engaged students in the study of political caricatures and gave them opportunities to discuss and compare images stemming from the contemporary context with images they were less familiar with, such as those produced by Daumier or Philipon, two iconic figures of 19th-century France. For these activities, the class used the site of the BnF (http://expositions.bnf.fr/daumier/index.htm), which features a virtual exhibit on Daumier and his successors and is an excellent starting point for the work on this topic, as it offers a wealth of information. Many satirical images from the famous journal published by Philipon are also available online in digitized versions, making pedagogical projects easy to set up (e.g., www.ub.uni-heidelberg.de/Englisch/helios/fachinfo/www/kunst/digilit/artjournals/caricature.html).

Finally, the course looked at iconic images and photographs, and students were asked to reflect on possible reasons for the wide circulation, success, and afterlives of some images by examining their formal features and their context of production and reception. The study of iconic images and their reappropriation and adaptation led to discussions on visual interdiscursivity and on the influence of iconic images on interpretations of events. It also allowed students to have a broader vision of the importance of visual representation throughout history. Students were asked to find examples of images referring to other ones and to reflect on the frequency and intensity of visual interdiscursivity enabled by new technologies.

At the end of the semester, students had to complete an individual research project. They selected two to three images related to a topic of their choice and had to apply the theoretical and methodological knowledge learnt during the course to the study of iconographic material. The choice of topics chosen by the students was very wide, ranging from analysis of 19th-century posters with a focus on the changing image of women, to propaganda material for children during World War II, to the visual representations of bankers in 19th-century caricatures, to analyses of satirical images during the Dreyfus Affair, to name a few examples. Students then presented their findings orally to the class for discussion and wrote a final term paper on their topic. This work served as a partial assessment for the course.

Outcomes

The course on *Reading Images* has received very high evaluations from students, who commented on its originality and interdisciplinary dimensions, and is, at printing time, in its fourth consecutive year. The didactic sequences were adapted to integrate a pedagogy of multiliteracies, in order to have students reflect on the human repertoire for meaning-making at a given point in a social, cultural, and historical context. The instructional sessions were designed in line with the sociocultural principles of mediation, scaffolding, and collaboration. Working in the ZPD meant articulating informative readings with the presentation of new concepts and guiding students to engage collectively with activities that required conceptual thinking and critical framing, while making sure the cognitive load was not too high and that they had the lexical tools and referential knowledge to accomplish the tasks they were given, first with the help of the instructor, then without.

At the end of the course, students showed an increased understanding of Design and its three components (Available Designs, Designing, and the Redesigned), as an active and dynamic process (NLG, 1996). They demonstrated a better comprehension of how bimodal discourses work, and how they can be constructed, deconstructed, and reconstructed. They also developed better abilities to describe and critique visual texts, referring to key conceptual terms learnt in the course. They engaged with bimodal texts with increased awareness of the importance of situating meaning-making in a historical, cultural, and social context. The contextualization of the images gave background cultural and historical knowledge and allowed students to make connections to literary works they had read in other courses on the particular time periods studied, thereby aligning with the humanistic tradition of the department.

Course participants were able to *experience* the known and the new (weaving between the known and the unknown), and to *conceptualize by naming and by theory* (making the tacit explicit and generalizing from the particular, making generalizations, putting key terms into interpretative frameworks, building mental models); they *analyzed* functionally and critically and they also *applied their knowledge appropriately and creatively* (Cope & Kalantzis, 2009, p. 185) to engage in activities.

Students also commented on the new perspective they had gained on their familiar environment: Parallels were drawn between "revolutions" brought about by new technologies in the 19th century (lithographs, photography, etc.) and the 21st century, which is seeing an explosion of new means of communication that are already having an impact on social and discursive practices. Students, who belong to the so-called "digital generation," appreciated these numerous opportunities to reflect on these issues and develop critical perspectives on multimodal communication and its impact on their daily lives. By contrasting past and present discursive practices, by highlighting how multimodal communication has been shaped by different technologies, the course helped students enhance their understanding of the process of meaning-making while enriching their cultural knowledge through the study of a wide range of iconic and textual material.

Although the course did not culminate with the production of "texts" as would be the case for didactic sequences on verbal discourses, the instructional principles of the didactic sequence remained intact. In the lower levels, the French Program is now experimenting with didactic sequences on multimodal material in which students, who normally have great command of multimedia tools, can create their own "discourses" on the genres studied.

Pedagogical portfolios are also being created, in which multimodal material is connected to textual material, and where images (still or moving) do not function as mere illustrations for a thematic unit, but as an object of analysis. Even with limited linguistic abilities, students have adult cognitive capacities (Swaffar et al., 1991) and are able to reflect on meaning-making if given the possibility within guided and scaffolded activities. In line with Vygotskian principles, instructors can conduct a didactic sequence after they have prepared the students adequately to start in the ZPD (by having covered lexical or grammatical notions, etc.).

The ability to scan interesting images to present them in class and the existence of image databanks with accurate references empower instructors, who do not have to rely so heavily on commercially published material and are able to design their own pedagogical tools and sequences. Although the sources given here are French, the ideas presented can easily be expanded and adapted to other language teaching contexts.

Toward a New Vision

The work conducted by SDI researchers and educators in the French-speaking world is complementary to the research on multiliteracies conducted in the English-speaking world. Theoretically and pedagogically, as briefly highlighted in this chapter, the two approaches have much in common and share many theoretical references. Together, they provide a comprehensive theoretical framework in which to rethink FL curricula.

One of the advantages of the concept of didactic sequence is that sequences can be introduced gradually into the curriculum, using short or long formats, as instructors get progressively trained and experiment with the new approach. Sequences on verbal and visual material can also simply be added to the existing pedagogical material, making it possible to implement reform gradually. The French Program at Princeton has found the concept of didactic sequence very useful for teacher training purposes also, as a template to engage Teaching Assistants in critical and conceptual activities on discourses. Once novice instructors understand the theoretical underpinnings, they can attempt to design their own sequences on texts and test them in the classroom.

In the new paradigm presented in this chapter, where language is understood as a socioculturally situated semiotic system (Bronckart, 1985; Halliday, 1978), the objective of the "integrative curriculum" is to help students "comprehend discourse while learning language" (Swaffar et al., 1991), to develop linguistic abilities while they develop skills to generate ideas (i.e., *design meaning*) and think critically about a wide range of cultural narratives. I will argue, as many others do (Allen & Paesani, 2010; Byrnes & Maxim, 2004; Kern, 2000, 2008; Kramsch, 2006; Maxim, 2006; Swaffar & Arens, 2005, to name a few), that a pedagogy of multiliteracies, that is, working on a wide range of discourses as early as possible in the curriculum, working on texts using *bottom-up* and *top-down* strategies and linking the notion of *text* to that of *context*, enables students to make connections between instances of discourse and to see links between literary and non-literary texts and between textual narratives and other forms of cultural expression.

As new generations of students enter university settings with diverse experiences regarding written and oral communication, shaped by the rapid advance of new technologies, it seems urgent to attempt to revamp and reinvent FL curricula. Innovative ways of (re)engaging students with texts in a conceptually integrated framework, in this age of mass communication dominated by images and screens could help meet the challenges ahead. By adopting a more intellectually grounded and analytical approach to multimodal texts, language educators can help students understand the many forms of human communication and how these become transformed and shaped by historical and social forces.

Reflecting on the various modes of communication, learning to analyze and interpret images and texts, and seeking to understand social, historical, and cultural connections in a foreign language setting help students distance themselves from their own cultural frames of reference and facilitate the cognitive and affective decentration processes that develop "translingual and transcultural competence" (MLA, 2007). Such activities can also provide a springboard for aesthetic reading and appreciation, as this chapter has attempted to demonstrate.

A more encompassing theory of text, as proposed by many researchers in the field, grounded in solid theoretical and pedagogical reflection, could help bring into productive conjunction the goals of the upper and lower levels of the curriculum. Aesthetically valued or culturally salient texts, as well as "mundane" textual and visual narratives can be analyzed, discussed, and compared to help students comprehend the many types of meaning-making that are available in a given context (Kress, 2003). In sum, the multiliteracies framework, with its rich and diverse proposals, can "bring coherence to language programs, and (re)locate these departments within the humanistic tradition to which they belong" (Kumagai & López-Sánchez, Chapter 1, this volume).

It is clear that much remains to be done. Issues such as training and professional development must be addressed if reform is to happen. New ideas must circulate and old dogmas be abandoned. If we, as educators, wish to reshape Foreign Languages and Cultures curricula, it is essential that we call for a meaning-oriented conceptualization of language in higher education, produce some new pedagogical material, and disseminate "seeds of change." It is hoped that this chapter will contribute to conversations about reform and help foster a renewed vision for foreign language departments.

Notes

1 I use the term "Bakhtinian" theory of discourse for the purpose of this chapter to facilitate understanding, in spite of the recent controversies about the authorship of some key texts on genre; see Bronckart and Bota (2011) for more details.

2 With the notable exception of the German Department at Georgetown University, under the leadership of Heidi Byrnes. See Warren and Winkler, "Developing Multiliteracies Through Genre in the Beginner German Classroom" (Chapter 2, this volume) for more information.

3 See Sagnier (2010, 2013) for more details.

4 Once the first reading in the selection of texts of a sequence has been examined and discussed collectively, it is possible to assign the study of the other remaining texts to pairs of students who synthesize the main remarks in a presentation to the class.

5 This work has unfortunately not yet been translated into English, which explains why SDI is not often referenced in publications in English, in spite of its strong contributions to the field.

6 According to the authors (Cope & Kalantzis, 2009), *visual representation* refers to still or moving image, sculpture, craft (representing meaning to another), view vista, scene, and perspective (representing meaning to oneself); *spatial representation* refers to proximity, spacing, layout, interpersonal distance, architecture/building, streetscape, cityscape, and landscape.

7 The material found in this chapter has been translated for an English-speaking audience.

8 In this undergraduate course conducted in a foreign language, I use this terminology of figurative (iconic) signs versus plastic signs for the sake of simplicity, because it is easy for students to understand, although it is not used as such by Kress and van Leuween (2001, 2006). My intention is to have students place visual and textual elements into broad categories and then discuss signs as fusion of form and meaning in a given context, exploring the situated character of meaning-making.

Bibliography

Adam, J.M. (1999). *Linguistique textuelle. Des genres de discours aux textes.* Paris: Nathan Université.

Adam, J.M., & Bonhomme, M. (2012). *L'Argumentation publicitaire.* Paris: Armand Colin.

Allal, L. (1999). Impliquer l'apprenant dans le processus d'évaluation: Promesses et pièges de l'autoévaluation. In C. Depover, & B. Noel (Eds.), *L'Evaluation des compétences et des processus cognitifs* (pp. 35–56). Bruxelles: De Boeck Université.

Allal, L., Bain, D., & Perrenoud, P. (Eds.). (1994). *Evaluation formative et didactique du français.* Neuchâtel: Delachaux et Niestlé.

Allen, H.W., & Paesani, K. (2010). Exploring the feasibility of a pedagogy of multiliteracies in introductory foreign language courses. *L2 Journal, 2,* 119–142.

Amossy, R. (1991). *Sémiologie du stéréotype.* Paris: Nathan.

Amossy, R., & Herschberg-Pierrot, R. (2011). *Stéréotypes et clichés: Langue, discours, société.* Paris: Armand Colin.

Bakhtin, M. (1986). The problem of speech genres. In C. Emerson, & M. Holquist (Eds.), *Speech genres, and other late essays* (pp. 60–102). Austin: University of Texas.

Bakhtine, M. (1984). *Esthétique de la création verbale.* Paris: Gallimard.

Bakhtine, M., & Volochinov, N.V. (1977). *Le Marxisme et la philosophie du langage.* Paris: Editions de Minuit.

Barthes, R. (1964). Rhétorique de l'image. *Communications, 4,* 40–51.

Barthes, R. (1977). *Image–music–text.* London: Fontana Press.

Bawarshi, A.S., & Reiff, M.J. (2010). *Genre: An introduction to history, theory, research and pedagogy.* Anderson, SC: Parlor Press.

Böck, M., & Pachler, N. (Eds.). (2013). *Multimodality and social semiosis: Communication, meaning-making, and learning in the work of Gunther Kress.* New York, NY: Routledge.

Boyer, J.Y., Dionne, J.P., & Raymond, P. (1995). *La Production de textes: Vers un modèle d'enseignement de l'écriture.* Montréal: Les Editions Logiques.

Bronckart, J.P. (1985). *Le Fonctionnement des discours: Un modèle psychologique et une méthode d'analyse.* Paris: Delachaux et Niestlé.

Bronckart, J.P. (1996). *Activité langagière, texte et discours: Pour un interactionnisme socio-discursif.* Lausanne: Delachaux et Niestlé.

Bronckart, J.P., & Bota, C. (2011). *Bakhtine démasqué.* Genève: Droz.

Bronckart, J.P., John Steiner, V., Panofsky, C.P., Piaget, J., Schneuwly, B., Vygotsky, L., & Wertsch, J.V. (1985). *Vygotsky aujourd'hui.* Neuchâtel-Paris: Delachaux et Niestlé.

Brown, A.L. (1987). Metacognition, executive control, self-regulation and other more mysterious mechanisms. In R.H Kluwe, & F.E. Weinert (Eds.), *Metacognition, motivation and understanding* (pp. 64–115). Hillsdale, NJ: Erlbaum.

Brown, A.L. (1992). Design experiments: Theoretical and methodological challenges in creating complex interventions in classroom settings. *The Journal of the Learning Sciences, 2*(2), 141–178.

Brown A.L., & Palincsar A.S. (1982). Inducing strategic learning from texts by means of informed, self-control training. *Topics in Learning and Learning Disabilities, 2*(1), 1–17.

Byrnes, H. (1998). Constructing curricula in collegiate foreign language departments. In H. Byrnes (Ed.), *Learning foreign and second languages: Perspectives in research and scholarship* (pp. 262–295). New York, NY: Modern Language Association.

Byrnes, H. (Ed.). (2006). Perspectives: Interrogating communicative competence as a framework for collegiate foreign language study. *Modern Language Journal, 90,* 244–266.

Byrnes, H. (2011). Reconsidering graduate students' education as scholars-teachers: Mind your language! In H. Willis Allen, & H.H. Maxim (Eds.), *Educating the future foreign language professoriate for the 21st century.* Boston, MA: Heinle.

Byrnes, H., & Maxim, H.H. (Eds.). (2004). *Advanced foreign language learning: A challenge to college programs.* Boston, MA: Thomson Heinle.

Byrnes, H., Maxim, H.H., & Norris, J. (Eds.). (2010). Realizing advanced foreign language writing development in collegiate education: Curricular design, pedagogy, assessment. *Modern Language Journal, 94* (Monograph Series, Issue Supplement s1), 1–235.

Cope, B., & Kalantzis, M. (2000). *Multiliteracies: Literacy learning and the design of social futures.* London: Routledge.

Cope, B., & Kalantzis, M. (2009). "Multiliteracies": New literacies, new learning. *Pedagogies: An International Journal, 4*(3), 164–195.

Dolz, J., & Schneuwly, B. (1996). Genres et progression en expression orale et écrite. *Enjeux 37/38,* 49–75.

Dolz, J., & Schneuwly, B. (1998). *Pour un enseignement de l'oral: Initiation aux genres formels à l'école.* Paris: ESF.

Dolz, J., & Schneuwly, B. (2010). *Des objets enseignés en classe de français.* Rennes: Presses Universitaires de Rennes.

Duprat, A. (2000). *Histoire de France par la caricature.* Paris: Larousse.

Duprat, A. (2007). *Images et histoire: Outils et méthodes d'analyse des documents iconographiques.* Paris: Belin.

Eco, U. (1972). *La Structure absente.* Paris: Mercure de France.

Eco, U. (1979 [1985]). *Lector in fabula.* Paris: Grasset.

Fairclough, N. (1989). *Language and power.* London: Longmans.

Fairclough, N. (1992). *Discourse and social power.* London: Polity Press.

Fairclough, N. (1995). *Critical discourse analysis.* London: Longmans.

Flavell, J. (1979). Metacognition and cognitive monitoring: A new area of cognitive-developmental inquiry. *American Psychologist, 34*(10), 906–911.

Flower, L. (1994). *The construction of negotiated meaning: A social cognitive theory of writing.* Carbondale: Southern Illinois University.

Flower, L., Stein, V., Ackerman, J., Kantz, M.J., McCormick, K., & Peck, W.C. (1990). *Reading-to-write.* New York, NY: Oxford University Press.

Forcadell, F. (1989). *Le Guide du dessin de presse: Histoire de la caricature politique française.* Paris: Syros Alternatives.

Fraenkel, B., Gouiran, M., Jakobowitcz, N., & Tesnière, V. (2013). *Affiche-action: Quand la politique s'écrit dans la rue*. Paris: Gallimard-BDIC.

Gee, J. (1998). What is literacy? In V. Zammel, & R. Spack (Eds.), *Negotiating academic literacies: Teaching and learning across languages and cultures* (pp. 51–59). Mahwah, NJ: Erlbaum Associates.

Gee, J. (1990). *Social linguistics and literacies: Ideologies in discourses*. London: Falmer Press.

Gervereau, L. (1991). *La Propagande par l'affiche*. Paris: Alternatives.

Gervereau, L. (1996). *Terroriser, manipuler, convaincre! Histoire mondiale de l'affiche politique*. Paris: Somogy.

Gervereau, L. (2000). *Les Images qui mentent: Histoire du visuel au XXème siècle*. Paris: Seuil.

Groupe μ. (1992). *Traité du signe visuel: Pour une rhétorique de l'image*. Paris: Seuil.

Halliday, M.A.K. (1978). *Language as social semiotic: The social interpretation of language and meaning*. London: Edward Arnold.

Halliday, M.A.K. (1993). Towards a language-based theory of learning. *Linguistics and Education, 5*, 93–116.

Hodge, R.I.V., & Kress, G.R. (1988). *Social semiotics*. Cambridge, UK: Polity Press.

Howells, R., & Negreiros, J. (2012). *Visual culture* (2nd ed.). Cambridge, UK: Polity Press.

Jakobson, R. (1963). *Essais de linguistique générale*. Paris: Editions de Minuit.

Jauss, H.R. (1978). *Pour une esthétique de la réception*. Paris: Gallimard.

Jewitt, C. (Ed.). (2009). *The Routledge handbook of multimodal analysis*. New York, NY: Routledge.

John-Steiner, V., Panofsky, C.P., & Smith, L.W. (1994). *Sociocultural approaches to language and literacy: An interactionist perspective*. Cambridge, UK: Cambridge University Press.

Joly, M. (2005). *L'Image et les signes*. Paris: Armand Colin.

Kern, R. (2000). *Literacy and language teaching*. Oxford, UK: Oxford University Press.

Kern, R. (2003). Literacy as a new organizing principle for foreign language education. In P.C. Patrikis (Ed.), *Reading between the lines: Perspectives on foreign language literacy* (pp. 40–59). New Haven, CT: Yale University Press.

Kern, R. (2008). Making connections through texts in language teaching. *Language Teaching, 41*, 367–387.

Kramsch, C. (1993). *Context and culture in language teaching*. Oxford, UK: Oxford University Press.

Kramsch, C. (2006). From communicative to symbolic competence. *Modern Language Journal, 90*, 249–252.

Kramsch, C. (2009). *The multilingual subject: What foreign language learners say about their experience and why it matters*. Oxford, UK: Oxford University Press.

Kramsch, C. (2012). The missing link in vision and governance: Foreign language acquisition research. *Profession 2012*, 119–127.

Kress, G. (2003). *Literacy in the new media age*. New York: Routledge.

Kress, G. (2010). *Multimodality: A social semiotic approach to contemporary communication*. New York, NY: Routledge.

Kress, G., & van Leuween, T. (2001). *Multimodal discourses. The modes and media of contemporary communication*. London: Arnold.

Kress, G., & van Leeuwen, T. (2006). *Reading images* (2nd ed.). New York: Routledge.

Lantolf, J. (Ed.). (2000). *Sociocultural theory and second language learning*. Oxford, UK: Oxford University Press.

Maxim, H.H. (2006). Integrating textual thinking into the introductory college-level foreign language classroom. *Modern Language Journal, 90*, 19–32.

Meunier, J.P., & Peraya, D. (2010). *Introduction aux théories de la communication*. Bruxelles: De Boeck.

Modern Language Association (MLA) Ad Hoc Committee on Foreign Languages. (2007). Foreign languages and higher education: New structures for a changed world. *Profession 2007*, 234–245.

Morgan, B., & Ramanathan, V. (2005). Critical literacies and language education: Global and local perspectives. *Annual Review of Applied Linguistics, 25*, 151–169.

New London Group (NLG). (1996). A pedagogy of multiliteracies: Designing social futures. *Harvard Educational Review, 66*(1), 60–92.

Norris, S. (Ed.). (2012). *Multimodality in practice: Investigating theory-in-practice-through-methodology*. New York, NY: Routledge.

Paesani, K. (2004). Using literature to develop language proficiency: Towards an interactive classroom. In C.J. Stivale (Ed.), *Modern French literary studies: Strategic pedagogies* (pp. 13–25). New York, NY: Modern Language Association.

Paris, S.G., Lipson, M.Y., & Wixson, K.K. (1983). Becoming a strategic reader. *Contemporary Educational Psychology, 8*, 293–316.

Paris, S.G., & Winograd, P. (1990). How metacognition can promote academic learning and instruction. In B.F. Jones, & L. Idol (Eds.), *Dimensions of thinking and cognitive instruction* (pp. 15–51). Hillsdale, NJ: Erlbaum Associates.

Prima, M. (2012). Bridging language and history in an advanced Italian classroom: Perspectives in medieval Florentine narratives within their context. *L2 Journal, 4*(1), 142–170.

Rose, G. (2001). *Visual methodologies*. London: Sage.

Sagnier, C. (2010). Objectifs littératie(s): Vers de nouvelles modélisations en didactique des langues étrangères. In F. Neveu, V. Muni Toke, J. Durand, T. Klinger, L. Mondada, & S. Prevost (Eds.), *Actes du Congrès Mondial de Linguistique Française, CMLF 2010*, pp. 609–621.

Sagnier, C. (2013). *Métacognition et interactions sociales en didactique des langues étrangères*. New York, NY: Peter Lang.

Sagnier, C. (n.d.). Reading images in the foreign language classroom: A social semiotic approach. Unpublished manuscript.

Schneuwly, B. (1998). Genres et types de discours: Considérations psychologiques et ontogénétiques. In Y. Reuter (Ed.), *Les Interactions lecture-écriture* (pp. 155–173). Berne: Peter Lang.

Schneuwly, B. (2008). Eléments d'histoire des 20 années passées et propositions conceptuelles pour la suite. In M. Brossard, & J. Fijalkow (Eds.), *Vygotski et les recherches en éducation et didactique* (pp. 19–34). Bordeaux: Presses Universitaires de Bordeaux.

Swaffar, J.K., & Arens, M. (2005). *Remapping the foreign language curriculum: An approach through multiple literacies*. New York, NY: Modern Language Association.

Swaffar, J.K., Arens, M., & Byrnes, H. (1991). *Reading for meaning: An integrated approach to language learning*. Englewood Cliffs, NJ: Prentice Hall.

van Leeuwen, T. (2005). *Introducing social semiotics*. London: Routledge.

Ventola, E., & Guijarro, A.J.M. (Eds.). (2009). *The world told and the world shown: Multisemiotic issues*. Basingstoke: Palgrave Macmillan.

Voloshinov, V.N. (1973). *Marxism and the philosophy of language*. (trans. L. Matjeka & I.R. Titunik). New York, NY: Seminar Press.

Vygotsky, L. (1986). *Thought and language*. Cambridge, MA: The MIT Press.

Warschauer, M. (1997). A sociocultural approach to literacy and its significance for CALL. In K. Murphy-Judy, & R. Sanders (Eds.), *Nexus: The convergence of research &*

teaching through new information technologies (pp. 88–97). Durham: University of North Carolina.

Weill, A. (2011). *Encyclopédie de l'affiche*. Paris: Editions Hazan.

Wells, G. (1999). *Dialogic inquiry: Towards a sociocultural practice and theory of education*. Cambridge, UK: Cambridge University Press.

Wertsch, J. (1985a). *Culture, communication and cognition: Vygotskian perspectives*. Cambridge, UK: Cambridge University Press.

Wertsch, J. (1985b). *Vygotsky and the social formation of the mind*. Cambridge, MA: Harvard University Press.

Wertsch, J. (1991). *Voices of the mind: A sociocultural approach to mediated action*. Cambridge, MA: Harvard University Press.

Willis Allen, H., & Paesani, K. (2010). Exploring the feasibility of multiliteracies in foreign language programs. *L2 Journal, 2*(1), 119–142.

Wlassikof, M. (2002). *Signes de collaboration et de résistance*. Paris: Autrement.

5

READING WORDS TO READ WORLDS

A Genre-Based Critical Multiliteracies Curriculum in Intermediate/Advanced Japanese Language Education

Yuri Kumagai and Noriko Iwasaki

In this chapter, we introduce the principles and the instructional sequence for a *Genre-Based Critical Multiliteracies* curriculum that we have designed and implemented for intermediate to advanced Japanese as a foreign language (JFL) courses. We collaboratively developed and refined the curricular ideas for more than eight years and have incorporated them in a textbook we produced, *The Routledge intermediate to advanced Japanese reader: A genre-based approach to reading as a social practice* (Iwasaki & Kumagai, 2015). What has motivated us to design the curriculum, and subsequently the reader, was the need to address various problems that college-level foreign language (FL) education, particularly JFL education, faces today. The problems we are concerned with are also discussed in the introductory chapter as well as many of the other chapters in this volume.

Below, we first summarize problems specifically related to the treatment of reading in JFL. We then introduce our approach and present its theoretical background. Next, we describe some unique features of Japanese literacy to clarify what the learning of Japanese literacy involves. This is followed by an overall description of our curriculum and a sample sequence of an instructional unit. We then analyze the classroom implementation and retrospective interviews with the students. Finally, we conclude the chapter by re-emphasizing the benefit of the Genre-Based Critical Multiliteracies approach in any FL instruction.

A Solution to the Problems with Japanese-as-a-Foreign-Language Reading Instruction: The Notion of Literacy

In mainstream approaches to teaching FLs, such as communicative language teaching (CLT), "communication" tends to be primarily associated with speaking and listening (Kumagai, Okuizumi, Naka, Muruyama, & Sato, 2013). Thus, in such CLT-based classrooms, particularly in lower-level courses, speaking/listening is emphasized and reading activities are often reduced to mere language exercises (i.e., learning vocabulary, expressions, grammar, etc.). This tendency creates a rift in the articulation with higher-level courses, where reading plays a central role, as also reported for other FLs (Kern, 2003; Kramsch, 2006; Swaffar, 2006).

Though intermediate to advanced JFL textbooks are organized around written texts that are typically selected based on the topics (i.e., topics of potential interest to learners) (e.g., Kamada, Beuckmann, Tomiyama, & Yamamoto, 2012; Oka et al., 2009; Toki, Seki, Hirataka, Shinuchi, & Ishizawa, 2001), their primary focus in dealing with the texts (e.g., post-reading exercises) tends to be on the language (i.e., vocabulary, expressions, grammar, and organizational structure, and *kanji*, Chinese characters), and the potential for intellectual engagement with the content tends to be secondary. Further, the social meanings and effects conveyed by the writers' textual choice (e.g., style, vocabulary, discourse structure) are rarely considered (Iwasaki & Kumagai, 2008; Kumagai & Iwasaki, 2011).

Moreover, the goals for reading instruction, regardless of the levels, are often to develop students' ability to accurately retrieve information from texts. This emphasis on literal comprehension rather than on interpretive or evaluative reading practices is especially marked in JFL instruction due to the perceived challenge that its writing system presents (Iventosch, 2012).

Furthermore, like other FL instruction, reading is often treated separately from writing, which tends to be regarded as a means for the learners to practice and demonstrate what they have learned, rather than as a means to communicate and interact with people (Kumagai, 2007). But reading and writing (and talking around the texts) are intimately interconnected social practices. Hence, rather than treating reading and writing as discrete skills/activities, we adopt here a notion of literacy that allows us to have "a more unified discussion of relation between readers, writers, texts, culture, and language learning" (Kern, 2003, p. 43), and expand this notion further.

Expanding the Notion of Literacy to Multiliteracies

Globalization and the spread of the internet have transformed the way people engage in literacy practices. Internet-based communication tools allow people to access various types of information and to communicate with familiar and unfamiliar others beyond the boundary of time and space. Newly developed communication technologies also bring to the fore the multimodal nature of communication. Therefore, as emphasized in the recent theories of literacy (i.e., New Literacy Studies), language is recognized as just one element of meaning-making, which gets combined with various modes, including visual, aural, spatial, and gestural (Kress, 2003).

Against such a backdrop, what is now important to develop in FL is not only the knowledge and proficiency of a particular target language/culture and "mere literacy"[1] (Cope & Kalantzis, 2000, p. 5), but also the ability to draw upon all languages/cultures one knows and to interpret multimodal meanings in making sense of interactional context and achieving understanding: *multiliteracies*.

The term "multiliteracies" was first coined by the New London Group (NLG) (1996, 2000). The NLG put two principal aspects of multiplicity at its core: first, "the multifarious cultures that [are] interrelated and the plurality of texts that circulate" in our culturally and linguistically diverse society and, second, the "burgeoning variety of text forms associated with information and multimedia technologies" (NLG, 2000, p. 9). In other words, the concept of multiliteracies regards both *societal* multilingualism/multiculturalism and multimodality/multimedia as important when thinking about a new approach to literacy pedagogy.

Moreover, it also acknowledges *individuals'* resources of multiple languages and cultures as the statement suggests: "When learners juxtapose different languages, discourses, styles, and approaches, they gain substantively in metacognitive and metalinguistic abilities and in their ability to reflect critically on complex systems and their interactions" (NLG, 2000, p. 15).

Echoing the NLG's argument above, the Common European Framework of Reference (CEFR) underscores the benefit of linguistic and cultural repertoires stemming from multiple languages and cultures that one possesses; namely, *plurilingual* and *pluricultural* competences are key competences (Council of Europe, 2001).

Although the NLG (1996, 2000), in its *pedagogy of multiliteracies*, uses the term "discourse," we believe that designing curricula around the notion of "genres" is effective as it provides a way to analyze conventionalized linguistic practices specific to discourse communities. The notion of "genre" adopted here is based on the writer's purpose and goal (social process), which are actualized in different types of texts (e.g., news reports and essays). Such genres can be characterized by their "lexicogrammatical choices for meaning-making ... which are available in a specific discourse community" (Goldoni, 2008, p. 70), and these lexicogrammatical choices are important for the writer and reader to successfully and efficiently communicate in society.

We thus suggest that FL curricula move beyond the comprehension-based, mono-modal approach, and adopt a genre-based, plurilinguistic/pluricultural multiliteracies approach that better prepares our students to become critical readers/ writers of words and worlds.

Genre-Based Critical Multiliteracies and its Theoretical Background

We have drawn on two theoretical notions above in designing our curriculum: *genre* and *multiliteracies*. We further adopt another pedagogical orientation to reinforce our approach: *critical literacy*. We call this approach *Genre-Based Critical Multiliteracies*. Below, we discuss the genre-based approach and describe critical literacy and how we incorporate them into our curriculum.

Genre-Based Approach

"Genre" is a notion that is variously defined. What we adopt here is a view that sees genre as goal-oriented social process, a view that is based on systemic functional linguistics (SFL) (Halliday & Hasan, 1989; Halliday & Matthiessen, 2004). According to SFL, the text in each genre has socioculturally recognizable textual patterns for achieving a particular social aim. Hence, a genre-based literacy approach focuses on text as a representation of semantic choices in social context and focuses on grammar as a meaning-making resource (Martin, 2009).

Traditionally, genre-based pedagogies are concerned mainly with teaching (academic) writing because of the role assigned to writing as an assessment tool in a school context. However, more recently, the notion of genre has also been incorporated into the teaching of reading, as writing and reading are fundamentally interconnected (i.e., literacy) (Martin & Rose, 2005; Rose, 2006). Cope and Kalantzis (1993) describe genre and its relations to learning literacy as follows:

> Genre is a category that describes the relation of the social purpose of text to language structure. It follows that in learning literacy, students need to analyse critically the different social purposes that inform patterns of regularity in language—the whys and the hows of textual conventionality, in other words. (p. 2)

Critically analyzing "the whys and hows of textual conventionality" not only teaches learners normative practices of various genres, but also allows them to recognize deviations from norms that writers intentionally take in order to create special effects suitable for their intentions. It also makes it more visible that, because of the changing communication landscape brought by new technologies, the boundary of each genre has become blurred, and new and hybrid forms of genres (i.e., "multigeneric, intergeneric and heteroglossic texts") are constantly being produced (Cope & Kalantzis, 1993, p. 16). Therefore, developing a keen sense of such deviation and recognition of hybridity would allow learners to become critical readers who can interpret and critique the writer's intention and assumptions as well as the underlying ideologies implicated in the text.

In the field of second language teaching (i.e., ESL), genre-based pedagogies (mainly focused on writing) influenced by SFL have gained some prominence (e.g., Hyland, 2004; Johns, 2002; Scheleppegrell & Colombi, 2002, to name a few). Yet, within the FL education, the model developed by Byrnes and her colleague remains the only approach that is clearly articulated and systematically developed (Byrnes & Sprang, 2004; see Chapter 1, this volume, for more detail; also, Chapters 2 and 3, this volume). Their curricular model aims at developing the learners' "genre-based capacities" across all levels of language instruction (Byrnes, 2012). They use a teaching cycle (or a "wheel" model) with four distinct stages proposed by Rothery (1996) (see Chapter 2, this volume).

Genre pedagogy (in a strict sense) has been criticized by critically oriented scholars as "too didactic, and as uncritically naturalizing the status quo"; also, "by reifying the features of these genres they inhibited creativity and possibility for subversive and/or transformative redesign" (Janks, 2010, p. 122; see also Benesch, 2001; Cope & Kalantzis, 1993; Kress, 1999; Luke, 1996, among others, for similar critiques). Cope and Kalantzis (1993) have also argued against the "wheel" model as, if not used critically, it simply "[tells] students how they should write . . . and help[s] students internalize the form . . . so that they can reproduce that form" (p. 15). However, as Janks (2000, 2010) has pointed out, genre pedagogy recognizes the importance of providing access to "powerful discourse" for learners of the language (Hasan, 1996; Hyland, 2003).

Providing access to "powerful FL discourses" is precisely the reason we have adopted the notion of genre as a way to organize the texts in our curriculum. For FL learners to interpret FL texts, it is vital to understand and become familiar with generic features (with their intended purposes and social effects) that are characteristic of various genres that are exemplified by texts (Derewianka, 1990). However, the goal of the genre-based approach should not be simply teaching the generic features so that the learners can reproduce them; it is rather to make learners recognize various textual features and use them as a tool to analyze the conventionalized nature of linguistic interactions and the way in which language both reflects and constructs certain relations of power and authority (Kress, 1993).

Our approach, then, is to adopt *genre* and *multiliteracies* with critical analysis, similarly to an approach adopted by Macken-Horarik, an Australian SFL scholar whose work is at the intersection of genre and multiliteracies (and critical literacy). She wrote with her colleague, Hammond:

> Systematic discussion of language choices in text construction and the development of metalanguage—that is, of functional ways of talking and thinking about language—facilitates critical analysis. It helps students see written texts as constructs that can be discussed in quite precise and explicit ways and that can therefore be analysed, compared, criticised, deconstructed, and reconstructed. (Hammond & Macken-Horarik, 1999, p. 529)

"Critical" Multiliteracies

The pedagogy of multiliteracies as proposed by the NLG (1996, 2000) considers *Critical Framing* as one of the four essential components in the instructional process (see Chapter 1, this volume, for details). Thus, one might think it is redundant to call an approach *critical* multiliteracies. However, we have decided to name it as such in order to foreground the importance and value we place on *critical literacy*. The word "critical" here "signals a move to question the naturalized assumptions of the discipline, its truths, its discourses and its attendant practices," rather than to mean "reasoned analysis based on an examination of evidence and argument" (Janks, 2010, pp. 12–13).

Critical literacy focuses specifically on developing awareness of the power relations that authors create in texts. Given that "[all texts] are positioned by the writer's point of view, and the linguistic (and other semiotic) choices made by the writer are designed to produce effects that position the reader" (Janks, 2010, p. 61), critical literacy uses a linguistic analysis of texts to help learners recognize how authors shape their messages for particular readers for particular purposes (Pennycook, 2001). As Lemke (1995) puts it, "our meanings shape and are shaped by our social relationships both as individuals and as members of social groups . . . The meanings we make define not only ourselves, they also define our communities, . . . and our era in history" (p. 1). In other words, meanings created through texts do not exist in a vacuum, but are historically, socioculturally, and ideologically contextualized. For readers to be able to engage critically with texts, understanding such historical and sociocultural backgrounds of texts is immensely important.

Critical engagement with texts is undoubtedly a challenging task for FL readers, since they read texts written by the author for their imagined audience/community, which most likely does not include FL learners and their home community (Kramsch, 1993; Wallace, 2003). FL readers need to interpret the text from the viewpoint of the writer's and imagined reader's perspective (which they are not familiar with), as well as from their own and their familiar communities' perspectives. To accomplish this complex task, the students need to mobilize their multiple linguistic and cultural repertoires. In the CEFR, learners with multiple linguistic/cultural repertoires are termed "plurilingual language users,"[2] who build up a communicative competence to which all knowledge and experience of language contributes and in which languages interrelate and interact"(Council of Europe, 2001, p. 4). And they "can call flexibly upon different parts of this competence to achieve effective communication with a particular interlocutor" (p. 4). As FL readers, then, by shuttling between languages and by negotiating the diverse linguistic resources (for situated construction of meaning), the students can play mediator roles between the languages and cultures.

By engaging in critical multiliteracies practice in FL, students begin to recognize that what is written in the texts is not indisputable fact but rather the author's views or interpretations of the event shaped by a particular ideology. Being mindful and extremely cautious toward such textual politics is particularly crucial for FL students because they tend to have "an overly deferential stance" (Wallace, 2003) toward authentic FL texts due to their subjectivity as "learners" of that language. Recognizing the choices that text authors make to accomplish their purpose with particular use of linguistic devices and other semiotic systems is an important step for them to become active agents in the world with their own words for their own purposes.

To this end, the *Genre-Based Critical Multiliteracies* curriculum we propose here provides explicit guidance for students to unpack underlying assumptions and implicit meanings embedded in texts. Our curriculum views FL learners as emergent plurilingual users, and encourages them to mobilize their knowledge and ability about languages and multimodality for further development of the target language and plurilingual communicative competence.

Literacy in the Japanese Language

In this section, we briefly describe some important features of the Japanese language to clarify Japanese literacy and what its learning entails.

Japanese has three distinctive orthographies: *hiragana, katakana*, and *kanji*. These systems (and occasionally the Roman alphabets) are all used in typical Japanese texts. *Hiragana* and *katakana* are sound-based scripts called syllabaries (46 symbols in each). The other system, *kanji*, Chinese characters is a meaning-based script where each character represents a meaning. Though more than 50,000 *kanji* are said to exist in the Japanese language, the list of the commonly used *kanji* characters revised by the Ministry of Education, Science and Culture in 2010, contains 2,136 characters.[3] One of the major difficulties that Japanese readers face regarding *kanji*—aside from their sheer number and complexities of some in scribing—is the multiple pronunciations (sounding out) assigned to a single *kanji* (Toyoda, 1995). For example, a character "生" can be sounded out as "sei/see" "syoo," "zyoo," "u," "i," "nama," or "ki" depending on which word it appears in. This poses great difficulty and creates much dismay for JFL learners.

Each writing system has its own function (i.e., *hiragana*, primarily for function words such as case markers and verbal/adjectival suffixes; *katakana*, mainly for foreign-origin words; and *kanji* for content words). Yet, a writer has some freedom for the choice of orthography. For example, the Japanese word *kotoba* [language] can be written in *hiragana* (ことば), *katakana* (コトバ) or *kanji* (言葉), and each choice evokes different images and effects (Iwahara, Hatta, & Maehara, 2003; Smith & Schmidt, 1996). In addition, words from three types of vocabularies often exist for (nearly) an identical referent: Japanese native words, Sino-Japanese words (Chinese origin), and loanwords from Western languages (predominantly from English). For instance, a writer can be referred to as *kakite* (書き手), *hissha* (筆者), and *raitaa* (ライター), respectively. Both the choice of orthography and that of vocabulary evoke different images of the reference and of the writer (e.g., social status, sophistication) that she/he wishes to present to the readers.

As for styles, Japanese has two primary styles: the plain style and the *desu-masu* style. The plain style (e.g., *mondai da*, [(it) is a problem]) is commonly used in impersonal writing such as newspapers and academic writing to address a group of people and also in informal messages such as emails along with the use of interactive particles such as *ne* [agreement seeker] and *yo* [assertion]. The polite *desu-masu* style (e.g., *mondai desu*, [(it) is a problem]) is often used in letters and in prose to address an audience as if they were being spoken to (Maynard, 1991). Writers sometimes mix these styles strategically (Makino, 2002; Maynard, 1991, 2004). For instance, although the default style in newspapers and magazines is the plain style, when authors express their views or opinions (e.g., readers' opinion columns) they may choose to mix the styles (i.e., shift to the *desu-masu* style) in order to address their readers with a touch of interactive tone. Moreover, Maynard (2004) argues that "style mixture in contemporary writings is a strategy through which the writer expresses multiple emotions in varying intensities, creates multiple identities, and enhances the creative use of language" (p. 387).

Further, Japanese texts can be written both horizontally and vertically. The way the texts are written often depends on such factors as the type of texts (e.g., academic vs. popular texts; literary vs. science texts; Japanese-style vs. Western-style, etc.), mediums (e.g., books, magazines, newspapers, web-based, etc.), and social purposes of texts (e.g., creating a desired image in advertising, instructing, etc.). Also, within the same page, both directions of text can coexist (e.g., while the default writing direction of newspaper articles on paper is vertical, the headline(s) for the same article can be written horizontally). The different direction of texts evokes different impressions and creates different impacts on the readers. According to Okamoto (2013), the vertical writings are seen as associated with traditional, formal, and Japanese styles, while the horizontal writings with casual and Western styles.

Considering these characteristics in Japanese language literacy described above, we have designed a Genre-Based Critical Multiliteracies curriculum to guide students to become aware of the effects of semiotic choices, particularly those of writing systems, lexis, styles, and grammatical structures.

The Genre-Based Critical Multiliteracies Curriculum

We designed a curriculum for intermediate to advanced JFL (Iwasaki & Kumagai, 2015) with the following four aims:

1. **To develop an awareness of the purpose and effects of the author's choices (language and visual information) that suit particular audiences and purpose of writing.**

    The curriculum helps learners explore language choices and textual patterns in various genres (defined by the writer's purpose) in different types of texts (e.g., news reports, essays, short stories). Under "Language choices" discussed below, students are asked to focus on the choice of scripts, vocabulary, and styles (plain, *desu-masu*, mixed; conversational/spoken vs. written), as well as grammatical structures (e.g., passive vs. active; transitive vs. intransitive) and overall textual organization. As the distinction between written and spoken texts is increasingly blurred (e.g., on the internet), it becomes important to be aware of the respective effects of features associated with spoken and written language. Learners are also guided to analyze the effect of visual information (e.g., reflected in different scripts, fonts, emoticons, pictures) to develop their multimodal competence in making meaning out of texts.

2. **To understand how texts are situated in society.**

    Learners need to understand the contexts in which each text is written and/or published in order to appreciate and analyze the writer's purpose of writing the text and its potential significance. Such contexts include the type of media (whether it is a newspaper article or literary work), the perceived status/role of the particular publication (liberal vs. conservative newspapers; magazines or books in a variety of genres and for targeted readers thereof), societal situations of the time when it was written/published, and the profile and historical background of the writer. We provide essential information about each text and writer and also guide learners to explore ways to situate texts in society (e.g., by looking up information using internet resources).

3. **To appreciate the content and how it connects to other disciplines and society.**

    Texts are selected on the basis of richness and value of their content. We provide guiding questions to stimulate the learners' intellectual curiosity about the topic and related issues, and encourage further enquiry into these issues. In particular, we consider that materials to counter essentialized linguistic and cultural representations are valuable following recommendations given by such scholars as Kubota (2003).

4. **To become self-actualized readers and build their individual reading agendas.**

    The curriculum framework attempts to promote learner autonomy and social agency by guiding JFL readers to critically evaluate each text by considering (1) and (2) above and to further develop their ability to make meaning of other texts on their own in the wider world beyond the classroom. Through scaffolded activities, learners are guided to recognize the textual structure of a given genre and employ different reading strategies depending on text type and purpose of reading, and are guided to represent their interpretations by discussing the texts. In addition, we suggest activities for the learners to learn about the writer, issues, and social backgrounds of the writer/texts and beyond (e.g., by doing research using the internet, etc.). These activities will then develop the learners' capacity to read what they want and to participate more actively in society; they will guide them to become "code breakers," "text participants," "text users," and "text analysts and critics" (Luke, 2000) who are aware of social and cultural issues.

Selection of Texts

We chose texts based on their genres and contents. Below are the genres of the texts we selected (and their associated social purposes in parentheses). In order for learners to become familiar with various genres, we selected genres that are important and highly visible in our textual world.

- Reporting texts (*informing*) in which authors report events and survey results.
- Opinion texts (*appealing; evaluating*) in which authors express their opinions to appeal to the society or their evaluation of a book/film/TV program.
- Fictions (*entertaining*).
- Spoken language texts (*engaging*) in which authors represent interviews or write scripts for speeches.
- Essays (*narrating; responding*) in which authors narrate or explain their personal experiences and express their thoughts (e.g., in response to the well-accepted views shared in the community).

The texts were used in their original format, allowing the learner to recognize the features of a genre (such as layout and organization, text directions, size and type of fonts, and use and placement of images, etc.).

In terms of the content, we selected texts that are not only of interest to JFL learners, but also those that allow learners to reflect critically on and question certain stereotypical, essentialized views of Japanese society, culture, people, and language and that promote students' awareness of diversity and fluidity (Kubota, 2003). To challenge the monolithic understanding of traditional culture, for example, we chose texts that represent the voices of "minorities" in Japan (e.g., Ainu, *zainichi* Koreans,[4] non-native Japanese writers).

Sequencing of Instruction Revolving Around Each Text Lesson

For learners to situate the text and the author in the historical and sociocultural context, we provide brief biographic information about each author and text (including a type of genre) at the beginning of each lesson. Such background information, which is often "common knowledge" among the readers living in Japan (i.e., imagined target readers), is essential to understand the social meaning and significance of the text. Below, we describe the sequence of activities for each lesson:

1. *"Pre-reading" activities* help learners activate their personal experience and knowledge related to the topic and the type of text. For example, learners are asked to conjecture what the text is about based on the background information given and from the title of the text. To alleviate the burden of

new vocabulary the learners encounter in the text, some of the key terms are introduced in these activities, allowing the learners to become familiar with them before reading the text. These activities help the learner to recognize its genre and field, which would facilitate the understanding and interpretation of the text they read.

2. *"While-reading" activities* ask learners questions to (a) look for the broader meaning, such as key sentences or the main point of the text, instead of seeking word-by-word, sentence-by-sentence meaning, and (b) to notice the author's choice of visual information and linguistic features that are important to understand the text (e.g., sentence-ending patterns, the use of quotes, or the organization of the text as a whole).

3. *"After-reading" activities*, which follow comprehension questions that confirm the learners' general comprehension of the text, consist of two types of discussions that focus on different, yet equally important, aspects of reading. The first type of questions guides learners to analyze semiotic choices, their intended effects, and their effectiveness. Features selected for discussion include: (a) style, (b) orthography, (c) vocabulary (*wago, kango, gairaigo*, onomatopoeia), (d) grammatical structure (e.g., causative, passive, intransitive, and transitive, whose forms students are assumed to have the knowledge of), (e) direct/indirect quotes, (f) text organizations (i.e., stages), and (g) other modes (e.g., layout, color, images, size and type of fonts, etc.). The second type of questions encourages students to discuss the content of the text, reflecting on their own thoughts and ideas about the issue presented in the text.

4. *Writing activities* allow the learners to write their own text using both their linguistic (i.e., vocabulary, style, genre, etc.) and content knowledge they have gained in the curriculum in order to achieve a specified social purpose.

In the remainder of the chapter, we describe the implementation of the instructional sequence that was put into practice using web-based news in a third-year (the fifth semester) college Japanese classroom in the US. This is both to illustrate the curriculum in concrete terms and to report the students' learning outcomes based on the analysis of classroom interactions (audio-recorded), students' writings, and interviews that were carried out after the instruction.

Sequence of a Sample Instructional Unit

The students in this class (the fifth-semester Japanese) had studied Japanese in the previous two years and had learned all the basic grammar structures including passive and causative. The data we share below were collected in the fall of 2010 and 2011. Seven and 11 students, shown in Table 5.1,[5] were enrolled in the course respectively.

We spent three sessions (70 minutes each) completing this unit. In this unit, students read two web-based newspaper articles about the same event: one published

TABLE 5.1 Students' Profile

2010: 7 students, age 19–21			2011: 11 students, age 19–24		
Name	Ethnicity/ Nationality	L1 (FL)	Name	Ethnicity/ Nationality	L1 (FL)
Betty	European-American	English, Italian (German)	Lisa	European-American	English (Spanish)
Wendy	African-American	English	Faith	European-American	English (Spanish)
Sophia	European-American	English (Russian, Korean)	Katia	European-American	English
Helen	Chinese-American	English (Mandarin)	Annie	European-American	English (Spanish)
Pat	European-American	English	Kristi	European-American	English
Cathy	Jewish-American	English (Hebrew)	Sonia	European-American	English (Italian)
Tami	Taiwanese	Mandarin, Cantonese (English)	Jana	Rwandan/American	English, Kinyarwanda (French, Mandarin)
			Julianne	Korean-American	English, Korean (Spanish)
			Angie	European-American	English (Spanish)
			Elena	European-American	English (French)
			Sarah	Korean-American	English, Korean

by *The New York Times* (www.nytimes.com) in English and the other by *Asahi Shimbun Digital* (www.asahi.com) in Japanese. Crucially, the articles (written in the two languages and, thus, targeting two different communities) differ in terms of the sociopolitical/cultural background knowledge of the writer and his/her imagined target readers. Such differences in target audiences lead to differences in the writers' selection of information and linguistic resources that may give readers differential impressions and ideas about the reported event. The activities aimed to take advantage of the students' linguistic and cultural resources in both languages, and to enhance the learners' agency as plurilingual users, allowing them to realize the important role they can play as cultural and linguistic mediators.

The event reported in the articles involves American teenagers from an American military base in Japan, who allegedly strung a rope across a road, toppling a Japanese female motorbike rider, and seriously injuring her. The articles report the event in a temporal sequence, and thus can be characterized as recounts. The event brings up different collective memories among the readers of two communities. In particular, among readers in Japanese communities, any episodes related to the US military bases in Japan are likely to remind people of other incidents and crimes that took place in the US military bases in the past.

Prior to the sessions, students were given opportunities at the college's library to become familiarized with the format (e.g., layout, sections) of the Japanese newspapers and to compare it with American newspapers that they were used to seeing and reading in the US.

In the first session, students engaged in *Pre-reading* activities, by first reading the *New York Times* article, to whose target audience community the students more or less belong (i.e., English speakers in the US.). Next, they summarized the event in Japanese, utilizing a list of key words taken from the *Asahi* article. In so doing, the students familiarized themselves with the gist of the event and with the language (i.e., vocabulary) that they needed to discuss the episode and to read the Japanese article. The students were instructed to read the *Asahi* article at home in preparation for the next session.

In the second session, the students discussed the textual features and content of the *Asahi* article based on *While-reading* and comprehension questions given to the students prior to reading. Among the *While-reading* questions were questions instructing the learners to find the most important paragraph in the article, and to underline the participants in the (series of) events. These questions are designed not merely to help learners grasp the main idea; crucially, they also provide the keys to recognizing the genre's structure ("stages") that are typical in news reports (recounts). Recount texts generally start with an *orientation*, which gives the information as to who was involved in the event and when and where it happened; it is followed by a *record of events*, presenting events in the chronological order; and it often ends with a *reorientation* that brings events into the present (Hyland, 2004, p. 33).

Other *While-reading* questions guided students to pay attention to textual features (e.g., sentence-ending epistemic modality) and direct quotes from the participants. This was followed by comprehension questions to check the students' understanding of the content.

In the third session, the students discussed their analyses of the text in depth based on *After-reading* questions, particularly paying attention to the effects of language choice on the reader. For example, the effect of the use of causative was discussed by comparing the two sentences below: one containing causative predicates (i.e., made [the woman] topple; made [her] get injured) and the other containing active intransitive predicates (i.e., [the woman] toppled over; got injured).

a.   ４人がロープを張り通りかかった女性を転倒させ、重傷を負わせた。
     Yo-nin-ga   *roopu-o*   *hari,*   *toorikakat-ta*   *josei-o*
     4-counter-nom rope-acc   string.ger   pass.by-past   woman-acc

     tentoo-sase,   *juusho-o*   *owa-se-ta.*[6]
     topple-cause   serious.injury-acc   inflict-cause-past

[The four strung a rope and made a passer-by woman topple over and caused serious injury.]

b.   ４人の張ったロープで通りかかった女性が転倒し、重傷を負った。
Yo-nin-no   hat-ta   roopu-de   toorikakat-ta josei-ga   tentoo-si,
4-counter-gen string-past rope-inst pass.by-past woman-nom topple-and

juusho-o   ot-ta.
serious.injury-acc   receive-past

[Because of a rope that the four strung, a passer-by woman toppled over and got seriously injured.]

The students also compared the information selected in the two articles, and the effect of the inclusion (and exclusion) of the information on the respective reader. For instance, while the *New York Times* article included a mention of a boy having sought help from a passer-by for the injured woman, the *Asahi* article contained two rather conflicting statements made by two of the four teenagers (one stating that two of the others strung the rope; the other stating that the action was decided by all four). The *Asahi* also mentioned that among the four teenagers were three high school students and one unemployed person, and that they originally gave the police fake names (see Appendix A for a comparison of information selected in the two articles). The *Asahi* article also included a drawing of the site of the accident, illustrating how the rope was strung.

Each student was then instructed to write an email message to her imagined Japanese friend, whose American colleagues only read *The New York Times*. The task was to inform her that her American colleagues' impression of the episode may differ due to the way the event is reported in *The New York Times*.

Illustration and Analysis of Classroom Discussions

We illustrate how students engaged in these activities by providing some excerpts from the classroom interactions. The interactions were nearly all carried out in Japanese and translated by the authors; words spoken in English are underlined. The parts important for our analysis below are in bold.

Effects of Language Choice and Information

In Excerpt 1 below, the ways in which the incident was treated differently by the two articles were discussed.

Excerpt 1
 1. T(eacher): Was the information contained in the quote also in the NY Times?
 2. Wendy: No. It wasn't.
 3. T: Why do you think it wasn't?
 4. Sophie: I think it's because **they have different purposes**. Asahi has more **detailed information**. But the NY Times article does not have that much **interest** (in the event).

5.	T:	Right. There are not as many details in *The New York Times*. What do you think, Helen?
6.	Helen:	I don't know.
7.	Tami:	It gives **a bad image** to readers.
8.	T:	Bad image if there is a quote?
9.	Tami:	About Americans.
10.	T:	You think quotes are there to give readers a bad image of Americans?
11.	Tami:	Yeah, <u>I feel like</u> ... *The New York Times* **does not regard the crime as a crime**.
12.	Betty:	Yes.
13.	T:	Then, what is it like?
14.	Tami:	**Like teenagers, like children or something. Make it look like it's just kids that are messed up**.
15.	Pat:	The **titles of the articles** also give that impression.
16.	Betty:	Yeah.
17.	Pat:	In *The New York Times*, "Four American Teenagers Arrested," but in *Asahi*, <u>"Four Teenagers Charged With Attempted Murder."</u>

The students readily interpreted and independently realized that the purpose of each article was shaped by the (imagined) readers' interest assumed by the writer, which consequently affected the details and types of information included in each article. Also, students made a point that the wording in the headlines and the use of quotes had created different impressions regarding the seriousness of the incident. Tami felt that the use of quotes in *Asahi* gave a "bad image about Americans" (lines 7 & 9) while *The New York Times* gave its readers an impression that the incident was as if it was just "kids [that] are messed up" (line 14). Agreeing with Tami's interpretation, Pat noted that the wording in the *Asahi* headline itself made the incident sound like a serious crime (lines 15 & 17). These interactions demonstrate that students were actively constructing meaning using their knowledge of both English and Japanese.

Effects of Causatives

As described above, we posed the question regarding the use of causatives: Compare the different nuances the readers get from two sentences describing the same event with and without causatives. The excerpt below shows students discussing the effects of causatives.

Excerpt 2

1.	T(eacher):	(Comparing the causative sentence (a) in the text with a sentence without causative (b)) What do you think?
2.	Tami:	in (a), **the woman became a victim**, and ...
3.	T:	What? Can you say that again?
4.	Tami:	<u>Like victim, victimized</u>.

5. T: Why do you think so?
6. Cathy: Because it uses causative. Um ... it shows the **woman's** <u>**tragic**</u> <u>**situation**</u>.
7. T: What do you think, Wendy?
8. Wendy: In (a), by putting up the rope ... <u>they intended</u>.
9. T: Right, intentionally.
10. Wendy: **They intentionally made the woman overturn**. In (b) ... um, <u>**innocent**</u>. <u>It's more like an accident</u>. In (a), they are guilty, but not in (b). In (a), because of the causative, the woman seems not to know.
11. T: In (b) she seems to know?
12. Betty: **In (a), something is done to her. She has no control over what happened to her.**

This excerpt shows students' active engagement in comparing different impressions that causative and non-causative statements had created. They articulated that while the sentence without the causative described the event as though it was "an innocent accident," the one with the causative highlighted the intention of the (evil) act done to the woman who had no control over the incident and became the victim. They recognized how a certain choice of grammatical structure (in this case, causative) evoked different nuances and images, and communicated different messages to the readers.

Writing Assignment

At the end of the instructional sequence, as noted above, each student was instructed to write an email message to her (imagined) friend, who may encounter a situation where a misunderstanding occurs between the Japanese-only readers and the English-only readers about the news.

Although students' writings were not always accurate or appropriate (in openings/endings), most of them showed clear awareness of what might help the Japanese acquaintance to avoid a misunderstanding with her colleagues. Our analysis shows the following characteristics in the content of many of the students' writing (the numbers in parentheses show the number of students who included the information in their writings):

- American colleagues may not be able to situate the event in the history and experience of the Japanese. (7)
- *The New York Times* does not have much information about the teenagers; there were no quotes from the teenagers. (15)
- *The New York Times* does not give an impression that the teenagers might have committed a serious crime. (10)

For the second point above (*Asahi* being more informative), one student (Tami) in particular focused in her "email" on the fact that *Asahi* included a visual image of the scene, which made it unexpectedly easier for her (the audience) to understand the event. This attention to the presence of the image and its effect shows the student's awareness that visual information makes a difference in the impression that the reader may have.

Overall, the ways the students wrote varied greatly (two examples in original Japanese are given in Appendix B). To exemplify their writing, the following is the authors' translation of what Lisa (a junior-year, European-American student of Engineering) wrote (see Appendix B):

> Hi,
>
> I've heard that you read the newspaper article titled "Four Children of US Military Personnel Arrested on Charges of Attempted Murder." It was interesting, wasn't it? I read that too. Actually, there is also an article about this incident in the *The New York Times*, in the US. The title is "Four American Teenagers Arrested in Japan." The article has a lot of the same information, but the details are a little different. You might be able to see it if you compare the titles.
>
> For example in the Japanese newspaper, they used quotes by the teenagers. Their responses were suspicious so they give a bad impression. But according to the *The New York Times*, one of the kids tried to find someone to help the woman who was toppled. This is not a quote, but it implies that the suspect is a good person.
>
> Further, the Japanese article said that the US military was initially resisting to cooperate, but in the *The New York Times*, it only reported that "US military is cooperating." It did not give much detail about this information.
>
> Why is the information a bit different? I think it's because they are writing for different readers and so there is a bias. So if you have a chance to meet and talk with Americans about this article, please tell them about what you know. And I think it would be good too if you listen to what they know about it. If you learn different opinions and perspectives, you will understand the incident better.

In her text, Lisa explained how each article created different impressions by comparing and contrasting the ways each article portrayed the incident. First, she informed her friend that the title and details reported in each article differed. Then she pointed out that *Asahi* highlighted how the teenagers were suspicious by including two direct quotes, which contradicted each other. Next, she mentioned that *The New York Times* tried to portray the teenagers as "good" by mentioning that they tried to seek help for the woman who was toppled. She also explained that *Asahi* reported that the US military was initially resisting to cooperate whereas *The New York Times* only mentioned that the US military was cooperating. With these examples, Lisa explained how each newspaper article created different impressions about the American teenagers and about the ways the American military authority dealt with the incident. She then gave her opinions that these discrepancies were due to differences in each newspaper's intended audience and different biases. In the end, she took up the position of a mediator and suggested that her friend shares with American colleagues different opinions and perspectives that are promoted in each newspaper.

In terms of her use of language, she began the email message with an appropriate greeting (*konnichiwa*, [hi]) and used the *desu-masu* style throughout as if she was speaking personally to her friend. She carefully chose modality expressions, which allowed her to express her opinions without being too assertive (e.g., use of . . . *kamo shiremasen*, [might] . . . *tara ii to omoimasu*, [it would be good if . . .]). Similarly, by using a rhetorical strategy of self-posing a question and answer (*dooshite sono joohoo wa chotto chigaimasuka?*, [why is the information a little different?]), instead of making her opinion sound authoritative, she positioned herself at the level of her friend (who may also wonder) maintaining a friendly tone. Her use of language demonstrates her ability to mobilize her linguistic resources to achieve the social goal of this writing task.

Interviews: Students' Thoughts About the Task

After the semester was over, the first author conducted interviews (in English) with all her students in order to learn their thoughts about the activities. What emerged from the interviews was that students' awareness of three key areas was heightened by class instruction.

First, students were led to recognize how different sociocultural perspectives are reflected in the ways news articles are written.

Excerpt 3

T: What do you think about the purpose of this activity?

Wendy: Um, I think, I think it was good because usually if I think about newspapers, I think about my hometown newspaper, and like *The New York Times*. Um, and I'm not really comparing them to, I guess, other perspectives? . . . **I never seriously thought about, um, how the perspectives can be different**, if it's not just along with political parties. **If it's cultural difference, like based on histories and experiences, it's good to think about who is writing, and who they are targeting** . . .

In Excerpt 3, Wendy says that originally she thought different perspectives were only born out of different political stances. But, through this activity, she came to realize different perspectives were also shaped by sociocultural differences resulting from different histories and experiences. She realized that such perspectives consequently affected how newspaper articles were written.

Second, students were guided to realize there is no clear line between "facts" and "opinions" in news reports. Namely, what appear to be reported as "facts" may embed opinions of the writer or the community that the writer (or the editor) belongs to, as shown in Sophia's statement in Excerpt 4.

Excerpt 4

T: So . . . what kind of perspective do you have now?

Sophia: Perspective . . . (laugh) Um . . . well, frankly, I have this scary perspective of . . .

T: Scary perspective? OK.

Sophia: You have to read all the accounts in order to get anywhere, you know, hear the truth.

T: All right? Explain to me more. What?

Sophia: Well, you know, **even in the account that seem to be dry and without any kind of opinion in there, are actually opinionated by grammatical structures and what facts are being reported**. So in order to keep the best perspective, you have to read more and more, like all the time, which isn't really possible but, um . . . that's sort of what this is teaching me.

Sophia came to recognize that even though something appeared to be non-biased, objective reporting of news, it was in fact implicated with the writer's perspectives—"opinionated," to use her word—marked by a choice of words and grammatical structures.

Third, when asked about what roles they could potentially play because of their ability to read in multiple languages with understanding of multiple cultures, most of the students considered their own roles to be significant. In Excerpts 5 and 6, in response to a question "As a person who can read both articles, what kind of role would you like to play?," Pat (Excerpt 5) and Sophia (Excerpt 6) discussed the importance of helping others become aware of cultural differences.

Excerpt 5

I think, a kind of **a mediator between the two viewpoints**, I guess. Since I know a lot of people who read one thing and they are like "this is how it is, I read an article about this." And it's like, well, there's always this other take on it, **there's always the more intense or less intense, more detailed or less detailed things. So I think just keeping people aware that there are different details . . . Just keep people's minds open to the cultural differences**. I think it's really important.

Excerpt 6

Well, just by **making them aware that another perspective exists** . . . a lot of my friends already sort of have this awareness, studying other cultures, but my family, for example, I think, would be really surprised to hear something like this (difference in news reports). **And you obviously can't force them to go and read another language or anything but just making them aware** that like, you know, Japan look at this in a totally different way.

Both Pat's and Sophia's comments clearly demonstrate their growing awareness that they could play the role of a mediator as a plurilingual/pluricultural social agent for those who do not have access or a desire to go beyond their language or cultural boundary.

   With the data collected from actual class sessions and from retrospective interviews with students, we have shown that encouraging students to draw on their knowledge of multiple languages/cultures (in this case, both English and Japanese) and guiding them to pay closer attention to the semiotic choices in the texts led them to engage in critical multiliteracies practices—the analytical disposition that "seeks to uncover the social interests at work, to ascertain what is at stake in textual and social practices" (Janks, 2010, p. 12). The students recognized that power relationships and political forces are at work in texts, which in turn shape how the readers of a particular text view reality. They also recognized that they could assume the role of a linguistic/cultural mediator by shifting between languages/cultures—that is to exercise their social agency to act on the world.

Conclusions

In this chapter, we introduced the principles and the instructional sequence for the Genre-Based Critical Multiliteracies curriculum that we have designed for intermediate to advanced JFL courses. The sample instruction sequence we described above focused on the multilingual/multicultural aspect (rather than the multimodal/multimedia aspect) that the *pedagogy of multiliteracies* proposes. We chose to do so because, even though the concept of multiliteracies refers to both multilingual/multicultural and multimodal/multimedia, existing studies tend to focus on the multimodal/multimedia aspect (see Chapter 1, this volume). We believe that, particularly for the FL education field, inquiries into how we can incorporate the multilingual/multicultural aspect of multiliteracies are indeed necessary.

   Although the curricular sample described here is for JFL courses, the benefit of proactively using the learners' other language(s) and cultures in interpreting a given text will be useful for any FL learning/teaching contexts. We suggest that, in FL education of any language, the curriculum should aim at developing students' understanding of the textual features of genres, guiding them to analyze critically the choice of semiotic systems and their effects, and encouraging them to "shift between languages and cultures." By so doing, we may be able to lead the students to read words in order to read and rewrite worlds.

Notes

1 "Mere literacy" refers to literacy that focuses on language only, and usually on a singular national form of language, which is conceived as a stable system based on rules such as mastering sound–letter correspondence (Cope & Kalantzis, 2000, p. 5).
2 Similarly, pedagogical discussions for translingual practice (Canagarajah, 2013) and the translanguaging approach (Garcia, 2009; Garcia & Wei, 2014) are evolving in the field of composition study and bilingual education in the US.
3 Originally, in 1981, the Ministry of Education issued a list of *tooyoo kanji* containing 1,945 characters. In 2010, they increased its number with additional 191 characters.
4 *Zainichi* Koreans are the permanent ethnic Korean residents in Japan, whose roots go back to the era of Imperial Japan. Even today they face various forms of societal and personal discrimination and hardships.
5 All students' names are pseudonyms to ensure their anonymity.
6 NOM: nominative, ACC: accusative, GER: gerund, INST: instrumental.

References

Benesch, S. (2001). *Critical English for academic purposes: Theory, politics and practice.* Mahwah, NJ: Erlbaum.

Byrnes, H. (2012). Of frameworks and the goals of collegiate foreign language education: Critical reflections. *Applied Linguistics Review, 3*(1), 1–24.

Byrnes, H., & Sprang, K.A. (2004). Fostering advanced L2 literacy: A genre-based, cognitive approach. In H. Byrnes, & H.H. Maxim (Eds.), *Advanced foreign language learning: A challenge to college programs* (pp. 47–85). Boston, MA: Heinle Thomson.

Canagarajah, A.S. (Ed.). (2013). *Literacy as translingual practice: Between communities and classrooms.* New York, NY: Routledge.

Cope, B., & Kalantzis, M. (1993). How a genre approach to literacy can transform the way writing is taught. In B. Cope, & M. Kalantzis (Eds.), *The powers of literacy: A genre approach to teaching writing* (pp. 1–21). Pittsburgh, PA: University of Pittsburgh Press.

Cope, B., & Kalantzis, M. (2000). Multiliteracies: The beginnings of an idea. In B. Cope, & M. Kalantzis (Eds.), *Multiliteracies: Literacy learning and the design of social futures* (pp. 3–8). New York, NY: Routledge.

Council of Europe. (2001). *Common European Framework of reference for languages: Learning, teaching, assessment.* Strasbourg: Language Policy Unit. Retrieved from www.coe.int/t/dg4/linguistic/Source/Framework_EN.pdf.

Derewianka, B. (1990). *Exploring how texts work.* Newtown, NSW: Primary English Teaching Association.

Garcia, O. (2009). Bilingual education in the 21st century: A global perspective. Malden, MA: Wiley-Blackwell.

Garcia, O., & Wei, L. (2014). Translanguaging: Language, bilingualism and education. New York, NY: Palgrave Pivot.

Goldoni, F. (2008). Designing a foreign language curriculum in postsecondary education drawing from the multiliteracy, functionalist, and genre-based approaches. *VIAL: Vigo International Journal of Applied Linguistics, 5*, 63–85.

Halliday, M.A.K., & Hasan, R. (1989). *Language, context, and text: Aspects of language in a social-semiotic perspective.* Oxford, UK: Oxford University Press.

Halliday, M.A.K., & Matthiessen, C.M. (2004). *An introduction to functional grammar.* London: Hodder Education.

Hammond, J., & Macken-Horarik, M. (1999). Critical literacy: Challenges and questions for ESL classrooms. *TESOL Quarterly, 33*, 528–544.

Hasan, R. (1996). Literacy, everyday talk and society. In R. Hasan, & G. Williams (Eds.), *Literacy in society* (pp. 377–424). London: Longman.

Hyland, K. (2003). Genre-based pedagogies: A social response to process. *Journal of Second Language Writing, 12*, 17–29.

Hyland, K. (2004). *Genre and second language writing.* Ann Arbor: University of Michigan Press.

Iventosch, M.S. (2012). Teaching Japanese written language. In K. Goodman, S. Wang, M.S. Iventosch, & Y. Goodman (Eds.), *Reading in Asian languages: Making sense of written texts in Chinese, Japanese, and Korean* (pp. 236–257). New York, NY: Routledge.

Iwahara, A., Hatta, T., & Maehara, A. (2003). Effect of compatibility feeling between types of scripts and words in writing Japanese. *Reading & Writing, 16*, 377–397.

Iwasaki, N., & Kumagai, Y. (2008). Towards critical approaches in an advanced level Japanese course: Theory and practice through reflection and dialogues. *Japanese Language and Literature, 42*, 123–156.

Iwasaki, N., & Kumagai, Y. (2015). *The Routledge intermediate to advanced Japanese reader: A genre-based approach to reading as a social practice.* London: Routledge.

Janks, H. (2000). Domination, access, diversity and design: A synthesis for critical literacy education. *Educational Review, 52*(2), 175–186.

Janks, H. (2010). *Literacy and power.* New York, NY: Routledge.

Johns, A.M. (Ed.). (2002). *Genre in the classroom: Multiple perspectives.* Mahwah, NJ: Lawrence Erlbaum Associates.

Kamada, O., Beuckmann, F., Tomiyama, Y., & Yamamoto, M. (2012). *Ikita sozai de manabu shin chukyu kara jokyu e no nihongo* [Authentic Japanese: Progressing from intermediate to advanced (new edition)]. Tokyo: Japan Times.

Kern, R.G. (2003). Literacy as a new organizing principle for foreign language education. In P.C. Patrikis (Ed.), *Reading between the lines: Perspectives on foreign language literacy* (pp. 40–59). New Haven, CT: Yale University Press.

Kramsch, C. (1993). *Context and culture in language teaching.* Oxford, UK: Oxford University Press.

Kramsch, C. (2006). From communicative competence to symbolic competence. *The Modern Language Journal, 90*(2), 249–252.

Kress, G.R. (1993). Genre as social process. In B. Cope, & M. Kalantzis (Eds.), *The powers of literacy: A genre approach to teaching writing* (pp. 22–37). Pittsburgh, PA: University of Pittsburgh Press.

Kress, G.R. (1999). Genre and the changing contexts for English language arts. *Language Arts, 32*(2), 185–196.

Kress, G.R. (2003). *Literacy in the new media age.* New York, NY: Routledge.

Kubota, R. (2003). Critical teaching of Japanese culture. *Japanese Language and Literature, 37*(1), 67–87.

Kumagai, Y. (2007). Tension in a Japanese language classroom: An opportunity for critical literacy? *Critical Inquiry in Language Studies, 4*(2–3), 85–116.

Kumagai, Y., & Iwasaki, N. (2011). What it means to read "critically" in a Japanese language classroom: Students' perspective. *Critical Inquiry in Language Studies, 8*(2), 125–152.

Kumagai, Y., Okuizumi, K., Naka, K., Maruyama, M., & Sato, S. (2013). Komyuni-keeshon: Komyunikeeshon kenkyuu to kotoba no kyooiku ni okeru komyunikeeshon gainen no hensen to genjoo [Communication: Its definitions in communication studies and language education]. In S. Sato, & Y. Kumagai (Eds.), *Gengo kyooiku ni okeru Ibunka-kan komyunikeeshon saikoo* [Problematizing the notion of intercultural communication: Towards transcultural communicative capacity] (pp. 33–69). Tokyo: Coco Shuppan.

Lemke, J. (1995). *Textual politics: Discourse and social dynamics.* London: Taylor & Francis.

Luke, A. (1996). Genres of power? Literacy education and the production of capital. In R. Hasan, & A.G. Williams (Eds.), *Literacy in society* (pp. 308–338). London: Longman.

Luke, A. (2000). Critical literacy in Australia: A matter of context and standpoint. *Journal of Adolescent and Adult Literacy, 43*(5), 448–461.

Makino, S. (2002). When does communication turn mentally inward?: A case study of Japanese formal-to-informal switching. *Japanese/Korean Linguistics, 10,* 121–135.

Martin, J.R. (2009). Genre and language learning: A social semiotic perspective. *Linguistics and Education, 20*(1), 10–21.

Martin, J.R., & Rose, D. (2005). Designing literacy pedagogy: Scaffolding democracy in the classroom. In R. Hasan, & C. Matthiessen (Eds.), *Continuing discourse on language* (pp. 252–280). London: Continuum.

Maynard, S.K. (1991). Pragmatics of discourse modality: A case of *da* and *desu/masu* forms in Japanese. *Journal of Pragmatics, 15*(6), 551–582.

Maynard, S.K. (2004). Poetics of style mixture: Emotivity, identity, and creativity in Japanese writings. *Poetics, 32*(5), 387–409.

New London Group (NLG). (1996). A pedagogy of multiliteracies: Designing social futures. *Harvard Educational Review, 66*(1), 60–92.

New London Group (NLG). (2000). A pedagogy of multiliteracies: Designing social futures. In B. Cope, & M. Kalantzis (Eds.), *Multiliteracies: Literacy learning and the design of social futures* (pp. 9–37). New York, NY: Routlege.

Oka, M., Tsutsui, M., Kondo, J., Emori, S., Hanai, Y., & Ishikawa, S. (2009). *Jokyuu e no tobira: kontentsu to marutimedia de manabu nihongo* [Gateway to advanced Japanese through contents and multimedia]. Tokyo: Kurosio.

Okamoto, N. (2013). Komyunikeeshon nooryoku o koeru "nooryoku" towa: maruchiriterashiizu ni okeru dezain gainen kara kangaeru [What is "competency" beyond communicative competency?: From the concept of design in multiliteracies]. In *Komyunikeeshon nooryoku no shosoo* [Various aspects of communicative competencies] (pp. 373–397). Tokyo: Hituzi Shoboo.

Pennycook, A. (2001). *Critical applied linguistics: A critical introduction.* New York, NY: Routledge.

Rose, D. (2006). *Learning to read, reading to learn: Scaffolding the English curriculum for indigenous secondary students.* Sydney, NSW: Erebus International. Retrieved from http://ab-ed. boardofstudies.nsw.edu.au/files/Scaffolding_Literacy_Evaluation_Rose.pdf.

Rothery, J. (1996). Making changes: developing an educational linguistics. In R. Hasan, & G. Williams (Eds.), *Literacy in society* (pp. 86–123). London: Longman.

Scheleppegrell, M.J., & Colombi, C. (Eds.). (2002). *Developing advanced literacy in first and second languages: Meaning with power.* Mahwah, NJ: Lawrence Erlbaum Associates.

Smith, J.S., & Schmidt, D.L. (1996). Variability in written Japanese: Towards a sociolinguistics of script choice. *Visible Language, 30*(1), 46–71.

Swaffar, J. (2006). Terminology and its discontents: Some caveats about communicative competence. *The Modern Language Journal, 90*(2), 246–249.

Toki, S., Seki, M., Hirataka, F., Shinuchi, K., & Ishizawa, H. (2001). *Nihongo Chukyu J501: chukyu kara jokyu e* [Intermediate Japanese J501: From Intermediate to Advanced (English version)]. Tokyo: Three A Network.

Toyoda, E. (1995). *Kanji* gakushu ni taisuru gakushu-sha no ishiki [Student perception toward *kanji* learning]. *Nihongo Kyoiku [Journal of Japanese Language Learning], 85,* 101–130.

Wallace, C. (2003). *Critical reading in language education.* Basingstoke: Palgrave Macmillan.

Appendix A: Information Differentially Selected

The New York Times (excerpts from the article)	*Asahi* (translations of excerpts and information summarized)
"One of the teenagers sought help from a passer-by for the injured women, according to news report."	Inclusion of pictorial description of the crime scene.
"The police said that American officials were cooperating in the investigation."	"US military base officials were initially reluctant to cooperate."

"The United States and Japan are still negotiating the relocation of another United States military base, the Marine Corps Air Station Futenma in Okinawa, in the aftermath of a public outcry over the rape of a local schoolgirl by three American servicemen in 1995."	Inclusion of:
	
	– Detailed information about the teenagers (e.g., 18 year old was unemployed; two are brother and sister of different ages but in the same grade level).
	– Quotes from teenagers:
	  1. "The other two put up the rope. We did not mean to harm anyone."
	  2. "We four decided to put up the rope, but we did not think we would be charged with attempted murder."
	– A report that they gave false names at the beginning.

Appendix B: Two Samples of Students' Writing

Lisa (Junior-year, Engineering major, European-American):

こんにちは、

　「米兵の子４人を殺人未遂容疑で逮捕バイク女性転倒事件」という記事を読んだと聞きました。面白いんじゃないでしょうか。私も読みました。実は、アメリカの「ニューヨークタイムズ」という新聞にもこの事件についての記事があります。タイトルは「４人のティーンエイジャーは日本で逮捕された」というタイトルです。記事は同じ情報がたくさんありますけど、詳しいはちょっと違います。タイトルを比べたらそれをわかるかもしれません。

　例えば、日本の新聞の記事で、ティーンエイジャーを引用しました。返事は不審に答えたから、ちょっと悪くしました。でも、ニューヨークタイムズによると、１人は転倒された女性のために手伝う人を探しました。それは引用じゃありませんけど、その情報は容疑者がいい人だという気持ちがあります。それに、日本の新聞で、米軍側は当初難色を示したという情報が書いてあって、ニューヨークタイムズは「米軍側が応じている」ということだけ書いてあります。その情報はありますが、詳しいことは書いてありません。

　どうしてその情報はちょっと違いますか？私は、違う読者のために書いているから、先入観が表せると思います。それで、アメリカ人と知り合ってこの記事について話したら、知っている詳しいが違ったら、悪いことを考えないで知っていることを教えてあげてください。それから、アメリカ人の知っていることについて聞いたらいいと思います。違う意見や視点を習えば、事件をわかるようになれます。

Karina (Junior-year, Japanese major, European-American):

ともだちチャン、

　お元気？さっき仕事でのアメリカ人は皆ニューヨークタイムズを読むと言ったね？あなたは朝日新聞だけ読むから、ちょっと注意したい事があると思った。新聞の違いのせいで誤解があるかもしれない。タイムズの中にアメリカ人の意見とか、日米関係の違いも入っている。例えば、日本に起こる事件は日本人に対して大事な詳しい事を教えるけど、同じ事件はアメリカの記事であまり詳しく説明しないかもしれない。なぜかというと、アメリカ人は日本のニュースにまあまあ興味があるし、事件の本当の説明はアメリカ人に悪いイメージをつけるし、アメリカ人は日米友情を信じたいし。そして、日本の読者が読みたいことはアメリカのと違う。だから、アメリカ人は朝日新聞にある詳しいことを読むと、関係ないと思うはずだ。これは、アメリカの新聞は嘘をつくとか、アメリカ人は日本に起こることに全然興味がないというわけじゃない。だけど、仕事でアメリカ人と話している時に、これに気をつけた方がいい。職場でニュースについていい会話ができるといいね。

PART II

Implementing Multiliteracies-Based Projects

6

FOSTERING MULTIMODAL LITERACIES IN THE JAPANESE LANGUAGE CLASSROOM

Digital Video Projects

Yuri Kumagai, Keiko Konoeda, Miyuki Nishimata (Fukai), and Shinji Sato

Multimodal Literacies and Video Production

In mainstream second language acquisition theory, which dominantly draws on psycholinguistic perspectives, language acquisition/learning is often conceived as an "internally driven, individual phenomenon that is largely independent of the context in which it takes place" (Kramsch, 2000, p. 314). From psycholinguistic perspectives, language is considered as a formalized and rule-governed system (e.g., grammar), which is best acquired by separating it from its context of use. In line with this "autonomous" or psycholinguistic view of language (Firth & Wagner, 1997; Street, 1984), "literacy" in the field of world language education is often understood as the ability to read and write a written text. This is a narrow view that does not adequately account for the variety of literacy practices that exist in different sociocultural contexts, and which are not limited to reading and writing. Literacy, from sociocultural perspectives, is considered a social practice that is embedded in historical, sociocultural, and political contexts (Gee, 2012; New London Group (NLG), 2000; Street, 1984) (see also Chapter 1, this volume). The sociocultural perspectives posit that people engage in different types of literacy depending on the purpose, the medium, and the audience (or the interlocutor) of a particular communicative event.

Given the changes in communication due to the recent advancement of new digital technologies, it is vital to expand the idea of literacy linguistically defined, with a view of multimodal, multimedia, as well as multilingual multiliteracies. The need to develop multiliteracies, particularly multimodal literacies, then becomes an important part of any educational endeavor, including world language education. Our daily life now involves digitally intense activities using new communication tools, such as email, texting, and/or chat, creating an individual homepage or blog, and participating in social networking sites such as Facebook and Twitter. These tools have not only impacted the literacy practices that we engage in but have also brought about changes to the ways we communicate with each other on a personal level as well as the ways we share information publicly. In such environments of advanced communication technologies, heightened awareness of the important role multimodalities play in our communication has become even more significant.

Language is not the sole means for meaning representations and communication; it is just one aspect of the multimodal nature of communication. In addition to language, people utilize other modes of communication such as visual, aural, spatial, and gestural (Kress, 2003). In world language education, where little weight has been given to such aspects, due to the privileged status of written and spoken language, there is an increased and urgent need to develop learners' "multimodal communicative competence" (Royce, 2007). Some may consider it natural that people use other modes such as gestures and visual prompts (both pictures or written scripts) to communicate in world language classrooms in order to compensate for the lack of linguistic resources. However, multimodal literacies do not constitute the supplementary use of non-linguistic modes just to assist the language instruction or communication in the language. Multimodal literacies instead pay attention to the new meanings created by the co-influences of multiple modes when language is just one of the resources available. What is critical in multimodal literacies is to foreground communication as the integrated use of all semiotic modes.

In world language education, video production is one such effort to enhance students' multimodal literacies. Video production dates back to the 1980s, when hand-held camcorders became available (Godwin-Jones, 1998). Earlier literature indicated the advantages of using video to focus students' attention to non-verbal communication such as gestures and intonation (Marsh, 1989). The literature also discussed students' application of their knowledge developed from watching TV (e.g., types of TV programs) to video production (Charge & Giblin, 1988; Coleman, 1992). These advantages still hold true in present day. However, further advancement of technology (e.g., online video sharing, video editing software, see Godwin-Jones, 2007) has added more pedagogical possibilities and challenges of video production.

First, online video sharing allows the final video product to have a wider audience than the teacher and the classmates (Brown & Green, 2007; Fukushima, 2002; Hafner & Miller, 2011). In addition to providing learners with the opportunity to use the language for authentic communicative purposes, online video creates instructional challenges to raise learners' awareness about their responsibility in deciding what and how to share video products with a wider public (e.g., appropriateness of the content, use of copyrighted materials, issue of privacy, etc.). As was the case in earlier studies (e.g., Charge & Giblin, 1988; Coleman, 1992), the relevance of video production to real life also allows students to draw on their "funds of knowledge" (González, Moll, & Amanti, 2005) and provides an opportunity to include elements that go beyond the textbook discourses (Nikitina, 2010).

Second, the user-friendly video editing software allows freer combination of such modes as speech, images, writing, background music, and movement. A new type of video production that takes advantage of this flexible combination is digital storytelling. Digital storytelling involves students' creation of a 3–5 minute digital video where "the creator narrates a deeply personal story with the help of video or a series of still images" (Godwin-Jones, 2012, p. 3). This multimodal composition allows students to showcase their familiarity with, and the use of, a variety of modes to communicate complex emotions (e.g., Castañeda, 2012; Hayes, 2011; Nikitina, 2011; Oskoz & Elola, 2014; Yang, 2012). However, it also presents challenges in multimodal orchestration (Nelson, 2008).

Although these studies have suggested that digital video technologies allow language learners to be producers of meaningful multimodal texts for a wider audience outside the classroom, published reports on such projects in Japanese-as-a-world-language are scarce, and there is almost none that focuses on the novice levels. To fill the gap, in this chapter, we report on two digital video projects conducted in first-semester and third-semester college Japanese language classes. Drawing on multiple data sources (e.g., classroom discussions, students' writing of drafts and final products, post-project surveys, and individual interviews), we discuss the significance of multimodal literacies in world language education.

Vodcast[1] Project in the First-Semester Japanese Classroom

Description of the Course and the Project

The video production project was conducted in four novice-level Japanese language classrooms (either the first semester of the intensive first year or the second semester of the non-intensive first year[2]), at a private university in the northeastern US in the fall semester of 2007. The project took place from early October to late November. When the project started, the students had knowledge of only the most basic grammatical patterns and were only able to produce simple sentences using a few adjectives and verbs.

The purpose of the project was to provide the students with an opportunity to communicate with a wider audience in a newly learned language (Japanese), actively integrating multimodal resources. In order to raise students' awareness of the fact that communication in the target language is not constrained within the classroom, the students were told that the intended audiences included both Japanese people and language learners at other universities in the US and elsewhere. The assigned topic was to introduce either their university, its neighborhood, or American college life in Japanese to those audiences.

Based on a view of learning as a sociocultural practice (Lave & Wenger, 1991), the project incorporated collaborative working processes (e.g., peer-editing and a self/peer-evaluation) along with teacher instruction. At the onset of the project, the students discussed the characteristics of good/bad videos and decided on the evaluation criteria for the final products. Next, students formed groups, wrote scripts, created "draft" videos, and exchanged feedback on each other's "draft" videos. Based on the feedback, the students revised and produced the final video products. Since this was the first video production project at the university and there were no videos made by students in previous years, the students participating in the project did not watch any sample videos.

Five to six class meetings were devoted to the project. These hours were used for group meetings and to watch classmates' videos for feedback. The actual filming and editing were done outside of the class. In order to expand the (possible) audience, the final products were published on iTunes as vodcasts and on a blog that the teachers set up. At the end of the project, the students and the teachers together evaluated each product based on the established criteria.

A total of 11 videos were produced. In this chapter, we analyze two of these videos, entitled: "大学紹介 [Introducing Our University]" and "このせいかつ [This Life]." We chose these videos because they provided insight into the ways students used multimodal resources in communicating messages.

Descriptions of the Two Videos

The first video "Introducing Our University" was produced by Jim, Son-ha, and Gina.[3] Jim was a graduate student of Japanese history, and both Son-ha and Gina were undergraduates. The video began with a question similar to those found in a quiz show followed by a series of hints about the university. The first scene featured an image of a child scratching his head, with a puzzled expression. The image was accompanied with a voice-over asking, "ここはどこでしょう。 [Where do you think this is?]" It was then followed by hints, for example, a photo of an antique doll, featured with the narration, "1754ねんからあります。 [It has existed since 1754]," and a photo of bundles of $100 bills with the voice-over, "でもとてもたかいです。 [But it is very expensive]." After revealing the answer to the question, Jim, Son-ha, and Gina introduced themselves (voice only) and took turns talking about the campus and the stores in the neighborhood. With the exception of one scene—in which Gina appears—the students are not seen, only heard.

The second video, "This Life," was produced by Allen, Sam, and Henry. The video introduced a college student's life. For their assignment, these students made a video clip of an original song they wrote. The video can be found on YouTube (www.youtube.com/watch?v=wwiiAZt16hM).

The song consisted of three verses, and Allen, Sam, and Henry each sang a verse (1, 2, and 3, respectively) and played the character in it. For example, in the part "まいにちおきます。あさごはんをたべます。[I wake up every day. I eat breakfast.]," Allen woke up, opened the pizza box on the floor, and ate a slice. Sam sang the second verse, and in the scene that depicted "ときどきともだち とでんわではなします。[I sometimes talk to my friend on the phone]," he held the receiver upside down, and the image of then-President Bush talking on the phone was inserted. Verse 3 was a rap performed by Henry, and some scenes from Verse 1 and Verse 2 filmed from the viewpoint of Henry were used. All verses ended with the scene in which the main character (singer) ran up the stairs to a Japanese classroom and took a seat.

Comparison of the Two Videos

The two groups created videos that addressed the assigned topic (i.e., to introduce the university, its neighborhood, or American college life, in Japanese to the audience). To complete the assignment, they adopted different genres, and seemed to have approached the assignment with different social purposes. In this section, we compare the two videos in terms of their genres and social functions, and their design resources (i.e., linguistic and non-verbal elements).

Genres and Social Purposes

These two videos can be interpreted as belonging to different genres with different social purposes. "Introducing Our University" created a "hybrid genre" (Fairclough, 1992) by combining a quiz show, documentary, and the instructional technique (i.e., vocabulary introduction) often found in world language classrooms. The use of the question at the beginning, "ここはどこ でしょう。[Where do you think this is?]," followed by a series of hints, resembles the quiz show. After revealing the answer (i.e., the name of the university), the various places in and outside the campus were introduced with still images accompanied by narration. Thus, this video seems to also belong to the genre of a documentary. In the last scene, where they described a nearby frozen yogurt shop, they used pictures of frozen yogurt and fruits, which functioned as scaffolding for the audience to understand vocabulary. This technique resembles the way language teachers introduce new vocabulary in classrooms, thus evoking the genre of schooling for world language learning. With the descriptions of various places in and outside the campus, this video functions to provide information to the audience. At the same time, the students' (active) use of interactional sentence-end particles and invitation forms contributes to creating and maintaining a friendly relationship between the producer and the audience. For example, they engage the audience by inviting the viewers to take some actions (e.g., "(name of a store) へいきま しょう。[Let's go to (name of a store)]," "(name of the university) へきま せんか [Why don't you come to (name of the university)?]"), and posing questions (e.g., "みなさんはどれがすきですか。[Which one do you like, everyone?]").

The genre of "This Life" is that of a music video. At the beginning and the end of the video, on the bottom-left corner of the screen, the written text "この せいかつ／ざんねんさんにん [This Life/Unfortunate Three]" appears. This format is strikingly similar to commercial music videos often seen on MTV, clearly communicating to the audience the genre of the video. As a music video, "This Life" seeks to entertain the audience, especially the students' classmates, with the inclusion of their Japanese teacher's name in the song. They sing "Xせ んせいはいちばん！[Professor X is the best!]" in the chorus accompanied by a scene where a student runs up to the Japanese classroom. This word of compliment for their Japanese teacher can be considered as an insider joke or humor that is only understood by their classmates, and its inclusion serves to create a sense of communal camaraderie.

To summarize, the open-ended and multimodal nature of the project allowed diversity in the genres, drawing on the students' funds of knowledge, in this case their life experiences with media (i.e., quiz shows, documentary films, and music videos).[4] The open-endedness of the assignment also seemed to have encouraged the students to add their own social purposes (i.e., to make an interactive presentational video, to create an entertaining video similar to commercial media, and to entertain their classmates).

Design Elements: Languages and Other Modes Used in the Videos

The video production project was conducted in the first-semester Japanese course as mentioned earlier. At that point, the students had studied Japanese for only a few months and knew only minimal grammatical patterns and vocabulary (e.g., greetings, using adjectives, talking about daily activities with several verbs). In "Introducing Our University," at the beginning of the video, the students used the question sentence pattern that they had learnt in order to stage a quiz show, and uttered short simple sentences as hints. In the video, locations such as the subway, various places on campus, and the neighborhood shops were introduced one after another. Each place was described in very simple declarative patterns, such as "Xです [it is X]," "あります [non-animated object exists]," and using some adjectives; thus, no detailed information about the places was offered verbally. However, taking advantage of the video format, which allows the use of modes other than language, particularly images (both still and moving), the students were able to communicate to the audience additional information that their minimal language could not convey. In other words, the images and language complemented each other, creating a coherent and informative text as a whole.

Similarly, in "This Life," the students illustrated an ordinary day in a college student's life in the simplest sentence structures, by using action verbs. The lyrics (see Verse 1 below as an example) only describe mundane information about college life:

"This Life" Verse 1:

まいにちおきます。 [(I) wake up every day.]
あさごはんをたべます。 [(I) eat breakfast.]
そして、 [And,]
おふろにはいります。 [(I) take a bath.]
ともだちとクラスにいきます。 [(I) go to class with friends.]
このせいかつはおもしろくないです。 [This life is not interesting.]
にほんごのクラスだけたのしみます。 [(I) only enjoyed Japanese class.]
Xせんせいはいちばん！ [Professor X is the best!]

Even though the lyrics were extremely basic in terms of both the language used and the information it provided, the combination of the lyrics with the visual—humorous enactment of the scenes—changes the impression of the song drastically. For example, Allen eats a slice of pizza from a cardboard box on the floor that looks like leftovers from the previous night's party, and Sam eats a fast-food hamburger he finds in the park. Further, the line describing the student taking a bath is accompanied by the image of Allen getting into a fountain on campus, and in Verse 3, when Henry sings about borrowing a notebook from a friend and sings "thank you," he shoves the friend away. By dramatizing and enacting the song in unconventional ways with humor, they bring comical elements to the fore, which results in a completely different mood between reading or hearing the lyrics alone and combining them with the images. This is to show the students tactically created completely different meanings of a song with the effective use of visual modes and language.

Finally, the two videos seem to reflect the students' own experiences as Japanese language learners or pop culture consumers. The use of still images to accompany words in "Introducing Our University" reminds us of a typical use of drawings/pictures when introducing new vocabulary in an elementary language classroom. In "This Life," the students' knowledge about music was evident. While Verses 1 and 2 have melody like pop songs, Verse 3 changes to a rap. In Verse 3, the character (singer) wears clothes that match the genre of the music; Henry, as a singer, wore a black hood and black sunglasses, popular fashion accessories among rap singers. As Henry danced, he moved his hands and arms in ways that resembled those of rap dancers, demonstrating his familiarity and expertise in rap singing and dancing.

In this section, we described the video project in the first-semester Japanese course and compared two of the student videos. The project allowed the students to draw on their life experiences by remixing genres, adding their own social purposes, while orchestrating various modes of communication such as images, music, movement, and written texts, which enabled novice language learners to express what they could not with language alone. Even though the project did not have the development of multiliteracies as an instructional goal, students took advantage of multiple modes of communication in order to create meanings beyond their linguistic level. It is important to emphasize here that the function of various modes is not merely assisting or replacing what students cannot communicate through language; the use of multimodality creates *new* meaning, as the addition of the visual modes completely altered the mood of the song in "This Life," for example.

In order to raise critical awareness of multimodal meaning-making, we designed a curriculum for a second-year (third-semester) Japanese course that aims at developing students' multimodal literacies, which we introduce next.

Digital Storytelling Project in the Second-Year Japanese Classroom

Description of the Course and the Project

The digital storytelling project discussed in this chapter was conducted in the second-year (third-semester) Japanese language classroom in fall 2013 at a private women's college in the US. The class met five days a week (50 minutes per day) for 14 weeks. The course curriculum was organized around an elementary Japanese textbook (*Genki II*, Chapters 18 to 23) (Banno, Sakane, Ohno, Shinagawa, & Tokashiki, 2011). Since 2009, the digital storytelling project has been incorporated into the curriculum as a way for students to use the language for authentic, meaningful purpose. The work for the project began on the fifth week and continued until the end of the semester. The assigned topic for this project was "An Important Thing in My Life" or "My Unforgettable Experience." The project sought to have students critically reflect on their own lives, and to think about and communicate a personal message based on their experiences. The objectives of the project were presented to the students as follows:

1. Understand the genre and register of first-person past narrative.
2. Analyze authentic media texts to understand the culturally significant designs presented in the texts.
3. Write/create one's own (multimodal) texts with clear purpose for a particular audience.
4. Reflect on the process of creating story and media and on the final digital video.

Participants

Eighteen students in two sections of the course participated in the project. They were all female students between the ages of 17 and 25. There were three first-year students, eleven sophomores, three juniors, and one third-year PhD student (from a nearby university). There were seven Chinese speakers, one Korean speaker, and the rest were English speakers.

Procedure and Instructional Steps

In order to raise critical awareness of multimodal meaning-making, the instructional steps for the project were carefully designed, incorporating the pedagogical features proposed by the *pedagogy of multiliteracies* (NLG, 1996)—i.e., *Situated Practice, Overt Instruction, Critical Framing,* and *Transformed Practice* (see Chapter 1, this volume, for details).[5]

Situated Practice (SP) refers to "immersion in experience and the utilization of Available Designs of meaning" that invokes and draws on students' funds of knowledge from their "lifeworlds" (NLG, 1996, p. 35). Overt Instruction (OI) is instruction and intervention by the teacher (or other expert members) to introduce students to explicit metalanguage that is necessary to raise students' conscious awareness and control over *Designs of meaning* and *Design process.*[6] Critical Framing (CF) guides students to stand back and frame what they have learned in relations to the historical, sociocultural, and political context of particular Designs of meaning. Transformed Practice (TP) refers to a revised practice in the context of SP that meets the students' own purposes, through the application of the understandings learned in OI and CF. According to the NLG, these four components are not linear steps, but are interrelated elements that may occur simultaneously and may be revisited at different stages. Figure 6.1 shows the pedagogical sequence of the digital storytelling project that took three phases: Critical Multimodal Reading, Critical Multimodal Designing, and Presenting and Re-Viewing Multimodal Design.

The Critical Multimodal Reading phase (phase 1) was designed to get students to reflect on their own media consumption and production practices and to engage them in a critical reading/viewing of multimodal texts (see Appendix A,

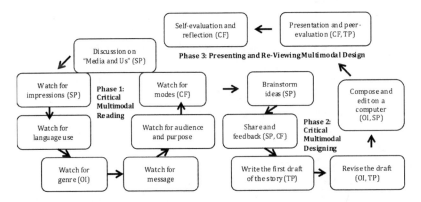

FIGURE 6.1 Pedagogical sequence of critical multimodal reading and designing.

for the overall procedure of the phases and steps; Appendix B for the Activity Worksheet used in the phase 1). Phase 1 started with a discussion of the students' own experiences and engagement with various types of media (such as TV, radio, newspapers, magazines, podcasts, blogs, YouTube, Twitter, Facebook, and others).[7] This discussion is Situated Practice (SP) in which students reflect on their prior experiences on texts and media by making connections to familiar lifeworld experiences before being introduced to a new text (Kalantzis & Cope, 2005; Mills, 2010). Then students watched a digital story created by a Japanese youth that was found on YouTube. After the first viewing of the digital story together as a class, students discussed their general impressions of the story and possible sources for such impressions (e.g., music, images). This discussion was placed before a comprehension activity in order to position the students as participants in making meanings and drawing on their media viewing practices, and thus encourage SP. Another purpose of the activity was to reflect on the multimodal effects of music, images, and the tone of voice, and to activate the students' multimodal meaning awareness brought from their various literacy practices.

Following the general discussion, students worked in pairs on a series of tasks (see Appendix B) while watching the story as many times as necessary. They were asked to first fill in the missing words in the transcript of the story provided by the instructor, playing, pausing, rewinding, and replaying the video, to identify the linguistic forms used in the digital story. This activity aimed to facilitate the understanding of the message with the transcript and the word list as scaffolds, while paying attention to the choice of words and textual composition. Second, the students were guided to identify each paragraph's function within the story, thus raising awareness of textual features such as discourse structure and genre moves. In order to provide students with the metalanguage, students were asked to match a paragraph function (provided as a list in English) to each paragraph as a way of Overt Instruction (OI). By identifying the functions such as "the author's main message," students became aware of the genre's features, such as chronological ordering, a substantial reflection to follow the description of the critical incident, and presenting a lesson learned from the experience toward the end. Next, the students discussed the overall message of the story. These tasks encouraged students to do a close reading of the story, which facilitated their understanding of the storyline, and of the style of language and the structure that are typical of the narrative genre.

Students then shifted their focus to the use of multimodal resources. They were asked to pay close attention to the use of pictures (the specific images, including the color and tone) and the background music. They discussed how different modes (i.e., narration, music, image, use of script, etc.) were and were not enhancing each other for the quality of the overall story. In other words, the students were guided to critically evaluate the multimodal design choices (CF).

Lastly, the students were asked to share their opinions on the authors' intended audiences and the reasons for telling the story. Shifting the students' attention to the social purposes of digital storytelling was meant to have them critically frame their understanding of the multimodal media (CF). Activities in this phase were to activate their Available Designs for designing their digital stories in the next phase.

In the Critical Multimodal Designing phase (phase 2), taking into account what they had learned about the genre of a personal narrative and the ways different modes enhanced the digital story as a whole, students began thinking about their own stories. First, each student brought ideas for her story to class, shared the ideas with her peers (in pairs) and received questions and feedback. The student who shared her story took on the position of author and knowledge producer, while the other student became an attentive audience, who would listen for meaning, comment on what she liked, and ask for clarification or details of what she wanted to hear more about (SP). Based on the peer exchanges, students expanded and/or modified their initial ideas for their stories (CF), and wrote their first drafts (TP). The instructor read the first drafts and provided feedback, guiding students to pay particular attention to the importance of communicating their feelings and emotions and the significance of the message, rather than to simply describe and recount the factual events (Hayes, 2011). The pedagogy at work here was Overt Instruction (OI) as the instructor guided students to get a more adequate conceptualization of the genre. Students, then, revised their stories reflecting on the questions and suggestions provided by the instructor (TP). The instructor read the second drafts and provided feedback, this time mainly for their use of language; rather than simply correcting linguistic errors and awkwardness, the feedback was to encourage students to be more conscious about their choice of words and expressions (OI), and the students further revised according to the instructor's feedback (TP).

Next, two in-class workshops were conducted at the college's computer lab. The first workshop, conducted by educational technology staff, taught students to use the software to create their digital stories (Photostory, a freeware, for the Windows-based computer users, and iMovie for the Macintosh users) and other matters that media producers need to be cautious about when/if using copyrighted materials from the internet (OI). Students learned how to import images and background music, how to insert written texts on to the images, how to create moving effects by different types of transition, how to record their voice, etc. (SP). The students started creating their stories in class and continued after class. They brought whatever technical questions or problems they encountered to the second workshop and continued working on their projects in and after class.

The Presenting and Re-Viewing Multimodal Design phase (phase 3) was the end-of-the-semester event where the students presented their finished digital stories in front of their classmates and guests. The students started their presentations by briefly introducing their videos in Japanese. After showing the videos, they reflected (again, in Japanese) on the process of the video-making and answered questions from the audience (CF). The students also evaluated each other's video in writing, commenting on the impression they received from watching the video, their thoughts on the message, and on any other aspects replicating the questions discussed in the Critical Multimodal Reading phrase (CF, TP).

As a conclusion of the project, the students wrote a self-reflection/evaluation (either in Japanese or English) about what they had paid conscious attention to in their digital storytelling (e.g., use of language and other modes), what they would do differently if they were to create another digital story, and rewarding/ challenging aspects of the project (CF), etc. This was done as homework due to the time constraints.

Discussion

In this section, drawing on the audio-recorded data from classroom discussions, we first discuss students' discovery and sharing of knowledge regarding the use and effects of multimodal elements in communicating messages during Critical Multimodal Reading. Then, we analyze how their understanding of multimodality gained in Critical Multimodal Reading was put to use in their stories and reflected in their final video products. To access the students' understanding and perspective of their use of multimodality, we used additional data we had collected, namely an open-ended self-evaluation questionnaire (i.e., post-project survey) and individual interviews.

Students' Meta-Knowledge and Discovery of Multimodality

During the Critical Multimodal Reading phase, all students in both sections actively contributed to the discussions and shared their thoughts and knowledge about the important role different modes, particularly pictures and music, played in the sample video.[8]

Excerpt 1 below is from the whole-class discussions (from Section 1 of the course) when students were expressing their opinions about the use of pictures:[9]

Excerpt 1[10]

1. T(eacher): *Shashin ni tsuite doo omotta?* [What did you think about the choice of photos?]
2. Iris: I think it was trying to invoke what she was talking at the time. Each one may not be completely accurate for her representation but it was symbolic . . . it gives you more the kind of feeling she has.
3. T: *Hoka no hito wa doo?* [How about other people?]
4. Amy: Some picture was directly related to what she was saying, like shoes (laugh). But a lot of them weren't related to directly. I don't know if she did filter pictures herself but many of them had sad color tone to them.

5. T: *Hoka ni kigatsuita koto wa?* [Anything else that you noticed?]
6. Yuki: I noticed that a lot of sky and tree images were used when she
              had a breakthrough and when she was self-reflective. Although it
              started off with more filtered images in the beginning, it ended up
              kind of more of flowers and fruits, like "I understand the world is
              a beautiful place." So I think we can see the progression pretty well
              through images, even though the music was constant through it.

In the above, the students noticed that many pictures in the video did not necessarily correspond to the words spoken, but rather they evoked and represented the narrator's feelings in a symbolic way. They also discussed that not only the object in the images, but also the color and tone of the images ("filtered"), communicated the mood of the story (line 4). Yuki also astutely noted that the shift in the selection of images from darker tones to colorful ones (such as flowers and fruits) captured the transformation of the author's feeling and thinking, thus contributing to storytelling (line 6).

During a discussion in the Section 2 class, as in the case of the Section 1 class above (Excerpt 1), they expressed opinions that the choice of pictures was seemingly "random," yet the pictures were more "abstract" and "symbolic." Like Yuki in Excerpt 1 (line 6 above), Tina also noted that the shift in the colors used in pictures symbolized that the "feeling of it changed. Like in the end when she was reflecting about her change from *waruiko-chan* [bad girl] to now, she made the picture more colorful." Students thought the music was "peaceful" (Nina), "monotone" (Amy), and "reflective" (Kathy); because it was "slow and it is piano so that you can listen to more of the words. The music wasn't overpowering with what she is saying" (Nina). Here, Nina touched on the importance of balancing volume of narration and the background music.

In response to the teacher's question as to whether the use of pictures and music was effective in conveying the message, students responded in the following way:

Excerpt 2
1. Jen: I think that music kind of helped enhance the mood, because it
              was acoustic and made the mood more mellow, so when she was
              talking about when she was a bad child, it kind of emphasized
              her reflectiveness of that time period through the music. And the
              pictures weren't so random. I did think of them as more symbolic;
              it symbolized all that happening within the story, so . . . I think that
              helped it more because it made more people who are watching and
              listening, think about it, like think more, like whole scenery pictures,
              that kind of, show like blue sky, like it shows how she was thinking.
2. Naomi: I agree with Jen-san that the sky, it is exactly talking about worldly,
              like world and people around you now. More worldly, abstract.
              I think it's very stylistic; in Japan it's very common to have that.

3. T: You notice it somewhere else too?
4. Naomi: I think (laugh) in many Japanese stuff. (Many students nod and laugh.)
5. T: *Honto? Okkee.* [Really? OK.]

From the above, we can see that the students were critically analyzing and inter-preting the design of the video and reached their own understanding of how different modes interacted with each other to create the desired meaning and to convey the message as a coherent whole.

Naomi's comment about "abstractness" as a common Japanese (cultural) fea-ture (line 2) was also agreed on by other students who said they had seen similar phenomena in television commercials and such (line 4). During the interview, Naomi explained that by "abstractness" she was referring to the use of Zen-like features that emphasize the importance of nature as symbolic to people's way of looking at life, knowledge she has learned from a philosophy course. Whether the sample video's use of abstractness and symbolic representation of life through nature is a Japanese cultural influence deserves further discussion; however, it suf-fices to say here that students actively drew on their own funds of knowledge to make sense of the texts they encountered.

Analysis of a Selected Video: Students' Use of Multimodality in Their Story Designing

In this section, we discuss how students' meta-knowledge of multimodality was utilized in their final video products by analyzing one student's video (out of 18 videos produced in total). We selected a digital story made by Genni as a good example of a video that reflected the multimodal awareness gained in the Critical Multimodal Reading phase. When appropriate, we also include her own reasoning of her choices, explained during her individual interview.

Genni's Digital Storytelling Video

Genni was a sophomore student and a Japanese major. She was a European-American and her first language was English. Genni's story, entitled "私のじょうねつを見つけている [Finding my passion]," was about her unforgettable childhood experience when she discovered her passion about books through her best friend's love for reading. Figure 6.2 shows the first five screens of her story.

Genni's story consists of four parts that can be summarized as: background, introducing her best friend, describing a critical incident, and reflecting on the experience. She used 20 still images in her story: 7 personal photos of her family and friends and 13 images taken from the internet (copyright-free materials). Soft piano music plays in the background throughout the story.

After the title slide, she begins telling the story with an image of a compass and the written words "Where will you go?" The series of images that follow—an

	Screen 1	Screen 2	Screen 3	Screen 4	Screen 5
Image		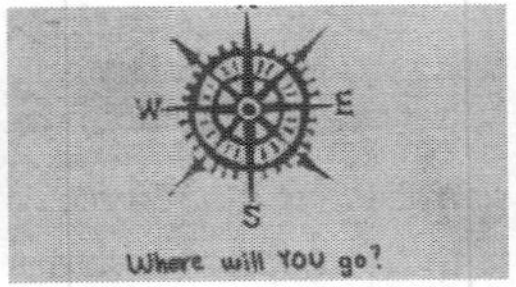	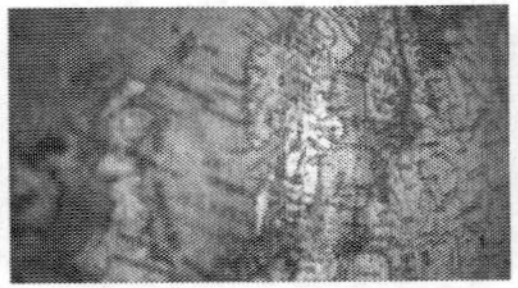		
Narration in original Japanese	(No narration)	子どもの時、私の情熱は何かが分からなかったから、私は本当にどうやって生活をするか分かりませんでした。	私は母と父と先生に私の情熱を見つけさせてくれませんでしたから、世界は「情熱を知らないほうがいいんですよ」と言っているみたいでした。	でも、幸せの道に迷っていたみたいでした。	私の中で何かは空でした。
Narration in English translation	(Title: Finding my passion)	When I was a child, I didn't know what my passion was, so I really didn't know how to live.	My mother, father, and teachers did not help me find my passion, so the world seemed to be saying "I better not know my passion."	But I seemed to have been lost in the road to happiness.	Something inside me was empty.
Zoom/ transition	Title fades in.	The image rolls down from the full figure of the compass to include the handwritten "Where will you go?"	The map slides in from the left, then zoom in.	Zoom out into black screen.	Black screen with red ray becomes clearer.
Music	Soft piano music plays throughout the story. The music started off as rather "sad" tune and shifted to more "uplifting" toward the end.				

FIGURE 6.2 First five screens of Genmi's story, "Finding My Passion."

antique map of Europe, a road in the woods, and a black blank screen—set the tone of the story, representing her feeling of "being lost" and "emptiness." She then introduces her best friend from her childhood as someone who shared and understood her feelings. Next, she describes a critical incident when her best friend brought a book, *Gone With the Wind*, for a sleepover at her house and read passages aloud from the book. Genni thought it was boring in the beginning, but when she saw the happiness in her friend's eyes, she herself wanted to start reading books. In the last part of the story, she reflects that the event was the most important unforgettable moment in which she was introduced to the world of novels, which became her passion in life.

In designing the multimodal text, Genni used her own photos minimally—just enough to make the story personal. The rest of the images were all abstract pictures (except for the cover of the book, *Gone With the Wind*) that symbolically captured the feelings and emotions of her story. She was keenly aware of the importance of the colors and tone of the images for communicating a message. For example, as described earlier, she chose to insert a black blank screen when she narrated "something inside me was empty" in order to evoke the emotion of "emptiness" (see Screen 5, Figure 6.2). Also, a sepia-colored image of a field with a carpet of dandelions at sunset was used to capture the feeling of nostalgic sadness; yet with some hopefulness (Screen 9; see Figure 6.3). Genni explained her choice of images by saying "I wanted it to be not completely bright but not dark; kind of in the middle."

	Screen 9	Screen 11	Screen 21
Image			
Narration in original Japanese	だから情熱を見つけたかったです。情熱を見つけたら、私はうれしくなると思いました。難しいと思いましたが、無理じゃないと思いました。	私の大親友はおなじ気持ちがありました。大親友は私と違う人でした。今も私達はとても違います。	今、生活の中でこの情熱が一番好きなことだから、この経験は全然忘れられません。
Narration in English translation	So I wanted to find my passion. I thought I would become happy if I found my passion. I thought it would be difficult, but I didn't think it was impossible.	My best friend had the same feeling. My best friend and I were very different people. We are still very different now.	Because this passion is my most favorite thing in life now, I can never forget this experience.

FIGURE 6.3 Three example screens with symbolic images from Genni's story.

In describing the friendship with her best friend, who Genni says shared her feelings, but who was different from her, Genni used a picture that depicted two trees with slightly different shapes standing next to each other with a moon and a sun as their background (Screen 11; see Figure 6.3). These images captured their friendship: They are similar yet different; they are complementary and indispensable to each other. She ends her story with an image of a sunset (Screen 21; see Figure 6.3) with her voice-over, "because this passion [for books] is my most favorite thing in my life, I can never forget this experience." She explained in her interview that the "sunset symbolizes the end of something," but at the same time it is also "the beginning of new things."

As an avid reader and an aspiring novel-writer, Genni was particularly aware and conscious of the importance of images and emotions that the story inspires. During the interview, she articulated the difference between language-based text writing and multimodal text designing:

> Video is easier to show what they mean because of physical representation. You are able to show what you want to say. In writing, you have to manipulate the words so that the readers can see what you mean . . . I captured the emotion (of what I'm saying) first, figure out what could symbolize the emotion in the right way, and then make sure the pictures match it.

By carefully choosing images (with an attention to tones and colors) as meaning-making elements to support her narration, Genni successfully communicated her message to the audience, as evidenced in her peers' comments on the peer-evaluations.

We shared the case of Genni to exemplify the students' growing awareness and understanding as to how the narration, pictures, and music worked together to effectively convey their message through their videos. During the question and answer sessions after their showing of the video at the presentation session, the audience (both students and guests) asked about the producer's choice of pictures and music in addition to the "usual" questions about the message of the story. Every student producer was able to articulate the reasons behind the choice she had made for various modes, from the tone of voice and the speed of narration, to the images, colors, transitions, and music. All these interactions were carried out only in the Japanese language.

Drawing on what they had learned during the Critical Multimodal Reading phase (e.g., color, tone, music, transition), linguistic knowledge learned from the language instruction, and their individual unique funds of knowledge from popular culture (e.g., anime, manga, computer games, movies, music videos, etc.), online resources (e.g., Facebook, Tumbler, etc.), and computer software (Photoshop, Garage band, etc.), all students created their unique, creative digital storytelling videos with a deeply personal message in Japanese. In many world language classrooms, the opportunity to use the language creatively for communicating meanings that are personally significant is often very limited.

Self-Reflection, Representation, and Investment in Designing Multimodal Texts

In light of the above discussions, what are the implications for world language education based on the *pedagogy of multiliteracies,* that positions students as designers of their own learning and of social futures?

In the digital storytelling project described in this chapter, because the selected topic involved the students' personal experience and because the story had to have an important message, the students were encouraged to reflect on and to negotiate what and how much of their life stories they were willing to share with the audience. The reflection processes, thus, began when thinking about the topics for their stories. Being self-reflective and reliving the significant experiences allowed them to learn about themselves: "I learned about myself" (Tina, self-evaluation), "I was also able to relive my Rwanda memories and define the highs and lows of the experience from a vantage of it happening two years ago . . . It felt like a cathartic experience to create something from some emotional and painful experience"[11] (Yuki, self-evaluation).

What students needed to self-negotiate was not only about what story they chose to tell (with how much detail to include); they also needed to negotiate the ways in which they wanted to represent themselves through their stories. During the interview, Genni said:

> I want them to think that I'm not totally superficial because I don't really act like how I wrote this; I don't act particularly thoughtful, like deep and serious. But I think people can be different when they are writing and speaking. When I write it's about figuring out what you don't talk about.

Negotiation of identity and self-representation are important functions of language and literacy practices, yet students often do not get many opportunities to practice these functions in a classroom setting.

The students' final video products and their comments on the self-evaluation clearly indicated that they had been highly invested in the project. Judging from the final video shown at the presentation, it was clear that they had revised their narrative scripts beyond what the instructor had suggested. They all reported that they re-recorded audios multiple times (some said as many as 80 times for some segments) to "make it sound 'perfect'" (Katherina, self-evaluation). That is, they took ownership of the project; they worked to "perfect" it to their satisfaction as time allowed. During the interview, one student said, "I didn't think I would put so much time into it, but I enjoyed the process, like telling a story . . . The most important and interesting part is that an idea becomes a thing and you can watch and share it with other people" (Ping, interview). Another student noted, "I really enjoyed when I recorded a section and played it back, and it almost sounded fluent, like I knew exactly what I was trying to say" (Iris, self-evaluation).

All of the students were proud of their videos and enjoyed sharing them with the audience. They also enjoyed watching their classmates' videos and learned something about them in the process. By doing this project, they gained confidence in using the Japanese language in a creative, meaningful, and personal way as the following comments illuminate:

> It was a great way to reflect on some of the important parts of my life, and to try out more challenging combinations of the grammar we've learned. I was able to teach myself new vocabulary, become proficient at using iMovie, and hopefully share something positive with my classmates. (Katharina, self-evaluation)

> It was a fun and interesting way of being able to use Japanese at my disposal. It was also rewarding to be able to talk more in depth about myself in Japanese and tell a story in Japanese. (Jackie, self-evaluation)

Conclusion

This chapter examined two video projects from Japanese language classrooms. Through their participation in these projects, students were able to position themselves as knowledgeable communicators, rather than "incomplete" world language learners (as they are often conceived as), by effectively accomplishing self-expression and exercising their agency. The change in student positioning achieved in these classes can take place in any world language classrooms that similarly encourage learners' multimodal literacies.

Both video production projects showed how the students creatively made use of a variety of Available Designs. This was true of even the very first semester learners, who were able to use language in a meaningful way to communicate messages and position themselves as knowledgeable and entertaining communicators, with support from other modes. For example, the students' expertise in the genres of music video, and rap music and dance became Available Designs in multimodal production, as did the grammar learned in the classroom such as simple expressions, question structure, interactional sentence-end particles, and functional phrases like invitation. This shows that the adoption of multimodal literacies should be considered for all levels, and especially in lower-level world language classrooms where such an aspect has often been downplayed.

Both projects positioned the students as designers from the point of view of the *pedagogy of multiliteracies*. However, starting with or without a sample seemed to influence the range of videos that students produced. On the one hand, the vodcast project without a sample encouraged a wide variety of genres that the students brought from outside the classroom. In other words, the lack of any model invited the creative use of the funds of knowledge (from Situated Practice). Also, with peer feedback and formative assessment (Critical Framing), the students were able to design meaningful and creative projects (Transformed Practice). On the other hand, the digital storytelling project started with a sample and encouraged the students to take it apart and critically analyze it. This approach allowed the students to access a model for a first-person past narrative (Overt Instruction) and the awareness of modal composition (CF). The advantage of presenting a model of an unfamiliar genre was to increase the students' genre expertise and encourage a new practice through which students could express reflections and emotions in a target language (TP). Even though presenting a genre model may have threatened to stifle students' creativity, the students creatively designed multimodal ensembles that communicated their emotions (TP).

It is worth noting that, in the digital storytelling project, the students also became critical evaluators of multimodal products through the explicit attention to multimodality. Their awareness of the effect of multimodal orchestration was observed not only in their own digital story products, but also in the questions they asked about other storytellers' modal choices. This heightened awareness suggests that the practice of watching multimodal media had been transformed. The students at this point indicated meta-awareness, as they were able to explain their intentions of their modal choices. The multimodal elements were used not just to "decorate," but to create a new meaning.

In this chapter, we demonstrated that the two multimodal projects afforded language learners the opportunity to draw on a wider range of Available Designs than they would have otherwise used in a single mode activity, and to design their language use for their own communicative purposes. We cannot emphasize enough the importance of projects that encourage students to be intentional and purposeful in designing a text, if we want our students to become the designers of their future selves and language use.

Notes

1 "Vodcast" refers to a video podcast.
2 Courses in the non-intensive track proceed at half the speed of those in the intensive track; therefore what the students learn in the first two semesters of the non-intensive Japanese is equivalent to the one semester of the first-year intensive Japanese. For this reason, we treat this course the same way as the first-semester course in the intensive track.
3 All students' names are pseudonyms.
4 Other types of genre the students used to complete the assignment include dramatized film.
5 In 2005, Kalantzis and Cope revisited their earlier proposal of the pedagogy of multiliteracies and reframed these pedagogical dimensions to "Experiencing," "Conceptualising," "Analysing," and "Applying," respectively (p. 17), shifting the focus from *pedagogical orientations* to *knowledge processes* of students (see also Chapter 1, this volume). In this chapter, we use the original constructs as they foreground the instructional designs.
6 In the pedagogy of multiliteracies, the NLG (1996) proposed treating "any semiotic activity, including using language to produce or consume texts, as a matter of Design" (p. 74), and described an act of "Design" as consisting of three aspects: *Available Designs,*

Designing, and *the Redesigned* (p. 20). For detailed explanations for each construct, see Chapter 1 in this volume.

7 Throughout the lesson, the students were encouraged to use as much Japanese as they could; however, the use of English (or other language, common to the the pair) was also allowed so that they could engage in deeper discussion that would not be possible using only Japanese language.

8 The sample video was selected according to the following criteria: It had to be (1) created by a Japanese person of a similar age group for the audience of other speakers of Japanese; (2) available on an online video sharing site (i.e., YouTube); (3) effective and engaging in its multimodal expression; and (4) about a topic that was relevant for students in the US.

9 In the discussions, both the teacher and students code-switched between Japanese and English. As described in the procedure section, in order to have a deeper discussion, the use of English was allowed. The teacher is represented as "T" and other discussants are students.

10 Excerpts of discussions and interviews are presented without any modification (e.g., grammar correction). When spoken in Japanese, we provide English translation in square brackets.

11 Yuki created her digital storytelling video about her school trip to Rwanda, where she learned about genocide and people's resilience in life.

References

Banno, E., Sakane, Y., Ohno, Y., Shinagawa, C., & Tokashiki, K. (2011). *Genki: An integrated course in elementary Japanese II* (2nd ed.). Tokyo: Japan Times.

Brown, A., & Green, T.D. (2007). Video podcasting in perspective: The history, technology, aesthetics, and instructional uses of a new medium. *Journal of Educational Technology Systems, 36*(1), 3–17.

Castañeda, M.E. (2012). "I am proud that I did it and it's a piece of me": Digital storytelling in the foreign language classroom. *CALICO Journal, 30*(1), 44–62.

Charge, N.J., & Giblin, K. (1988). Learning English in a video studio. *ELT Journal, 42*(4), 282–287.

Coleman, J.A. (1992). Project-based learning, transferable skills, information technology and video. *The Language Learning Journal, 5*(1), 35–37.

Fairclough, N. (1992). *Discourse and social change.* Cambridge, UK: Polity Press.

Firth, A., & Wagner, J. (1997). On discourse, communication, and (some) fundamental concepts in SLA Research. *The Modern Language Journal, 81*(3), 285–300.

Fukushima, T. (2002). Promotional video production in a foreign language course. *Foreign Language Annals, 35*(3), 349–355.

Gee, J.P. (2012). *Social linguistics and literacies: Ideology in discourse* (4th ed.). New York, NY: Routledge.

Godwin-Jones, R. (1998). New developments in digital video. *Language Learning & Technology, 2*(1), 11–13.

Godwin-Jones, R. (2007). Digital video update: YouTube, flash, high-definition. *Language, Learning & Technology, 11*(1), 16–21.

Godwin-Jones, R. (2012). Digital video revisited: Storytelling, conferencing, remixing. *Language Learning & Technology, 16*(1), 1–9.

González, N., Moll, L.C., & Amanti, C. (2005). *Funds of knowledge: Theorizing practice in households, communities, and classrooms.* Mahwah, NJ: Laurence Erlbaum Associates.

Hafner, C.A., & Miller, L. (2011). Fostering learner autonomy in English for science: A collaborative digital video project in a technological learning environment. *Language Learning & Technology, 15*(3), 68–86.

Hayes, C. (2011). "*Nihon to watashi: Japan and myself*": Digital stories to enhance student-centered Japanese language learning. *Electronic Journal of Foreign Language Teaching, 8*, 291–299.

Kalantzis, M., & Cope, B. (Eds.). (2005). *Learning by design*. Melbourne, VIC: Victorian Schools Innovation Commission and Common Ground.

Kramsch, C. (2000). Second language acquisition, applied linguistics, and the teaching of foreign languages. *The Modern Language Journal, 84*(3), 311–326.

Kress, G.R. (2003). *Literacy in the new media age*. London & New York: Routledge.

Lave, J., & Wenger, E. (1991). *Situated learning: Legitimate peripheral participation*. New York, NY: Cambridge University Press.

Marsh, C. (1989). Some observations on the use of video in the teaching of modern languages. *British Journal of Language Teaching, 27*(1), 13–17.

Mills, K.A. (2010). *The multiliteracies classroom*. Tonawanda, NY: Multilingual Matters.

Nelson, M.E. (2008). Multimodal synthesis and the voice of the multimedia author in a Japanese EFL context. *Innovation in Language Learning and Teaching, 2*(1), 65–82.

New London Group (NLG). (1996). A pedagogy of multiliteracies: Designing social futures. *Harvard Educational Review, 66*(1), 60–92.

New London Group (NLG). (2000). A pedagogy of multiliteracies: Designing social futures. In B. Cope, & M. Kalantzis (Eds.), *Multiliteracies: Literacy learning and the design of social futures* (pp. 9–37). New York, NY: Routledge.

Nikitina, L. (2010). Video-making in the foreign language classroom: Applying principles of constructivist pedagogy. *Electronic Journal of Foreign Language Teaching, 7*(1), pp. 21–31.

Nikitina, L. (2011). Creating an authentic learning environment in the foreign language classroom. *International Journal of Instruction, 4*(1), 33–46.

Oskoz, A., & Elola, I. (2014). Integrating digital stories in the writing class: Toward a 21st-century literacy. In J.P. Guikema, & L. Williams (Eds.), *Digital literacies in foreign and second language education* (pp. 179–200). San Marcos, TX: CALICO Monograph Series, 12.

Royce, T.D. (2007). Multimodal communicative competence in second language contexts. In T.D. Royce, & W. Bowcher (Eds.), *New directions in the analysis of multimodal discourse* (pp. 361–390). Mahwah, NJ: Lawrence Erlbaum Associates.

Street, B. (1984). *Literacy in theory and practice*. New York, NY: Cambridge University Press.

Yang, Y.D. (2012). Multimodal composing in digital storytelling. *Computers and Composition, 29*(3), 221–238.

Appendix A: Overview of the Phases and Steps

Phase 1: Critical Multimodal Reading
1. Project overview and "Media and Us"; classroom discussion on media production and consumption; watch and analyze two sample digital stories for their genres, language use, structure, message, audience, purpose, and non-verbal modes (SP, OI, CF).

Phase 2: Critical Multimodal Designing
2. Brainstorm ideas for own digital story; sharing ideas and peer feedback (SP, CF).
3. Write own story (first draft) (TP).

4. Revise the first draft based on the feedback from the instructor (second draft) (OI, TP).
5. Workshops 1 and 2 (learning how to use computer software; creating own digital story) (OI, SP).

Phase 3: Presenting and Re-Viewing Multimodal Design

6. Class presentation of the digital story and peer evaluation (CF, TP).
7. Self-evaluation and reflection on the process and the product of the project (CF).

Appendix B: Activity Worksheet Used in Phase 1 (Critical Multimodal Reading) (Original in Japanese)

1. Discuss your media experiences (consumption and production).

    – What types of media do you often watch and/or listen to, when and why?
    – Have you ever produced any media products?
    – What are some of the good things and bad things in various media (such as TV, radio, newspapers, magazines, podcasts, blogs, YouTube, Twitter, Facebook, and others)?

2. Watch and analyze a digital story.

    – What general impression did you get from it?
    – What elements of the story contributed to creating that impression?

3. Understanding the story.

    – Fill in the missing words to complete the transcript.
    – Match the function of each paragraph from the list.
    – Discuss the message of the story.

4. Close reading/examination of the story. Pay attention to the use of images and music.

    – Discuss the reasons for and evaluate the effectiveness of the use and choice of the particular modes.

5. Discuss the possible reasons (audience perceptions) for creating the story and intended audience of the story.

7

IMPLEMENTING MULTILITERACIES IN THE KOREAN CLASSROOM THROUGH VISUAL MEDIA

Lucien Brown, Noriko Iwasaki, and Keunyoung Lee

Introduction

The notion of "multiliteracies" challenges the idea that language, communication, and meaning are stable entities. Instead, language is seen as constantly being transformed, reinvented, and contested (Kress, 2000a). This conceptual leap mandates several changes in the way that language and literature are treated in the second language classroom, including three that are crucial to the current chapter. First, it demands that we go beyond "mere literacy" (New London Group (NLG), 1996, p. 4) as the consumption of printed texts and toward the acceptance of film, new media, and other multimodal materials as valid "texts" that can be created and interpreted in the classroom setting (see Chapter 6, this volume). Second, it requires that we adopt a social-semiotic perspective on language (Halliday & Hasan, 1985), which features a broader understanding of linguistic knowledge as including the creation and interpretation of meanings conveyed through multiple channels. In more recent years, this broader understanding of language is talked of as "multimodal competence" (Royce, 2007). Teachers need to engage visual, gestural, spatial, and other semiotic modes within their everyday classroom teaching (see Chapter 4, this volume). As argued by Kress (2000b), such a shift is required due to the increasing prominence of visual elements in the contemporary communication landscape, with interpretation of such visuals being key to successful social interaction. Third, and most crucially, the notion of multiliteracies moves us away from a "curriculum-as-neutral stance" to a "critical pedagogy stance" that encourages learners to design their own meanings, develop their own voices, and discover—and indeed create—their own versions of the target language culture. This, in turn, will allow learners to participate more fully in society and become active in negotiating equity and social justice (Crafton, Silvers, & Brennan, 2009, p. 31).

Although the acceptance of the multiliteracies framework may be growing within the US school system and in the pedagogy of more commonly taught European languages, the approach has not been widely discussed by educators who are working with less commonly taught languages (LCTL), such as Korean. The reasons for this have not been empirically established; however, we believe that certain conceptual and ideological factors may render it particularly difficult for LCTL and, in particular, Korean language educators to adopt a multiliteracies framework. Most crucially, the idea that the mission of education is to promote critical thinking, empower learners, and take a social justice stance appears to differ from how education is conceptualized in South Korean society, where the emphasis is on rote learning and teaching to the test (Li, 2012; Seth, 2002). In addition, as pointed out by Silva (2010), one prevailing ideology in Korean society is "homogeneity." Korean society displays a "strong normative bias," in which the acceptance of different varieties, interpretations, and worldviews is suppressed rather than encouraged. Since the vast majority of Korean language educators working in the US are native to South Korea, the importance of these ideologies in shaping practices in Korean as a second language (KSL)[1] courses should not be overlooked.

The lack of discussion of multiliteracies in the Korean context is particularly regretful in light of two emerging factors in South Korean society and its global projection. The first of these is the meteoric rise of South Korean popular culture on the global stage—a phenomenon known in South Korea as *hanlyu* [the Korean wave]. Due to the cultural power of *hanlyu* and its availability in online media, American students of non-Korean heritage now have a point of access to Korean culture that was not available just a few years ago. For heritage learners, *hanlyu* paves a way for them to (re)connect with their Korean heritage, (re)construct their Korean identities and (re)evaluate the place of their heritage culture on the global stage (Park, 2004). As the profile of Korean popular culture heightens, interest in Korean language learning at US colleges has been booming. Elementary Korean courses are often largely populated by students who are hooked on Korean popular culture and want to connect with the culture on a deeper level. Multiliteracies represent an ideal framework to engage these students with the "texts" of Korean popular culture and to provide the scaffolding needed to negotiate the meanings of these texts in a culturally situated way.

The second factor that heightens the need for multiliteracies frameworks in KSL is the emerging discourses of globalization and multiculturalism in South Korean society. These discourses have been fueled by the emergence of a global Korean diaspora now numbering around 7 million and by an influx of "foreigners"[2] to the Korean peninsula. These population shifts have resulted in a destabilization of what are considered to be traditional Korean discourses of homogeneity in terms of culture, language, and ethnic identity (e.g., Han, 2007). With these shifts, existing identities (such as *hankwuk salam* [Korean] and *oykwukin* [foreigner]) become problematized and new(er) identities emerge (such as *kyopho* [overseas Korean] and *honhyelin* [person of mixed blood]). The discourses surrounding these identities (that to various degrees connote foreignness) are complex and frequently feature racialized narratives. And this change has also triggered a transformation in the Korean television landscape (e.g., Ahn, 2014). Students who are learning Korean are going to encounter these narratives and indeed are going to be positioned within them. Therefore, students need to be given the tools to question, negotiate, and ultimately "redesign" (NLG, 1996, p. 13) the narratives of race within which they will find themselves positioned. A *pedagogy of multiliteracies* represents the vehicle by which learners of Korean can gain this level of social justice.

Against this backdrop, this chapter reports on a project that uses Korean visual media sources to develop multiliteracies within the remit of a Korean college program. Specifically, clips from a Korean television drama and a talk show (as well as background reading material in English) were selected to explore discourses surrounding different categories of foreigners in Korean society and how they are represented in Korean popular culture. Using pedagogical practices based on those suggested by the NLG (1996, pp. 18–22), we attempted to foster among learners a critical understanding of how foreigners are positioned as the "other" (meaning here "the foreigner, the unknown, the opposite of we or I" (Capetillo-Ponce, 2003, p. 122)) by means of different modalities such as their appearance, gestures, behavior, cultural knowledge, and, most crucially, their language use and the perceptions of it. We also explored with our learners how cinematic features are employed to modulate the degree of foreignness portrayed. The goals of the project were to enhance learners' multimodal competence, promote critical literacy, and empower students in their use of the target language and development of "second language identities" (Block, 2007). In particular, we placed emphasis on giving learners the opportunity to "redesign" the foreigner category (which they belonged to themselves) and empowering them to resist and transform the status quo.

Background: Foreigners in South Korea

The Identities and Social Positions of Foreigners

In recent years, South Korea has started to transition from "one of the most ethnically and linguistically homogenous countries in the world" (Brown, 2011, p. 103), to a multicultural society. This movement has been fueled by an increasing number of overseas residents in the country. In particular, there has been a rapid rise of so-called "international marriages" (*kwukcey kyolhon*), most typically involving "mail-order brides" from South East Asia and rural farmworkers and fishermen who are unable to find Korean partners due to the migration of young women to urban centers and a high sex ratio caused by son preference (see Kim, 2008). In 2013, the number of foreigners residing in Korea topped 1.5 million for the first time (Yonhap News, 2013).

A public discourse on multiculturalism (*tamwunhwa*) has quickly emerged, including efforts by the government to replace potentially discriminatory language in public spheres. In government documents, the term "mixed-blood children" (*honhyela*) was replaced by "multicultural-family children" (*tamwunhwa-kaceng chanye*). School textbook descriptions of Korea were changed from a "nation unified by one bloodline" to a "multiethnic and multicultural society" (Shin, 2006).

Despite this emerging awareness of multiculturalism, different groups of foreigners are subject to various forms of prejudices, stereotypes, and racism. The Korean word for "foreigner" (*oykwukin*) is most readily associated with the image of a Caucasian, typically American foreigner. White foreigners are afforded preferential treatment of sorts, due to positive associations with English language and modernity (Lee, 2006). However, they are also associated with negative images of the imperialistic American soldier (*mikwun*) and the cowboy English teacher (*yenge sensayng*). The latter is sometimes portrayed in the Korean media as an illicit drug user, womanizer, and carrier of sexually transmitted diseases (Glionna, 2009).

Foreigners of darker skin color may encounter more direct forms of racism. As noted by Tikhonov (2010), non-white native-speaker English teachers may be denied work because the employer would prefer a white teacher. Foreign laborers (*oykwukin kunloca*) from South East Asia suffer from workplace discrimination and a lack of workers' rights (Gray, 2007).

Perceptions of those of mixed Korean and foreign race appear to depend greatly on the ethnicity of the non-Korean parent. A recent trend has been the rise of mixed-race celebrities, who typically have one Caucasian parent. Daniel Henney (who features in the media materials used in the current project), the US-raised son of a Korean adoptee and an Irish-American father, has become a "mega superstar" and "heartthrob" (Lo & Kim, 2011, p. 443). Interestingly, the popularity of Henney can be attributed to his success in aligning himself with "high-class whiteness" rather than Koreanness. With limited Korean ability, he is positioned as an "elite white learner of Korean" (p. 444) and his efforts to use the language are framed as "cool and cute" (p. 446). According to Ahn (2014), the popularity of mixed-race celebrities "reveals the hypocrisy of the current Korean multiculturalism" in which "Koreans accept mixed-race Koreans only if they are successful and proud" (p. 16).

Overseas Koreans (*kyopho*) who return to South Korea face an unusual form of inverted racism. The societal expectation is that these returnees, as ethnic Koreans, should possess a high level of linguistic and cultural competence. When this expectation is not fulfilled, they are positioned as "defective citizens" or as "inauthentic and illegitimate South Koreans" who are linguistically and culturally inept (Lo & Kim, 2011). Returnees are the victims of various forms of discrimination. These may include being openly scolded by taxi drivers or shopkeepers for not being able to speak Korean (Paik, 2010, p. 132) and being verbally or even physically assaulted for speaking English in public.

How Foreigners Speak Korean

Korean people may hold preconceived ideas of what the speech of foreigners sounds like and what areas of the language can and cannot be perfected by foreigners. One such preconceived idea (which to some extent is specific to Korean) is the belief that foreigners fail to use honorifics correctly (Brown, 2010, 2013).

The Korean language has a complex system of honorific language, known colloquially as *contaymal* [respect-speech] and *nophimmal* [raised-speech], involving the addition of verb endings and a special lexicon when addressing or referring to status superiors (see Brown, 2011, pp. 19–58, for a full description). However, intimates of equal or lower status are addressed in a register of speech lacking such honorific devices, which is known as *panmal* [half speech].

As argued in Brown (2013, pp. 275–276), the correct use of honorific speech is closely tied up with performing Korean identity in that it evokes Korea-specific cultural beliefs such as respecting the elderly and upholding hierarchical social structures. Perhaps due to this strong link between using honorifics and performing Korean identity, foreigners are sometimes portrayed in Korean popular culture as being unable to use honorific *contaymal*.[3] In addition, Brown (2013) shows that some Koreans believe that *contaymal* is not required when addressing foreigners.[4]

The Study

The research project described here involved the design, implementation, and evaluation of a lesson plan for a third-year college course (a course where learners have intermediate high or advanced low level on the ACTFL (American Council on the Teaching of Foreign Languages) proficiency scale). The lesson used visual and printed media sources to analyze the positioning of "foreigners" in Korean culture. We designed the materials with the goals of enhancing multimodal competence, promoting critical literacy, and empowering students in their negotiation of their identities.

In this section, we present the teaching materials and the research project we formed around them. We begin by introducing the research context and the methods of data collection. Next, we describe the materials and classroom activities we used. The final two sub-sections analyze the data that we collected from video recordings of classroom interactions and retrospective interviews.

The Research Context

The lesson plan was implemented with a group of third-year learners at a mid-sized state university on the West Coast of the United States. The 1.5 hour lesson was designed by the authors of this chapter and taught by the third author, who is a native speaker of Korean with two years' teaching experience.

The class had four learners: Robert, Brian, Su-bin, and Devin.[5] Three of the learners were of Korean heritage (Robert, Brian, Su-bin) and one was Caucasian American (Devin). The three heritage learners had quite distinct backgrounds. Robert (aged 18) and Su-bin (21) identified as Korean Americans, with Robert being born in the States to immigrant parents and Su-bin moving to Hawaii at age 7. Both reported high usage of Korean with their parents (90–100%). In contrast to this, Brian (22) was Korean Chinese and had come to the US to attend college. His family lived in the Yanbian Korean Autonomous Prefecture in the Jilin region of China, where Korean is a co-official language (Park, 2003, p. 1). Brian reported speaking 50% Korean and 50% Mandarin at home. The non-Korean heritage learner Devin was older than the other learners (aged 31) and had worked and studied in South Korea. He had first spent time in Korea as a Mormon missionary, before returning later as an English teacher.

Collection of Data

Data regarding student reactions to the teaching techniques were collected using two methodologies: analysis of video recordings and retrospective interviews.

The class session was video recorded using a handheld Flip F260N Ultra Series Digital Camcorder. The recording was transcribed in full, including the notation of paralinguistic features such as gesture. Episodes in which learners appeared to be engaged in expression or negotiation of identity were then identified and subjected to discourse analysis.

The retrospective interviews took place 3–7 days after the class session and were conducted in English by the first author. During these interviews, the learners were asked for their opinions on the teaching techniques used and were quizzed in more detail about their identities (vis-à-vis the topic of "foreigners") and how they felt about the fact that the class session allowed them to question (or simply to express) these identities. Finally, using a stimulated recall technique (Gass & Mackey, 2000), the learners were shown video extracts from the class sessions and were asked to recall the thought processes and emotions they were experiencing at that time. In our analysis of these interview transcripts, we treat learner comments as situated and contested accounts, which are nevertheless "symptomatic" (Kvale, 1996) of the experiences and emotions of the participants.

Design and Implementation of Materials

Media Sources

The lesson plan included two visual media sources—a clip from the 2005 MBC drama *My Lovely Sam Soon* (*Nay ilum-un Kim Sam-swun*; 2005, MBC) and a clip from the talk show *Taykwukmin thokuswo annyenghaseyyo* (2013, KBS). In addition, an academic article written in English about perceptions of mixed-race actors in Korean (Lo & Kim, 2011) was given to the learners as background reading.

My Lovely Sam Soon is a hit drama series that features a romantic struggle between four characters, one of whom is Doctor Henry Kim (Henry hereafter), played by megastar mixed-race actor Daniel Henney. Interestingly, Henry is not supposed to be mixed race, but an ethnic Korean adopted by American parents and raised in the US speaking only English. Henry becomes romantically involved with Hee-Jin (Jung Ryeo-won). However, he has to deal with the advances of her ex-boyfriend Jin-heon (played by top star Hyun Bin), who is now becoming involved with the show's main character, Sam Soon (Kim Suna).

In the clip, Jin-heon (Hyun Bin) visits Henry (Daniel Henney) at his guest house. They go to play basketball together, although only Henry participates, and then go swimming. Finally, they go to a restaurant to eat *sellengthang* [ox-bone soup]. Plot-advancing dialogue in the scene is fairly minimal, although Jin-heon does ask Henry about his feelings for Hee-Jin ("Do you love Hee-Jin?").

The clip is interesting for the way it uses linguistic and visual cues to render Henry (Daniel Henney) "foreign," whereas Jin-heon (Hyun Bin) is portrayed as "Korean." The dialogue features regular code-switching between Korean and English. Henry sticks mostly to English (10 utterance units in English; 2 in Korean[6]), whereas Jin-heon prefers Korean (8; 23). Henry's two Korean utterances are simple stock phrases (*kwiyewe* [you're cute] *way?*, [why?]), positioning him as a learner of the language only familiar with some of the basics. As for Jin-heon, his use of English mostly occurs in interrogatives, imperatives, and hortatives addressed directly to Henry ("Do you play basketball?"; "Do you love Hee-jin?"), whereas he uses Korean to comment on Henry's actions and appearance, sometimes using casual or derogatory slang expressions such as referring to Henry as *casik* [dude]. Given Henry's low level of Korean, the viewer assumes that Henry is unable to understand Jin-heon's derogatory comments, thus further positioning Henry as a foreigner who can be taken advantage of by a native speaker in this way. All Korean utterances from both characters are in *panmal* [half speech], which given that they are adults who hardly know each other is quite marked. The use of *panmal* works to cast Henry as a foreigner unfamiliar with (or undeserving of) the fineries of Korean etiquette and adds to the feeling that Jin-heon is taking advantage of Henry's linguistic and cultural ignorance.

Visual elements further render Henry "foreign." A striking contrast is established between the ways that Jin-heon (as the Korean) and Henry (as the foreigner) are dressed. With long hair and a pink shirt, Jin-heon typifies the *kkochminam* [pretty flower boy] identity preferred by younger Koreans (Maliangkay, 2010). In contrast, Henry represents the casual and sporty American dressed in T-shirts, shorts, and sneakers. The sense that Henry does not fit into the Korean background of the drama is heightened by the use of traditional Korean locations, such as a traditional Korean *hanok* house for the guesthouse in the opening scene. Henry is also contrasted with Jin-heon by being cast in the role of cultural novice, whereas Jin-heon appears as the expert. In the restaurant scene, Jin-heon shows Henry how to add rice, green onions, salt, and kimchi juices to his *sellengthang*, with Henry diligently following Jin-heon's lead.

The treatment of foreigners in Korean society is also salient in the extract from the talk show *Taykwukmin thokuswo annyenghaseyyo*. In this show, viewers send in their personal problems, which are then discussed with the presenter and guests. In this particular episode, a viewer named Choi Sang-il complains that he is frequently addressed in *panmal* by strangers. As more of the story is revealed, it emerges that the reason for this is that he has a darker complexion and is thus often mistaken for a foreign laborer from South East Asia. This leads to discussion of what the use of *panmal* says about the way Korean people treat foreigners.

Sequence of Activities

The sequence of activities built around these media sources was designed according to the pedagogical principles of multiliteracies set out by the NLG (1996) and further developed by Kalantzis and Cope (2000). In particular, we adopted their framework of including four factors in the lesson plan: *Situated Practice* (the students are immersed in meaningful practices), *Overt Instruction* (the teacher provides interventions that guide practice and focus the students on important features of their experiences and the activities), *Critical Framing* (the students stand back from the study materials and interpret them critically), and *Transformed Practice* (the students put new knowledge to work in other contexts, integrating it with other knowledge and coping with the tensions that develop).

Another important principle we followed was the promotion of multimodal competence. Activities targeted both language and visual images, thus following the underlying philosophy that visual images are "socially and culturally constructed products which have a culturally specific grammar of their own" (Stenglin & Iedema, 2001, p. 195).

Before the in-class session, students were asked to read the English academic article and to submit a "reading note" summarizing the article and giving their critical reflections (three out of the four learners completed this task). The decision to provide English language material was inspired by Byrnes' observation (1991) that this can help learners to build native-culture schemata that they can then apply to target-language texts. Without this step, learners exposed directly to target-language texts on unfamiliar subjects are prone to interpret them through their native-culture schemata and miss the way that the materials represent the target culture.[7]

The opening section of the class (23 minutes) was devoted to introducing the general topic of foreigners in Korea. It began with a Situated Practice activity during which the teacher asked the learners whether they saw the term *oykwukin* [foreigner] as having positive or negative connotations and whether they considered themselves to be *oykwukin* in Korean society. The teacher then used PowerPoint slides containing statistics to show the rapid growth of the foreigner population in South Korea (overt instruction), and asked learners to critically evaluate them (Critical Framing). Then, as the next Situated Practice activity, learners completed a ranking activity in which they had to decide which out of a group of six foreigners (a white American English teacher, a white American soldier, a black British English teacher, a mixed-race American-Korean bartender, a Japanese journalist, and a Filipino laborer) Korean people would treat with the most kindness.

The next section of the class (37 minutes) consisted of viewing the clip from *My Lovely Sam Soon* and analyzing the use of language and visual cues in the construction of the identities of Henry (Daniel Henney) and Jin-heon (Hyun Bin). On the second viewing of the clip, learners had to note down observations on the visual representation and language use of these two characters. This Critical Framing activity targeting multimodal competence was followed by a Situated Practice activity in which learners answered discussion questions regarding the portrayal of Henry and Jin-heon and related issues regarding the perception of foreigners in Korean society.

In the third and final section of the class (20 minutes), students viewed the clip from the talk show *Taykwukmin thokuswo annyenghaseyyo*. After viewing the opening frames, students were asked to predict the identity of the viewer who was complaining about receiving *panmal*. They then watched the remainder of the clip. This led to a final pair and class discussion (Transformed Practice), which involved the learners applying the observations about the use of *panmal* in the video clips to wider questions of what this tells us about the social position of foreigners in Korean society. In addition, the learners discussed how the content of the videos related to their own experiences of interacting with Korean people. This final discussion encouraged learners to engage and negotiate their own identities and to express resistance to their environment.

Teaching visual media through the techniques used in our study has a number of learning outcomes, all of which are relevant to multiliteracies. First of all, learners will be more aware of different text types and different modalities of meaning-making, thus boosting their multimodal competencies (Kress, 2000b; Royce, 2007). Second, learners will learn how to engage critically with these texts and the semiotic systems within them. This critical aspect of language learning is often ignored in the language classroom until students have reached advanced levels of proficiency; however, the current chapter has shown some ways in which it can be successfully done at third-year level. Third, students will learn culture-specific aspects of how these modalities are represented and inter-preted in the target language, which will improve their awareness of cultural and linguistic diversity—also a key concern recognized by the NLG (1996). Fourth, and of most importance, learners will negotiate their own identities vis-à-vis the thematic focus of the class, in this case the positioning of foreigners in South Korean society. Students will redesign the topic (i.e., give their own meaning to it) and become empowered to actively negotiate their subject positions vis-à-vis the target language.

Although the lesson plan here is limited to one topic ("foreigners") and specific to one language (Korean), the topic is undoubtedly relevant to all learners of second languages. Moreover, the basic types of activities and their sequence can be applied to other topics. The techniques described here would relate best to topics that involve areas of identity that can be contested by language learners in their contact with the target language culture. Examples would include gender identities, age-based identities, religious identities, regional or dialect-based iden-tities, student identities, workplace identities, identities within the family, and identities within friendships. Rather than addressing these identities directly, the class could pinpoint the social contexts, activities, or discourses in which these identities are negotiated. For example, family identities could be addressed through a class that focuses on birth- or wedding-related customs; and workplace identities could be addressed through a class that looks at drinking culture (which forms an important part of workplace culture in societies such as South Korea and Japan). We provide a template for teaching multiliteracies through visual media in Table 7.1.

Analysis of Classroom Talk

We now analyze selected extracts from the video recordings of the class. These extracts represent episodes in which learners appeared to be expressing or negotiating their identities in relation to the class theme of "foreigners." In particular, we selected episodes in which learners seemed to realize something new about their identities through their reactions to the teaching materials. These episodes provide evidence for how the multiliteracies approach allows learners to create their own meanings, redefine their own identities and, ultimately, redesign the narratives that they are confronted with. Our discussion of these episodes follows the chronological progression of the class outlined in the previous section.

As stated above, the introductory section of the class began with the teacher asking the learners whether they considered themselves foreigners in Korean society. Thus, from the very outset of the class, learners were asked to define their identity in relation to this foreigner label. Understandably, the heritage learners (Robert, Brian, and Su-bin) were conflicted about this:

TABLE 7.1 Template for Teaching Multiliteracies Through Visual Media

Stage	Activity	Type of Pedagogy	Application in Current Project
0 (Pre–class)	Students perform a critical reading of a related (academic) article and submit a critical reading note (may be done in target language or native language)	Critical Framing	Students read English article on mixed-race actors in Korea
1	Students are asked to give initial definition of "self" in relation to the class topic	Situated Practice	Students were asked if they were "foreigners"
2	Students are given further (factual/statistical) information on the topic and asked to critically evaluate it	Overt Instruction; Critical Framing	Students were given statistics on the increasing number of foreigners in Korea
3	Students engage in initial discussions of the topic. Spoken activities such as ranking, brainstorming, sequencing, and classifying may be used at this stage. These activities may also act as preparation for media viewing	Situated Practice	Students completed a ranking activity asking which category of "foreigner" would receive best treatment in Korean society
4	Students view visual media and complete activities that target the social significance of different modalities of meaning (linguistic, visual, etc.) in relation to the class topic	Critical Framing	Students viewed *My Lovely Sam Soon* clip and noted down observations on how Henry and Jin-heon were represented linguistically and visually
5	Students discuss the different modalities of meaning noted in stage 4	Situated Practice; Critical Framing	Students discussed questions regarding the way that Henry and Jin-heon were represented in relation to notions of foreignness
[4,5]	Repetition of stages 4 and 5 using further media materials		Students viewed talk show clip and discussed
6	Students discuss the wider implications of the linguistic and visual elements analyzed in the class in relation to their own experiences and identities	Transformed Practice	Students discussed wider issues of foreigners being addressed in *panmal* and their personal experiences

Excerpt 1

24. T(eacher): 저는 한국에 가시면 외국인은 아닐것같다– 외국인 아니다 하시는 분들 계세요?

    [When I go to Korea, I don't think I am a foreigner—I am not a foreigner, is there anyone here who thinks this?]

25. 한국에 가면 외국인은 아닐 것 같다.

    [When I go to Korea, I am not a foreigner.]

    (Robert and Brian look at each other and smile; Robert shakes his head once.)

26. 솔직하게.

    [Honestly.]

27. Su-bin: 저는 안 느끼는데 사람들이 미국에서 온 걸 알아요. 화장이나 얼굴 까무잡잡한 거 보고, 미국에서 오셨어요, 물어봐요.

    [I don't feel it myself, but people know I am from America. When they see my make-up and dark complexion, they ask me "are you from America?"]

28. T: 그럼 수빈은 스스로 한국에서는 외국인이 아니라고 느끼세요?

    [So you feel yourself that you are not a foreigner in Korea?]

29. Su-bin: 네.

    [That's right.]

30. T: 로버트는 어때요?

    [How about you, Robert?]

31. Robert: 저도 그래요.

    [I'm the same.]

    근데 옷하고 신발하고 사람들이 보면 외국인이라고 느낄 수도—

    [But when people see my clothes or shoes they might feel that I am a foreigner—]

In this extract, the students are slow to respond, leading the teacher to rephrase the question in line 25. Robert and Brian (who know each other well) exchange glances and smiles, with Robert shaking his head. In the retrospective interviews, Robert and Brian reported that this question of identity was one that they had discussed previously. "We were like 'not this again,'" said Robert, observing that although the question was important and interesting, the answer to it was elusive: "we can never choose a side." However, both Robert and Brian commented that the class had "helped" them develop a better understanding of the ways in which "Korean" and "foreigner" identities could be negotiated and had made them more aware of how these identities were visually presented in Korean visual media.

It is Su-bin who eventually answers the question (line 27) with the observation that she does not see herself as a foreigner, but that Korean people may perceive her as one due to her appearance (style of make-up, dark skin). Robert aligns with this, noting that Koreans may feel he is a foreigner due to his clothes and shoes.

Throughout the class, the three heritage learners continued to orient to the question of appearance (hair, make-up, clothes), whereas Caucasian American Devin notably did not. For the ranking activity, the pair of Su-bin and Brian justified all of their rankings in relation to notions of appearance such as "white," "blonde hair," "blue eyes," "good looking," and "cool." Contrary to this, Devin and Robert defined their answers in terms of how much these different foreigners were "needed" by Korean society (e.g., the American English teacher was needed for the education system, the American soldier was needed for defense, etc.). Although Robert is of Korean heritage, during the interview sessions he noted that he and Devin had "similar thinking" due to the fact that they were both American born and raised, hinting that Robert oriented to his American identity for this task. Here, it is evident that the learners (as Caucasians and overseas Koreans) were well aware of the comparatively privileged positions that they themselves held in the hierarchy of foreigners in Korean society.

Similarly, for the activity where learners had to make notes on the visual representation of Daniel Henney and Hyun Bin, the heritage learners quickly picked up on questions of clothing. Su-bin noted contrasts in the colors that the two actors wore. "Hyun Bin wore a pink shirt," she commented, "but in America men don't wear pink very often." Discussions on the importance of physical appearance in the popularity of Daniel Henney culminated with Brian describing Korean society in a one-word utterance: *oymocisangcwui* [appearance-obsessed] (Extract 2). Note how this observation is ratified by the teacher's repetition in line 536 and then by Robert nodding his head and running his hand down his face in a gesture that signaled facial appearance (Figure 7.1).

FIGURE 7.1 Robert runs his hand down his face to signal the idea of facial appearance.

Excerpt 2

535. Brian: 외모 지상주의.

[Appearance obsessed.]

536. T: 외모 지상주의, 한국은!

[Appearance obsessed, Korea!]

[Robert nods his head, then runs his hand down his face; Devin begins to raise his hand.]

537. 그래서 한국은 영어를 써서 친절한 게 아니고, 친절해도 잘 생긴 사람에게 친절하다?

[So in Korea it's not that people are kind to you if you use English, but they are kind to someone who is good looking?]

The orientation of the heritage learners to questions of physical appearance reflects the fact that these were narratives that they were involved in during their daily lives. During the interviews, when asked about the contrasting clothing styles of Henney, the American, and Hyun Bin, the Korean, Su-bin described this as "normal for me" and something that she encountered not only when she visited Korea, but among the Korean population on the US campus: "I pretty much see two kinds of people walking around every day." All three of the heritage learners reported a tendency for Korean people to associate them with their non-Korean identity and that clothing was one vehicle for this. "The way I dress," noted Su-bin, "I guess it is more provocative, more showy." They could also use clothing to modulate their identities, with Su-bin reporting that she would sometimes wear less make-up, flat shoes, "nothing showy" and "try to cover myself up" when she was in Korea. By orienting to the question of appearance, the heritage learners successfully provided their own meanings to the teaching materials and critically questioned the role of clothing, hair, and make-up in the way they negotiated their subject positions as "Koreans." However, this is not to say that the heritage learners did not learn anything new from the materials, as shall be commented on below.

The way that Devin oriented to the materials was notably different and constituted another kind of identity performance. Discussions regarding Daniel Henney's lack of Korean ability led to comments by Brian and Su-bin that Henney, in the privileged position of being an English-speaking American foreigner, did not need to learn Korean quickly and that sticking to English was an advantage of sorts as it made him appear cute. However, when the question of speaking English rather than Korean being an advantage for foreigners in Korea was put to Devin, he expressed disagreement (Extract 3). His expression of disagreement and his introduction of some of the disadvantages of being a monolingual English-speaking foreigner are accompanied by him rubbing his hands together slowly and puffing out his cheeks, which seem to mark anxiety or uncertainty (line 579; Figure 7.2).

Extract 3

578. T: [...] 외국인이 한국에 갔을 때 한국어를 말하지
않고 영어를 말했을 때 더 많은 이득을 얻는다고 생각하세
요, 여러가지 면에서?

[When a foreigner goes to Korea and doesn't use Korean but only English, do you think they gain more advantages, in many ways?]

579. Devin: 아니오, 그렇게 생각하지 않아요.

[No, I don't think so.]

영어 말하면 [rubs hands together slowly and puffs out cheeks], 교사 될수 있지만, 그, 단점이 많을 것 같아요.

[If you speak English, you can become an instructor [i.e., an English teacher], but I think there are many disadvantages.]

580. 한국어 배우려고 하면, 문화도 언어 같이 배워야 되잖아요.

[If you are to learn Korean, you learn culture with the language.]

581. 그래서 한쪽만 배우면 100퍼센트 못 배워요.

[If you only learn one aspect, you cannot learn 100%.]

582. 그래서 잘 살리지 못하고, 단점이 많아요.

[So you can't live well and there are many disadvantages.]

We analyze Devin's decision to explicitly list some of the negative aspects of the English-speaker identity as an expression of his own subject position as a Caucasian American who has invested considerable time and effort reaching an advanced level in Korean and establishing a target language identity of sorts with his Korean peers. During the interview, Devin talked of how, during his time in Korea, he "wanted a greater separation from his Western self" and particularly from the association of his appearance with speaking English and/or being an English teacher. He felt that he was continually trying to convince Korean friends to "take

FIGURE 7.2 Devin rubs his hands together and puffs out his cheeks.

me on to your team" and let him "be part of your crowd." "If you just speak English, you can never be in that group," commented Devin, "you might be popular, but in some circumstances you will be the outsider." By stating the need for foreigners in Korea to speak the language, Devin legitimized his own identity as an English-speaking Caucasian learner of Korean, which was threatened by the idea that someone such as himself would not need to learn the language.

Devin was notably more careful than the other three learners not to explicitly criticize Korean society during the class session. When discussing the tendency for Koreans to address foreigners in *panmal*, Devin dismissed it as just "a way of talking easily" (*swip-key iyakiha-nun pangpep*) not dissimilar to foreigner talk in other languages—"we [Americans] don't have *contaymal* and *panmal*, but we also speak to foreigners like we are using *panmal*" (*wuli-ka contaymal panmal-un eps-ciman wuli-to oykwukin-hanthey panmal ha-nun kes kath-ayo*). In addition, when asked if he would feel bad if he was addressed in *panmal* himself, he answered strongly that he would not, claiming that for him the difference between *panmal* and *contaymal* created no "deep feeling" (Extract 4).

Excerpt 4

728. Devin: 네, 기분이 나쁘지 않아요.
      [That's right, I don't feel bad.]
      (laughs; classmates and teacher also laugh)
729.   저 괜찮아요.
      [I'm okay.]
      반말 들을 때 반말하고 존댓말하고 어떻게 다른지 배웠는데, 그래서 깊은 느낌은 안가요.
      [When I hear *panmal*, I learned how *panmal* and *contaymal* are different, but it does not affect me deeply.]

Devin's claim that he lacks sensitivity to *panmal* and *contaymal* should be taken at face value. As noted quite perceptively by Devin during the interview session, unlike the heritage learners who had been socialized into the cultural meanings of *panmal* from an early age, "being offended by it [the inappropriate use of *panmal*] is something that I have had to learn." However, his orientation to this lack of sensitivity in this classroom context plays an obvious social function. As the only non-ethnic Korean in the classroom, Devin may have been strategically avoiding any overt criticism of Korean society and claiming to be the foreigner who lacks sensitivity to Korean culture helps him to accomplish this. The feeling that Devin's utterances are playing a social function is heightened by Devin's use of laughter directly after his statement in line 728. Here, Devin's laughter works to make light of his experiences and to bond with the teacher and classmates, who join in with it.

During the interview sessions, Devin advanced more negative opinions about the inappropriate use of *panmal* toward foreigners than he had done during the class session. "The more I thought about it and hearing what some of the other students said, I think that [the use of *panmal* toward foreigners] does bother me," said Devin. "It feels like impatient language to me. [. . .] Like Chris Tucker talking to Jackie Chan."[8] This comment hints that the class session and the multiliteracies techniques were effective in making Devin aware of the possible negative social implications of such patterns of *panmal* use. However, it is also possible that Devin simply felt more able to express such concerns frankly during the interview sessions, which were after all conducted in English with an English native speaker (the first author).

In contrast to Devin, all three of the heritage learners expressed degrees of discomfort regarding being addressed in *panmal* due to their foreigner identity. In Extract 5, Robert narrates an incident in which he was addressed in *panmal* by one of his Korean teachers. As can be seen in Figure 7.3, on first mention of the episode, Robert smiles nervously and touches his head. This kind of self-touching is considered an expression of negative affect, occurring when the speaker feels anxiety or a sense of conflict (Harrington, 1985). Here, the fact that Robert is relaying an episode involving a Korean teacher known by his audience is a probable source of discomfort, with the self-touching working to provide reassurance and to focus attention on how to convey this potentially problematic narrative.

Excerpt 5

739. Robert: 저는 그게 그, 처음 만난 사람이랑 반말 들으면 되게 기분 나빠요.
[I, well, when I hear panmal from someone I am meeting for the first time, I feel very bad.]

740. 근데 되게 웃긴 거는, 윤 선생님 아시죠?
[The funny thing is—you know teacher Yun?]
(touches head and smiles)

741. 윤 선생님 처음 만났을 때 선생님이 저한테 반말 했거든요.
[When I first met her, she used *panmal* to me, you see.]

742. 선생님 입장은 그게 맞는 거죠.
[From the teacher's standpoint, that's correct, of course.]

743. 나이가 훨씬 많으시니까.
[Because she's much older than me.]

744. 근데 제 입장에서는 그때는, 나이도 안 깠는데 왜 반말하지? 이런 생각을 했어요.
[But from my point of view, at that time I thought we haven't even revealed our ages, so why is she speaking *panmal*?]
근데 되게 기분 나빴어요.
[And I felt very bad.]

745. 나이가 더 많아도 우리 나이 밝히지도 않았고, 친하지도 않은데, 왜 나한테 반말 쓰지?

[Even though you are older, we have not revealed our ages and we are not close so why is she speaking *panmal?*]

746. *T:* 외려 한국적인 …

[You are so Korean …]

Despite the potentially problematic nature of this section of talk, it ultimately works to position Robert as someone who is sensitive to the social factors that legitimize the use of *panmal*. This position is ratified by the teacher, who describes his line of thinking as being "Korean" (line 746). Thus, unlike Devin who happily creates a non-Korean identity through his assumed lack of sensitivity to the social meanings of *panmal*, Robert successfully claims a Korean identity, which is legitimized by the teacher—a native speaker of Korean.

In sum, this analysis has shown that even during one isolated class session, the multiliteracies approach allowed learners to become actively engaged in creating their own meanings and designing their identities, in this case vis-à-vis the label of "foreigner." For Devin, the identity of foreigner was one that he was happy to accept, at least in this classroom environment. However, he was keen to argue against the idea that an identity such as his own was always beneficial in South Korean society, especially when it was suggested that it may preclude learning Korean altogether. As for the three ethnic Korean learners, they were quick to express that they saw themselves as Korean, although this viewpoint was not always shared by others in South Korea. Here, the three heritage learners created "appearance" as a (superficial) narrative that prevented them from gaining full access to Korean identities. They were critical of the importance of appearance in Korean society, framing Korea as "appearance-obsessed." Ultimately, in the final discussion, Robert (as well as Brian and Su-bin) positioned themselves as being

FIGURE 7.3 Robert touches his head and smiles.

sensitive to the workings of *panmal* and it was this that allowed them to engineer Korean subject positions of sorts.

Learners' Reactions

Finally, we briefly discuss the reactions and opinions that the learners expressed regarding the class session during the retrospective interviews. These discussions cover three areas: (1) use of English language background reading, (2) use of activities highlighting visual as well as linguistic elements, and (3) the suitability of the topic in general.

The learners expressed highly positive views of the background reading activity, which involved reading an English language academic text on the discourse surrounding mixed-race actors. Robert and Devin noted how the use of English made the text accessible, particularly since their Korean was not yet at a level where they could read an academic article at ease. "It really gave me a lot of the information I needed to prepare for the class," noted Devin, "it provided good background on the topic."

However, the interviews hint that the extent to which learners were able to apply this background knowledge to critical discussions in the language class-room may depend on their level of competence, particularly their knowledge of related vocabulary items. Whereas Robert noted that he was able to "process all of the English and translate it back [into Korean]," Devin found that he lacked the Korean vocabulary needed to do this, including key terms such as *honhyelin* ("person of mixed race").

Another limitation of providing English language reading materials is that it may be of limited assistance to learners whose L1 is not English, such as Korean-Chinese Brian in this class. In fact, Brian failed to submit a reading note for the article, complaining that his "poor English" rendered the task difficult. This reflects the challenges that educators face due to the diverse literacies of students. Given the increasing numbers of Chinese students populating Korean language classes in the US college system, teachers need to be aware of the needs of these learners when incorporating English language materials into the curriculum.

The learners also made positive and important observations regarding the use of activities that highlighted visual elements in the clip from *My Lovely Sam Soon*. All learners noted that they enjoyed these activities and felt that doing such activities made them consciously aware of visual factors that would normally go unnoticed for them: "I didn't catch it [the importance of visuals in the character-ization of Henry and Jin-heon] until you guys told me to do it," noted Su-bin. On the one hand, notably, the heritage learners performed well on these tasks, managing to note down many visual differences between Henry and Jin-heon. As previously stated, this was due to the familiarity these heritage learners held with narratives of appearance in South Korean society. Non-heritage Devin, on the other hand, admitted during the interview that he had "performed poorly" and that he had relied heavily on the observations of the other students, who he described as "more perceptive." These observations hint that although visual exercises are useful for both heritage and non-heritage learners, the latter may need more scaffolding and practice in order to perform well.

Finally, the learners expressed largely encouraging opinions regarding the selection of the topic of "foreigners." Both the heritage and non-heritage learners felt that the topic was relevant to them; for example, Robert commented: "Because I'm like a Korean American too, so it's kind of like 'am I a *oykwuksalam* [foreigner]?'" Importantly, the class not only widened their understanding of the topic through discussion of the discourses surrounding mixed-race actors ("I had never really thought about the American actors in Korea too"—Robert), but allowed them to reflect on their own identity and, as shown in the previous section, renegotiate their subject positions.

In sum, learners expressed positive opinions toward the teaching techniques and materials used. This fact alone is perhaps of limited significance given the social context of the interview (i.e., the fact that they were talking to the first author, who is a Korean linguistics professor). However, analysis of the interview transcripts has revealed interesting and important insights into what parts of the lesson plan were particularly effective and also how different techniques suited the individual identities and learning styles of each student.

Discussion and Conclusion

In this chapter, we have analyzed the design, implementation, and evaluation of a lesson plan using Korean visual media sources to develop multiliteracies in a Korean college program. Analysis of the classroom video and learner retrospective interviews revealed that the class was effective in the promotion of learner competence in key areas of multiliteracies, such as sensitivity to multimodal cues, critical thinking, and identity negotiation. Regarding the last of these, analysis of classroom discourse highlighted the ways that learners were active in positioning themselves and redesigning their self-images in relation to the teaching materials and the notion of what it meant to be a foreigner in Korean society. Thus, the analysis provides strong indications that the multiliteracies approach can be effective in encouraging learners to create their own meanings and transition toward becoming active members of the target language community (see Chapter 6, this volume).

The success of this project has obvious implications for teaching in Korean and other language programs in US college settings. First and most generally, the chapter makes a strong case for moving language teaching toward "a broader and more coherent curriculum in which language, culture and literature are taught as a continuous whole" (MLA, 2007, p. 3) and in which the teaching of communication is reconciled with the teaching of textual analysis (Kern, 2003, p. 43). This will allow language programs to be reconnected with the larger academic missions of language and literature departments, which extend "beyond the teaching of verb conjugations and cultural generalities" (Allen & Paesani, 2010, p. 119).

The second implication is more specifically connected to the selection of the topic of "foreigners" and the observation that similar lesson plans could be developed to address other identity-related issues such as gender, age, religion, and dialect. By engaging learner identity, this approach encourages students to develop critical perspectives on the target language culture, as well as their own. As mentioned briefly in the introduction, the use of media and the teaching of culture in the Korean classroom frequently stick to "safe" and accepted generalizations about Korean language and culture, with the focus often on educating learners regarding traditional observed culture (i.e., Korean food, dress, traditional customs—see, for example, Cho, 2003; Park, 2005). This of course is not a problem that is limited to Korean. Cutshall (2012, p. 33) caricatures the traditional approach to culture as being limited to "reading over the cultural points that pop up in the occasional [textbook] sidebar," "offer[ing] 'Culture Fridays'" and "celebrating a holiday, learning a few dances, or tasting some authentic food now and then." This treatment of culture lacks a critical angle and keeps the learner forever in the subject position of an external observer. In contrast, by addressing topics related to identity in increasingly multicultural South Korea, this chapter has shown that learners can engage with culture not only in a critical way, but also in a way that involves their very own subject positions in relation to the target language culture. By adopting such an approach, we can indeed fulfil one of the ultimate goals of the multiliteracies pedagogy: to transform learners and to make them problem solvers, active and informed citizens, meaning makers and code breakers (Anstey & Bull, 2006, pp. 23–44).

Notes

1 We use KSL as a general term that encompasses the learning of Korean as an additional language in all contexts.
2 In this chapter, we use the word "foreigner" as a direct equivalent of the Korean term *oykwukin* to refer to those who have (or are perceived as having) non-Korean nationality and/or ethnicity. We are aware that this differs from the typical English usage of the term (which is indeed increasingly considered pejorative).
3 Two examples of this are the drama series *My Lovely Sam Soon* (2005, MBC) and *I'm Sorry, I Love You* (2004, KBS). The former drama is used as classroom materials for the current study, so more information can be found later in the chapter. In the latter, a Korean adoptee raised in Australia (played by So Ji-sub) is portrayed as addressing all interlocutors using *panmal* and being taught by other characters how to use *contaymal*.
4 Although we focus here on the assumption that *panmal* is considered appropriate in interactions involving foreigners, it should be noted that the alternative assumption (i.e., that foreigners use and should be addressed in *contaymal*, or at least a simplified version of it) also exists (see Brown, 2010).
5 All names of the students and others mentioned in the classroom discussion are pseudonyms.
6 We exclude here one Korean utterance, *kamsahapnita* [thank you] spoken by Henry, as this was addressed toward the server in the restaurant and not directly to Jin-heon.

7 Byrnes (1991) actually suggests a four step process: (1) reading about an aspect of the student's own culture in his/her native language, (2) reading about an aspect of the student's own culture in the target language, (3) reading about an aspect of the target culture in the student's native language, and (4) reading about an aspect of the target culture in the target language.

8 This is a reference to the movie *Rush Hour*.

References

Ahn, J. (2014). Rearticulating black mixed-race in the era of globalization: Hines Ward and the struggle for Koreanness in contemporary South Korean media. *Cultural Studies, 28*(3), 391–417.

Allen, H. W., & Paesani, K. (2010). Exploring the feasibility of a pedagogy of multiliteracies in introductory foreign language courses. *L2 Journal, 2*(1), 119–142.

Anstey, M., & Bull, G. (2006). *Teaching and learning multiliteracies: Changing times, changing literacies*. Newark, DE: International Reading Association.

Block, D. (2007). *Second language identities*. London: Continuum.

Brown, L. (2010). Questions of appropriateness and authenticity in the representation of Korean honorifics in textbooks for second language learners. *Language, Culture and Curriculum, 23*(1), 35–50.

Brown, L. (2011). *Korean honorifics and politeness in second language learning*. Amsterdam/Philadelphia: John Benjamins.

Brown, L. (2013). Identity and honorifics use in Korean study abroad. In C. Kinginger (Ed.), *Social and cultural aspects of language learning in study abroad* (pp. 269–298). Amsterdam/Philadelphia: John Benjamins.

Byrnes, H. (1991). Reflections on the development of cross-cultural competence in the foreign language classroom. In B. Freed (Ed.), *Foreign language acquisition research and the classroom* (pp. 205–218). Lexington, MA: D.C. Heath.

Capetillo-Ponce, J. (2003). Defining the other. *Human Architecture: Journal of the Sociology of Self-Knowledge, 2*(2), Article 18.

Cho, H. (2003). Hankwukemwunhwa kyoyuklon-uy cwuyo cayngcem-kwa kwacey [Major issues and themes in Korean culture education]. In Y. Park (Ed.), *21-seyki hankwukekyoyukhak-uy hyenhwang-kwa kwacey* [The present situation of and issues in Korean language education] (pp. 441–472). Seoul: Hankwukmwunhwasa.

Crafton, L., Silvers, P., & Brennan, M. (2009). Creating a critical multiliteracies curriculum: Repositioning art in the early childhood classroom. In M. Narey (Ed.), *Making meaning: Constructing multimodal perspectives of language, literacy, and learning through arts-based early childhood education* (pp. 31–51). New York, NY: Springer.

Cutshall, S. (2012). More than a decade of standards: Integrating "cultures" in your language instruction. *The Language Educator* (April), 32–37.

Gass, S., & Mackey, A. (2000). *Stimulated recall methodology in second language research*. Mahwah, NJ: Erlbaum.

Glionna, John. (2009). Trying to teach South Korea about discrimination. *Los Angeles Times*, February 24. Retrieved from http://articles.latimes.com/2009/feb/24/world/fg-korea-teach24.

Gray, K. (2007). From human to workers' rights: The emergence of a migrant worker's union movement in Korea. *Global Society, 21*(2), 297–315.

Halliday, M.A.K., & Hasan, R. (1985). *Language, context and text: Aspects of language in a social-semiotic perspective*. Oxford, UK: Oxford University Press.

Han, K. (2007). The archaeology of the ethnically homogeneous nation-state and multiculturalism in Korea. *Korea Journal, 47*(4), 8–31.

Harrington, J. (1985). Self-touching as an indicator of underlying affect and language processes. *Social Science & Medicine, 20*(11), 1161–1168.

Kalantzis, M., & Cope, B. (2000). A multiliteracies pedagogy: A pedagogical supplement. In B. Cope, & M. Kalantzis (Eds.), *Multiliteracies: Literary learning and the design of social futures* (pp. 239–248). Abingdon, UK: Routledge.

Kern, R. (2003). Literacy as a new organizing principle for foreign language education. In P. Partrikis (Ed.), *Reading between the lines: Perspectives on foreign language literary* (pp. 40–59). New Haven, CT: Yale.

Kim, A.E. (2008). Global migration and South Korea: Foreign workers, foreign brides and the making of a multicultural society. *Ethnic and Racial Studies, 32*(1): 70–92.

Kress, G. (2000a). Design and transformation. In B. Cope, & M. Kalantzis (Eds.), *Multiliteracies: Literary learning and the design of social futures* (pp. 153–161). Abingdon, UK: Routledge.

Kress, G. (2000b). Multimodality. In B. Cope, & M. Kalantzis (Eds.), *Multiliteracies: Literary learning and the design of social futures* (pp. 182–202). Abingdon, UK: Routledge.

Kvale, S. (1996). *Interviews*. London: Sage.

Lee, J.S. (2006). Linguistic constructions of modernity: English mixing in Korean television commercials. *Language in Society, 35*, 59–91.

Li, D. (2012). "It's always more difficult than you plan and imagine": Teachers' perceived difficulties in introducing the communicative approach in South Korea. *TESOL Quarterly, 32*(4), 677–703.

Lo, A., & Kim, J. (2011). Manufacturing citizenship: Metapragmatic framings of language competencies in media images of mixed race men in South Korea. *Discourse & Society, 22*(4), 440–457.

Maliangkay, R. (2010). Effeminacy of male beauty in Korea. *IIAS Newsletter, 55*, 6–7.

Modern Language Association (MLA) Ad Hoc Committee on Foreign Languages. (2007). Foreign languages and higher education: New structures for a changed world. *Profession 2007*, 234–245.

New London Group (NLG). (1996). A pedagogy of multiliteracies: Designing social futures. *Harvard Educational Review, 66*(1), 60–92.

Paik, Y. (2010). "Not-quite Korean" children in "almost Korean" families: The fear of decreasing population and state multiculturalism in South Korea. In J. Song (Ed.), *New millennium South Korea: Neoliberal capitalism and transnational movements* (pp. 130–141). Abingdon, UK: Routledge.

Park, J. (2004). Korean American youths' consumption of Korean and Japanese TV dramas and its implications. In K. Iwabuchi (Ed.), *Feeling Asian modernities: Transnational consumption of Japanese TV dramas* (pp. 275–300). Hong Kong: Hong Kong University Press.

Park, K. (2005). *Kwukekyoyuk-kwa hankwukekyoyuk-uy sengchal* [Reflections on the education of Korean as a first and second language]. Seoul: Seoul National University.

Park, Y. (2003). A preliminary study of ethnic Koreans in China: Towards a sociolinguistic understanding. *Kyoto University Linguistic Research, 22*, 1–21.

Royce, T. (2007). Multimodal communicative competence in second language contexts. In T. Royce, & W. Bowcher (Eds.), *New directions in the analysis of multimodal discourse* (pp. 361–390). Mahwah, NJ: Lawrence Erlbaum Associates.

Seth, M. (2002). *Education fever: Society, politics and the pursuit of schooling in South Korea*. Honolulu: University of Hawai'i Press.

Shin, H. (2006). Korea greets new era of multiculturalism. *The Korea Herald*, August 3

Silva, D. (2010). Out of one, many: The emergence of world Korean(s). Paper presented at the 2010 meeting of the International Circle of Korean of Korean Linguistics, July 6–9, Ulaanbaatar, Mongolia.

Stenglin, M., & Iedema, R. (2001). How to analyse visual images: A guide for TESOL teachers. In A. Burns, & C. Coffin (Eds.), *Analysing English in a global context* (pp. 194–208). London: Routledge.

Tikhonov, V. (2010). Race and racism in modern Korea. Paper presented at SOAS (University of London), October 29, London, UK.

Yonhap News. (2013). Cheylyu oykwukin 150 man myeng ches tolpha . . . tamwunhwa, tainconghwa kasok [Resident foreigners exceed 1.5 million for the first time . . . accelerating toward multiculturalism, multi-ethnicism]. *Yonhap News*, May 28. Retrieved from www.yonhapnews.co.kr/compatriot/2013/05/28/1703000000 AKR20130528133900372.HTML.

8

EMPOWERING STUDENTS IN THE ITALIAN CLASSROOM TO LEARN VOCABULARY THROUGH A MULTILITERACIES FRAMEWORK

Barbara Spinelli

Introduction

The technologies of the 21st century have created new challenges for education programs and curriculum development. These challenges emerge from the need to analyze how information, ideas, and knowledge are structured in the multi-modal new media and in different genres, and how these new structures can affect people's readings and uses of that information (Saravanan, 2012). The new technologies demand the development of a critical literacy that hinges not only on the ability to interpret existing texts, but also the ability to create new ones.

In fact, people need to be able to develop what Freebody and Luke (1990) call "reproductive literacy," that is, the ability to identify the social and cultural features of texts and create their own multimedia texts through the use of different modes of communication—image, writing, music, etc. To achieve these literacies, education programs need to shift from traditional approaches to a curriculum reform that takes into account the development of knowledge based on today's complex society (Kress, 2000; Saravanan, 2012; Unsworth, 2001; see also Chapter 1, this volume).

New approaches to the curriculum, such as the *multiliteracies* approach (New London Group (NLG), 1996), have been developed to respond to these new challenges and to enhance learning and teaching. This new literacy model calls for a move away from an authoritarian pedagogy where the textbook plays the main role, to pedagogy of multimodalities (New London Group, 2000; Kress, 2000, 2003; Saravanan, 2012) that recognizes the different ways of meaning-making—visual, aural, textual and a multiplicity of semiotic resources. It is a model that promotes "literacy empowerment," by integrating social interaction, motiva-tion, and multiple forms of knowledge and strategies (Cope & Gollings, 2001).

This chapter discusses how these multiliteracies principles can be implemented in L2 vocabulary learning within a Web 2.0 environment such as Wiki, increasing learner autonomy and agency, and providing a common ground to develop the learning process as "a process of design" (Hampel & Hauck, 2006).

Multiliteracies and Communication Technologies

New and innovative technologies in today's digital era have created changes in education that call for new ways of teaching and learning. In this challenging time literacy needs to be understood in broader terms and to be viewed, as mentioned above, in a "plural" sense. The multiliteracies framework emphasizes the changing of literacy practices due to the emergent technologies within the evolving of the global environment. The NLG (1996) and Cope and Kalantzis (2000) take into consideration the growing significance of the cultural and linguistic diversity in the world and of the effects of the multiplicity of communication channels. They recognize that, in order to be literate, an individual needs to engage with and use different means of representation to empower his/her actions, feelings, and thinking in the context of purposeful social activity and to construct different dimensions of meaning: linguistic, visual, and digital (NLG, 2000; Kress, 2000).

The use of technology represents one type of these literacy models. Today, students need to develop computer literacy, which includes the mastery of technology devices, and more importantly electronic literacy, that is, the "use [of] computers to interpret and express meaning" (Warschauer & Shetzer, 2000, p. 173). Web 2.0 tools and environments—which have become increasingly popular in both language learning and teaching and in telecollaborative exchanges (Dolci & Spinelli, 2005, 2007; Guth & Helm, 2010)—empower users to design, edit, and publish through a wide spectrum of information delivery and exchange, including video, visual, aural, and graphic representations of reality. Social network tools, such as Wiki, blogs, etc., can extend language learners' opportunities for meaningful, creative language processing and for using multiple representational modes. Wiki, the content authoring tool that was selected for the project described in this chapter, can facilitate interaction, allow learners to share meaningful content embedded in their personal experiences, and seek and generate relationships between lesson content and their prior knowledge.

Hooper and Rieber (1995) argue that using technology to reproduce existing materials is unlikely to improve educational quality. In this respect, the benefit of Web 2.0 technology is not simply its potential to replicate existing educational practice, but that it enables students to combine ideas and products by engaging them in deeper cognitive activity. The technical functionalities offered by these new online media are, among others: artifact creation, artifact manipulation, displaying/storing/retrieving artifacts, clickable icons for interaction, asynchronous sending and receiving (e.g., Forum), and simultaneous use of different channels

(Lamy & Hampel, 2007, p. 36). These online "packaged resource kit[s]" allow learners to develop what Royce (2002) defines as "multimodal communicative competence" and provide them with the opportunity to become "creator[s]" of texts (Hampel & Hauck, 2006, p. 11). In fact, these mediational tools determine a mutual shaping process, namely "they can help to create the learning, and in turn, the learner may shape these tools or exploit them for his or her own purposes" (Lamy & Hampel, 2007, p. 32).

As Unsworth (2001) points out, teachers recognize the relevance of shifting from reproduction literacies that provide only rigid repetitive classroom activities to more interpretative literacy activities which provide opportunities to develop critical thinking approaches. The interpretative literacy activities can allow students to be "effective learners" because they will be autonomous and self-directed designers of their own experiences, in collaboration with others as well as by themselves (Gee, 2000).

However, in order to achieve this autonomy, they need to develop multiple strategies for tackling a task and to possess a flexible solution to problems (Cope & Kalantzis, 2000).

A Wiki environment, thus, seems to be an ideal space to replace the static representation of vocabulary and the print-based activities commonly used in the classroom setting with a dynamic representation such as "design" (Cope & Kalantzis, 2009, p. 175) that emphasizes and fosters language learners' *agency*, *creativity*, and *collaboration*. A classroom project was therefore conceived around its use and within a general multiliteracies pedagogical framework. In the following section, I will describe the main principles in which the project was grounded, the different phases of its development, and its results.

L2 Vocabulary Instruction and Acquisition

The importance of lexical knowledge for overall language learning is the focus of much research. There is a multitude of studies on the effectiveness of various types of vocabulary learning methods and instructional techniques that can inform second language pedagogy. These studies show that learners can acquire vocabulary through L2 reading and listening (Laufer, 1992; Laufer & Ravenhorst-Kalovski, 2010; Nation, 2006; Schmitt, 2008; Webb & Rodgers, 2009), through translations (Nation, 2001), making inferences in which a word is compared to other words (Hulstijn, 1992), encountering words in isolated sentences (Laufer & Shmueli, 1997; Webb, 2008), and processing words in an enriched context through visual and aural codes (Diao & Sweller, 2007). These studies show that the efficacy of these methods is mixed (Prince, 2012, p. 104). However, they emphasize the effectiveness of the multimodal approach in recalling words (Barcroft, 2009; Finkbeiner & Nicol, 2003) and, most importantly, they highlight the benefits of vocabulary learning when associations at a thematic level, and links between form and meaning, word and context, are intentionally generated *by learners* (Atay & Ozbulgan, 2007; Nikolova, 2002; Prince, 2012; Schmitt, 2000).

These findings suggest that a *combinatory teaching/learning approach* and the *quality* of mental processing involved play a crucial role in vocabulary acquisition. In fact, many studies point out that the quality of word processing is crucial for retention. More complex processing can be achieved by doing meaningful, personalized activities connected to the target word (Gairns & Redman, 1986; Laufer & Shmueli, 1997; Palmberg, 1988), by using verbal and imagery mnemonics (Atkinson & Raugh, 1975; Avila & Sadoski, 1996; Cohen, 1987b; Kelly, 1986), or by using text/context both for working out the meaning of unknown words and for memorizing them (Schouten-van Parreren, 1989). All these activities can develop what in the field of psychology has been called *deep levels of processing* (DOP). According to the *DOP hypothesis*, the more one manipulates, thinks about, and uses mental information, the more likely it is that one will retain that information. In terms of vocabulary learning, that means: the more a learner is engaged with the target word, the more he/she will remember it for later use. In contrast, techniques that involve shallow processing (e.g., repeatedly writing a word on a page) seem to not facilitate such good retention (Schmitt, 2000, p. 121). This finding supports the *involvement hypothesis* proposed by Hulstijn and Laufer (2001), for whom word learning and retention are dependent upon the amount of mental effort or *involvement* a word task imposes.

Researchers have identified the vocabulary learning techniques that can require this active manipulation of information. Examples of these techniques are forming associations (Cohen & Aphek, 1981) or using imagery such as in the Keyword Method[1] (Hulstijn, 1997). Researchers have also provided a theoretical rationale to support the use of these techniques which involves the *dual-coding theory* perspective (Paivio, 1971, 1979, 1986). According to this theory, when both verbal and visual materials are presented, learners can construct connections between these two forms of mental representation and learn more effectively. It also highlights the importance of visual memory: words dually coded (i.e., with mental images, pictures, or video) are better learned than words with only text definitions.

Finally, Schmitt (2000, pp. 137, 146) admits that word associations and imagery techniques are crucial for involving elaborative mental processing, while pointing out that further deep processing techniques should be explored in light of the multimedia capabilities that computers provide.

In the study described in this chapter, students explored these techniques using the multiple and multimodal resources that the Web 2.0 environment offers.

Authoring of Multimedia Materials to Promote Learners' Engagement

As mentioned above, allowing learners to make their own connections between the verbal and visual system while organizing the new information in their working memory can facilitate its retention in the long-term memory (Chun & Plass, 1996, p. 517). The pedagogical implication of this is that, because exposing learners to different modalities of representation through the multiple sensory components of the multimedia tools can have a real impact in their learning, it should be encouraged.

One way of encouraging learners to work with the new lexical items in order to create a link between form and meaning is asking them to build their own multimedia materials for vocabulary learning. As shown by Nikolova (2002, p. 103), learners' direct involvement in creating their own product increases their motivation and leads to enhancing content knowledge. Other benefits of authoring learning materials are the topic of numerous studies (Arnett, 1995; Bowman & Plaisir, 1996; Channell, 1988; Dörnyei, 2001; Kubota, 1999; Kramsch, A'Ness, & Lam, 2000; Nikolova, 2002). Channell's (1988) research states that giving learners an active role facilitates their vocabulary acquisition process. She also suggests that "learners should be encouraged to make their own lexical associations when they are actively learning new vocabulary" (p. 94). Dörnyei (2001, p. 104) adds that involving learners in the design of certain aspects of their own course can be both motivating and effective. The generative theory of multimedia learning (Mayer, 1997) posits that the multimedia design affects the degree to which learners engage in the cognitive processes required for meaningful learning within the visual and verbal information processing system. In vocabulary learning, storing information in memory seems not to be a difficult task, but retrieving it is expected to be difficult (Al-Seghayer, 2001). Media tools can provide learners with multiple retrieval cues by integrating different forms of mental representations.

The multiple modalities of representation available online (sound, picture, video, etc.) allow learners to experiment with *personal modes* or *combinations of modes* that work best for them as individuals (Pusack & Otto, 1997); thus, different learners will show preferences for different types of representations and types of information for defining a word, which, in turn, mirror differences among students in terms of strategy use. Research, which has increasingly focused in the learner's active role in the learning process, has shown that successful vocabulary learners are active strategy users who are conscious of their learning, while unsuccessful learners display little awareness of making connections with the new target word (Ahmed, 1989; Sanaoui, 1995). Cohen (1987a) indicates that the goal of instruction is to assist learners in becoming more effective learners by allowing them to individualize the language learning experience and to facilitate their awareness of the broad range of strategies that can be used in the learning process. It seems clear, then, that self-direction is essential in the active development of adults' abilities in learning, and that autonomy is important for learners since it is difficult to provide them with guidance outside the classroom.

The vocabulary strategies learners adopt in the classroom while learning new target words will be combined with the strategies that are activated in the Wiki multimodal environment. In this online learning context, learners need also to develop a set of skills and competences that include: using critically the different modes (developing competence and familiarity with new codes such as visual, aural etc.), dealing with affective demands (affective challenges due to the use of unfamiliar tools, which can generate anxiety and cognitive overload), and recognizing intercultural differences (the fact that modes are influenced by cultural conventions) (Hampel & Hauck, 2006).

The Classroom Project

The goal of the project described in this chapter was to create a classroom interactive dictionary with the use of Wiki to collect the vocabulary studied during the fall semester of an Italian Intermediate Conversation I course in 2009, 2010, 2012, and during the spring semester of an Italian Intermediate Conversation II course in 2013 offered at one of the universities of New York City.

Participants and Setting

The total number of students involved in the project was 43. All of them were students (undergraduate and graduate level) of Italian as a foreign language (FL) at one of the universities of New York City. Although the majority of the students were American (35)—with six being Italian-American students, there were also eight students who came from other countries, including New Zealand (1), Ecuador (1), Mexico (1), England (1), Australia (1), Egypt (1), Russia (1), and Croatia (1). Among them, three students were non-traditional students.[2]

Within the Italian Language Program of this university, conversation courses are particularly focused on oral skills. In order to register for the Intermediate Conversation I and Intermediate Conversation II classes, students need to have completed two or three semesters of regular Italian language courses[3] respectively. Conversation classes are 1 hour and 15 minutes long and meet two days/twice a week for 14 weeks.

Materials and Instruction

The topics and learning objectives of the two conversation classes were identified using the Common European Framework of Reference (CEFR) (Council of Europe, 2001) descriptors and the related lexical items were selected according to the word frequency list for the Italian language of the *Profilo della lingua italiana* (Spinelli & Parizzi, 2010).[4] The goal of the course was to enhance speaking skills (spoken production and spoken interaction[5]), skills that foster the development of language competence and socio-pragmatic competence.

Estaire and Zánon's (1994) task-based approach model was adopted for both courses. This approach includes a "task cycle," which leads learners to complete a final task at the end of every unit. The task cycle includes a combination of "enabling tasks" (which provide learners with the linguistic tools) and "communication tasks" (which are smaller-scale tasks focused on the theme of the final task). In the Intermediate Conversation classes the "enabling tasks" included word-focused tasks that developed explicit learning on different "core meaning aspects" of the target word (Schmitt, 2000, p. 22), such as word meaning(s)[6] and word relations (e.g., collocation), as well as on the written and spoken form of the word. During the "communication tasks," instead, incidental learning[7] of lexical items occurred through speaking, reading, and listening.

For these courses, only handouts and online materials were used; no specific textbook was adopted. The classroom project consisted of a "problem-solving task," which asked students to create an online dictionary using Wiki. To create this dictionary, at the end of every unit, students collected all the lexical information and pragmatic formulae related to the unit theme from the materials used in the classroom, and organized them on the online space. They were also encouraged to integrate extra, relevant information they could find on the internet. Students were asked to find a way to make this electronic lexical repository an effective instrument of reference for the two oral tests included in the course: a midterm and a final exam.

The project included three main stages: (1) discussing in an initial forum, as a class, which lexical information should be included in the electronic space and how to define and categorize it; (2) building, in groups, the webpage related to the thematic area assigned by the teacher approximately every two weeks; and (3) evaluating, individually, peers' webpages and providing suggestions for amendments once a month.

Instructional Techniques and Vocabulary Retention

Many studies have shown that the use of the dictionary is beneficial for vocabulary learning (Aust, Kelley, & Roby, 1993; Hulstijn, 2000; Knight, 1994; Laufer & Hill, 2000), but this is a very controversial topic. One of the main problems is that dictionary use can become boring for L2 learners (Nikolova, 2002, p. 113). However, if consulting the dictionary is perceived by learners as a tool for the creation of a product that they are responsible for and it represents part of a more adventurous experience (i.e., making their *own* dictionary), it can bring good results in vocabulary learning (Nikolova, 2002, p. 115). Chun and Plass (1996, p. 185) state that students learn new words when they can establish a direct connection with a word in their L1, or can make associations with the corresponding image of an object or action. When such links are deliberately generated by learners, these links can be classified as mnemonic devices and they can aid vocabulary recall (Prince, 2012, p. 105). The main way of establishing links is by finding some pre-existing information in the long-term memory to "attach" to the new information. The selection of appropriate vocabulary learning strategies and the type of associations produced depend on a number of variables, among which are students' proficiency level, motivation, and purpose of learning (Atay & Ozbulgan, 2007, p. 40; Schmitt, 2000, p. 41). It is because of those reasons that the project was developed for this kind of course, a course where students' motivation is high and proficiency levels are quite advanced. Additionally, as mentioned before, a computerized dictionary offers the possibility of creating multimedia annotations that entail multiple retrieval cues by integrating different forms of mental representations (Al-Seghayer, 2001). As already stated, according to several scholars (Danan, 1992; Hulstijn, 1993; Knight, 1994; Underwood, 1989), the richness of information with which the material is created together with the more elaborated processing of the lexical item lead to higher vocabulary retention.

However, the retention of the new information does not depend only on the quality of the attention that individuals pay to the various aspects of words, but also on the amount of exposure to the word (Chun & Plass, 1996; Coady, 1993; Nagy, 1997; Nation, 1990; Schmitt, 2000).[8] In these intermediate conversation courses words were processed several times: students were exposed to the target word through reading, listening, or speaking activities (first encounter), then they were asked to: (1) carry out word-focused activities during the "enabling tasks" (second encounter); (2) use the words during the "communication tasks" (third encounter); (3) revise them while carrying out review activities before the beginning of a new unit (fourth encounter); (4) organize and define them on the webpage or check their definition during the peer's work evaluation stage (fifth encounter); and (5) go back to the online dictionary as many times as necessary to add additional information about the words (more encounters). Therefore, learning activities were designed to require multiple manipulations of a word and, through incidental and explicit learning, the online dictionary project worked as a recycling task.

Instruments

According to Wiersma and Jurs (2009, p. 284), the types of data that can be collected for a qualitative research project include, among others, artifacts. In this study, extracts from the online dictionary function as students' artifacts. Students' comments retrieved from self-evaluation forms, used in the middle and at the end of the course, were also analyzed. These self-evaluation forms (which included a combination of selected response and open-ended items) were aimed at enhancing the strategies used by students as well as at developing learners' awareness of their attainment of vocabulary learning objectives. As stated earlier, many researchers (Cohen, 1996; Cohen, Weaver, & Li, 1998; Oxford, 1990, 1993, 1996) point out how essential it is to promote self-direction in adults' abilities in learning and to develop awareness of strategies they can use after they leave the language classroom. These self-evaluation tools were adopted to reach these goals.

Discussion

Allen and Paesani (2010, p. 135) suggest that one of the main aspects of multiliteracies-based instruction is providing students with regular opportunities for *reflection* on the process of language learning and *self-reflection* on their engagement in this process. Besides the use of the self-evaluations mentioned above, more of these opportunities were provided by the Wiki forum discussion used at the beginning of the classroom project.

The forum provided an opportunity for students to activate metacognitive skills while planning their work by identifying thematic areas to group their words, deciding ways of categorizing them, discussing the need of defining them in sociolinguistic terms (e.g., different registers), and providing contexts of use, etc.

Another aspect of a multiliteracies curriculum is to provide suggestions as to how language learning can be maximized, and these include familiarizing students with the instructional approach being used and giving them concrete ideas for succeeding in such an approach (Allen & Paesani, 2010, p. 135). For this project, excerpts from selected vocabulary learning strategies literature were provided for a twofold reason: (1) to develop students' awareness of strategies they can use on their own after they leave the classroom; and (2) to sustain their motivation while accomplishing the classroom project.

However, according to Politzer and McGroarty (1985), strategies are not necessarily good per se; their effectiveness depends on the context in which they are used, which may include: proficiency level, tasks, background knowledge, and context of learning. The multisensory environment offered by Wiki and the tasks required by the classroom project described in this chapter allowed students to explore a wide range of strategies.

Schmitt (Schmitt & McCarthy, 1997) proposes a comprehensive Vocabulary Learning Strategies (VLS) taxonomy that classifies 58 strategies. These strategies are classified into two macro-categories: the *Discovery strategies*, which support learners in the initial discovery of the new word, and the *Consolidation strategies*, which allow them to remember the word once it has been presented. These strategies are further classified into five subgroups: *Determination strategies* (DET), *Social strategies* (SOC), *Memory strategies* (MEM), *Cognitive strategies* (COG), and *Metacognitive strategies* (MET). Some of these strategies are shown below (from Schmitt & McCarthy, 1997):

Discovery strategies

- (DET) Determination
   - Analyze part-of-speech
   - Analyze affixes, roots
   - Check for L1 cognate

- o Guess from the context
- o Consult dictionary
- o Use word list
- o Ask teacher.

- (SOC) Social
  - o Ask classmates
  - o Group work.

Consolidation strategies

- (SOC) Social
  - o Group study practice
  - o Teacher check word lists
  - o Interact with L1 speakers.

- (MEM) Memory
  - o Image of word meaning
  - o Connect related words
  - o Group words together
  - o Study word sound/spelling
  - o Use physical action
  - o Use cognates
  - o Paraphrase word meaning
  - o Use physical action
  - o Use cognates
  - o Paraphrase word meaning.

- (COG) Cognitive
  - o Verbal/written repetition
  - o Note-taking
  - o Put L2 labels on objects.

- (MET) Metacognitive
  - o Use L2 media
  - o Test yourself
  - o Continue study over the time
  - o Skip/pass new word.

The nature of the electronic space and tasks, which asked learners to define the word encountered in the classroom by adding information about its form and meaning, and categorize it in the online dictionary, made the division between the two macro-classes of strategies (Discovery and Consolidation) more flexible. For instance, some DET strategies such as "analyze affixes, roots" or "check for L1 cognates," which are generally classified as Discovery strategies in Schmitt's

Pubblico- I (gli) spettatori, Le persone che seguono uno spettacolo

Molto vocabolario per i film e il cinema è molto vicino a inglese, o proviene direttamente da inglese (ess: *documentario*, un film *romantico*, una *commedia*, *azione*, *horror*, ecc.)

MA! Ci sono alcuni falsi amici:

actor = *attore* MA **to act** non è *agire*, ma *recitare*

impersonare non è **to impersonate**, ma significa anche **to act, to personify**

FIGURE 8.1 Example of DET strategy used during the consolidation phase.

inventory, were actually activated by the learners as Consolidation strategies while working on the online dictionary (see Figure 8.1).

Figure 8.1 shows that when reflecting upon some words related to the thematic area of "cinema" the student noticed similarities in form and meaning between the L1 and the L2 lexical items and he also focused on differences (i.e., the word *actor* in English corresponds to the word *attore* in Italian with a shared root, while the English related verb with the same root *to act* has a corresponding verb in Italian with the same meaning but with a different form, *recitare*). This observation had not been made in the classroom; the learner made it by himself and presented it to his peers. This showed that Discovery strategies were not necessarily used to familiarize oneself with the new word when it was introduced, but that they were activated by the learner, in the online environment, while seeking better ways to remember the word.

Students have personal modes and strategies that work best for them as individuals (Pusack & Otto, 1997). Additionally, the same strategy can have different effects on different students. In this project, the online learning environment made these differences fruitful because the shared multimedia materials built by the "class as group" facilitated cooperation between the stronger learners, who were conscious of their learning and used a variety of strategies, and the weaker learners who lacked this awareness and control (Ahmed, 1989; Sanaoui, 1995).

Learners' collaborative work also allowed the integration of more traditional strategies, such as "word list," with those that require a deeper cognitive process (e.g., the use of L2 media). An example of this combination is shown in Figure 8.2.

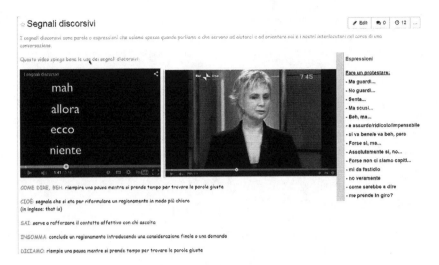

FIGURE 8.2 Comparison between "word list" (DET and COG strategies) and the use of "Italian language media" (MET strategy).

The data from the project showed that, although Wiki is a multimodal environment, non-traditional students seemed to prefer more conventional and single-mode strategies, such as a "translation to L1" and a "word list" that they typically used in the face-to-face context of the classroom, while younger students' choices reflected their technology literacy and their non-linear progression of learning. As Prensky (2001) states, today's students "develop hypertext minds. They leap around. It's as though their cognitive structures were parallel, not sequential" (p. 10). Wiersma and Jurs (2009, p. 249) add that the hypertext is based on a multidimensional geometry which mirrors multidimensional human mental processes. The hypertext imitates these processes, creating different links on the structural representation of the information. Figure 8.2 shows that a non-traditional student classified the discourse markers to elicit different language functions through a list (DET and COG strategies), while a younger student used a multi-code with audio, verbal, visual, and video aids (MET strategy). This combination of strategies was particularly fruitful for non-traditional students' vocabulary learning, as mentioned below.

Another example of collaborative learning was the students' variety of network-building while adopting MEM strategies, across the duration of this project. MEM strategies involve relating the word to be retained to some previously learned knowledge, using some form of imagery or grouping (Atay & Ozbulgan, 2007, p. 41).[9]

Even though a number of studies demonstrate the effectiveness of memory strategies (Carlson, Kincaid, Lance, & Hodgson, 1976; Fang, 1985; McDaniel & Pressley, 1989, among others), the majority of learners seem to favor some form of mechanical strategy, such as repetition (Segler, Pain, & Sorace, 2010). However, the Wiki multimodal and multimedia learning context seemed to facilitate the implementation of MEM strategies, which turned out to be the most commonly used by learners.

The analysis of the data showed that the task allowed learners to activate many mental linkages between the word to be defined and the students' values, background knowledge, and world perception. Some learners seemed to favor linkages that rely on the recoding and relating of the new word, with, for instance, their knowledge in other disciplines. Figure 8.3 shows how a student defined the core meaning[10] of words, related to a subjective and objective description of a person, using associative recall through Art History, Literature, and Philosophy, and by means of cinematic and pictorial codes. For instance, in order to describe the meaning of the Italian word *scortese* (in English [rude]), a student used the character of Mr Darcy from Jane Austen's book *Pride and Prejudice* (and he added: "except when Mr Darcy proposed to Elizabeth"), while his/her peers used iconic images of different fields to contextualize the meaning of other adjectives.

This mnemonic route also involved the student's knowledge of the target culture. As shown in Figure 8.4, information about an Italian director and rapper provided the link to the meaning of the new word: *incomunicabilità* (in English [incommunicability]). The learner used a combination of visual and aural codes. He provided the description of the word meaning, linking it to one of the most famous themes illustrated by the Italian director Michelangelo Antonioni's cinematography, and to a video that shows the last years of his life when, due to a disease, he lost his voice. The student also made use of a second mnemonic device: the Italian rapper Fabri Fibra's song illustrating miscommunication between generations.

As a matter of fact, learners' mental linkages sometimes involved not only the core meaning of a word, but also their *Encyclopedic Knowledge*,[11] which was linked

Penetrante: Mona Lisa ha uno sguardo penetrante.

curioso:
Socrate ha interrogato tutto.Era molto curioso

FIGURE 8.3 Example of mnemonic devices through different disciplines.

FIGURE 8.4   Example of using target culture as mnemonic device.

to their personal experiences and beliefs (that is, they activated the MEM strategy "Connect the word to a personal experience").

In the next example (see Figure 8.5) a student filled the core meaning of the lexical collocation *reinserimento sociale* ("social reintegration") with information she could retrieve from her personal experience as a volunteer in her social community. She linked the White House rehabilitation program to the corresponding program of the Italian Ministry of Justice (which had been discussed in the classroom), making a cross-cultural comparison. In this case, the student's Encyclopedic Knowledge was recalled via *schema*. According to Schmitt (2000, p. 28) the schema "is the knowledge of how things in a specific area of the real word behave and are organized." MEM strategies within the Wiki context, then, enable a more complex manipulation of words and activate a deep processing through the integration of the new word with many kinds of learners' pre-existing knowledge.

In the context of multicultural classrooms, while dealing with aspects of word meaning that are more encyclopedic in nature, a wider range of associations can be activated. For instance, the core meaning of the lexical collocation *tempo libero* [free time] corresponds to how people spend time while not working or studying

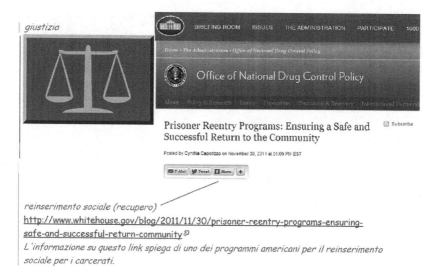

FIGURE 8.5 Example of the use of Encyclopedic Knowledge.

(i.e., leisure time), but in different cultures that might be associated with quite different rituals and interpretations of the sense of time. In the next example (Figure 8.6) two different students (an Italian–American student and a Russian student) compare the meaning(s) of free time in the Italian cultural setting, recalling the Latin concept of Roman "*otium*" (not laziness but creativity) and in

FIGURE 8.6 Example of cross-cultural comparison of rituals.

the Russian context in which people spend several hours of their spare time socializing through eating and drinking.

Another MEM strategy widely used in the Wiki was "Study word with pictorial representation of its meaning." The dual-coding theory of Paivio, previously mentioned in this chapter, suggests that it is the combination of modes or media that contributes to greater learning success. However, some researchers (Avila & Sadoski, 1996; Boers, Piquer Píriz, Stengers, & Eyckmans, 2009; Chun & Plass, 1996, among others) underline the need to further investigate the effect of combination of code: for instance, pictorial and text; video and text, etc. An area of research of particular interest concerns whether abstract ideas, adjectives, adverbs, or idioms can be visualized or represented by non-textual annotations or with an association of verbal and pictorial information. In particular, Boers et al. (2009) examine if the association of concrete images (drawing, photographs, etc.) with figurative phrases might facilitate idiom learning by exploring the literal roots of their meaning. One may wonder if learners themselves might spontaneously make use of the literal meaning of words to identify the figurative use of L2 idioms. The study by Cieslicka (2006) actually confirms that they do. In this classroom project, Wiki tools seemed to support and enhance students' creativity in finding such connections.

Figure 8.7 provides an example of how a learner used a verbal and pictorial code to interpret the figurative use of the Italian idiom, *prendere fischi per fiaschi* (whose figurative meaning is [to misunderstand]), retrieving it from the literal meaning of constituent words.

The figurative sense of this Italian idiom is based on the misunderstanding that can emerge from the orthographic similarity of the constituent words (*fischi* [whistles]) and (*fiaschi* [flasks]), which the student represented through pictorial aids. Thus, the electronic context created an opportunity to explore an additional pathway for recalling the verbal information. Boers and Lindstromberg (2008) suggest that the connection between idioms and literal roots, when constituent words contain sufficient clues for interpretation, is an effective pedagogical

prendere fischi per fiaschi: capire una cosa per un'altra

FIGURE 8.7 Example of using a combination of codes to explore the figurative use of idioms.

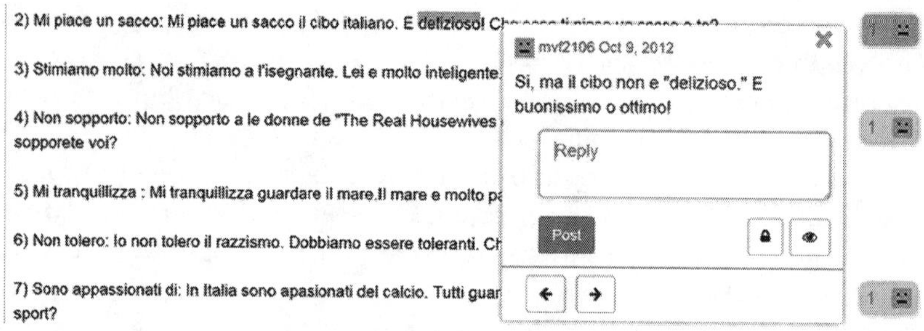

2) Mi piace un sacco: Mi piace un sacco il cibo italiano. E delizioso! Ch~~~~~~~~~~~~~~

3) Stimiamo molto: Noi stimiamo a l'isegnante. Lei e molto inteligente.

4) Non sopporto: Non sopporto a le donne de "The Real Housewives sopporete voi?

5) Mi tranquillizza : Mi tranquillizza guardare il mare.Il mare e molto pa

6) Non tolero: Io non tolero il razzismo. Dobbiamo essere toleranti. Ch

7) Sono appassionati di: In Italia sono apasionati del calcio. Tutti guar sport?

mvf2106 Oct 9, 2012

Si, ma il cibo non e "delizioso." E buonissimo o ottimo!

Reply

Post

FIGURE 8.8 Example of MET strategy.

technique. Pictorial aids may not be more useful than verbal definitions for some learners, but they definitely help visualizers.

An additional critical component of the project was the activation of students' MET strategies throughout their work online, particularly during the initial forum discussion mentioned above and peers' evaluation, which took place periodically. An example of feedback provided by peers is shown in Figure 8.8. In this extract a student provides feedback on a frequent negative transfer from English to Italian (*cibo delizioso*, a translation from English [delicious food,] is used; the peer comments that there are more appropriate adjectives than *delizioso* to describe food in Italian).

MET strategies were also activated when students produced on their own initiative testing items for their peers (see Figure 8.9). The testing items created by the students provided extra materials for practice, while also putting them in the role of "experts" (rather than novices) and, more importantly, of "authors."

One of the reasons to involve students in the design of some of multimedia materials was to measure if their levels of motivation and enthusiasm would increase, as argued by Nikolova (2002, p. 103). A semester-long qualitative study that relied on self-evaluation tools was carried out for this purpose. As mentioned above, students had to fill out self-evaluation forms periodically in order to develop

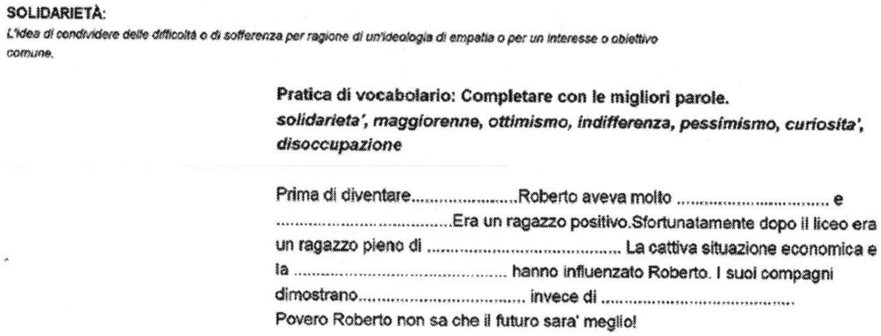

SOLIDARIETÀ:
L'idea di condividere delle difficoltà o di sofferenza per ragione di un'ideologia di empatia o per un interesse o obiettivo comune.

Pratica di vocabolario: Completare con le migliori parole.
solidarieta', maggiorenne, ottimismo, indifferenza, pessimismo, curiosita', disoccupazione

Prima di diventare...................Roberto aveva molto ....e
...............................Era un ragazzo positivo.Sfortunatamente dopo il liceo era un ragazzo pieno di .... La cattiva situazione economica e la .... hanno influenzato Roberto. I suoi compagni dimostrano................................... invece di ....
Povero Roberto non sa che il futuro sara' meglio!

FIGURE 8.9 Example of fill-in exercises created by the students for their peers.

self-awareness of their own work and vocabulary learning progress. Findings of these self-evaluations were compared with those of a final questionnaire which was submitted in order to collect students' feedback on their online learning experience and suggestions for further improvements. This comparison demonstrated that students' motivation increased throughout the project, as shown below.

The learners' final questionnaire comments were analyzed and grouped in four main categories: (1) Motivation, (2) Self-awareness, (3) Self-direction, and (4) Collaborative work. According to students' feedback, their work on the online dictionary was driven by both intrinsic and extrinsic motivation, as the following comments highlight:

> "*The online dictionary was a good method to learn the vocabulary creatively; it was more useful to create a multimedia dictionary rather than writing down words to memorize them.*"

> "*It is well-known that doing something helps you to remember better, and when the exam is coming up the online dictionary is a precious resource.*"

The intrinsic motivation was developed as a result of a two-fold process of self-awareness: (1) self-awareness of the efficacy of the qualitative and quantitative elaboration of the new word; and (2) self-awareness of the students' most useful strategies. Students highlighted the value of various (quantitative) and rich (qualitative) associations with their existing knowledge and identified their preferred strategies:

> "*The activities helped very much, in their repetition as well as in providing many contexts for us to learn the vocabulary.*"

> "*Being exposed to words many times is very useful.*"

> "*The online dictionary helped me a lot, it was easier to learn the vocabulary because I had to define the words and then put them on the Wiki and that helped me to memorize the new vocabulary.*"

> "*The strategies I have used were very helpful; I did not use them before this class.*"

> "*It helped me to associate pictures, songs, articles and synonyms to many of the words we learnt in class, I was able to better identify their meaning.*"

> "*It let me think on how to recall vocabulary [. . .] I think it is very useful to group words in categories.*"

> "*It really made me think about the vocabulary word <u>critically</u>[12] [. . .] When I spent time looking for how to represent the new vocabulary word (through definitions, pictures, etc.), it really made me think about and then learn the word.*"

Some students stressed the importance of self-direction ("*I can better recall words I worked on.*"; "*I found it more useful doing the work than reading.*"), while others pointed out the importance of the collective work ("*Sometimes seeing a good presentation of a word by another student helps me because I see the word in a different context and then become more familiar with it."; "The strategies my classmates used were very helpful."; "The work of my classmates was very helpful . . . they are very creative.").* (The latter was a comment from a non-traditional student.)

From a quantitative point of view, the questionnaire showed the following: 95% of the students found the online dictionary very useful, 4% not particularly useful and only 1% found it not useful. The 4% includes two non-traditional students of which one stated:

> "It was not so effective because of the time I spent doing it; it is possible that students with more computer expertise can better benefit from the Interactive Dictionary."

Conclusion

The present study investigated some qualitative parameters of the implementation of a multiliteracies pedagogy for the purposes of L2 vocabulary learning. The study showed that a pedagogy of multiliteracies had an effect on the *self-direction* and *agency* of students participating in multimedia authoring. First, the data showed that the multiple representational modes and communication channels offered by the Wiki provided students with further opportunities, beyond the classroom setting, to experiment with *personal paths of learning* aimed at vocabulary retention. Second, the data showed that the use of relevant literature on vocabulary learning strategies developed students' awareness and autonomy in finding form-meaning connections in lexical items. In particular, the electronic environment allowed students to experiment with deep processing techniques for vocabulary retention (such as word associations and imagery techniques, not commonly used in the face-to-face learning context), which turned out to be most efficient for their learning.

In this project, findings confirmed Schmitt's (2000, pp. 137, 146) intuition about the role that multimedia environments can play in the development of students' elaborative mental processing for vocabulary learning. The Wiki environment, in fact, affected students' choice of strategies and determined a more complex web of information interlinking these strategies. Students were able to use multiple strategies at the same time while using the multimodal tools offered by the multimedia environment. In fact, the artifacts created by the learners in the study showed that different inventories of strategies described by Schmitt's taxonomy seem to overlap; for instance, students used imagery strategy (one MEM strategy) jointly with the pictorial code (another MEM strategy) and with other media (MET strategy). However, the development of this electronic literacy did not seem to be fruitful for all students; non-traditional learners seemed not to benefit particularly from the multimodal environment. They used the same vocabulary learning strategies in both face-to-face and virtual contexts.

However, because of the collaborative nature of the tool, non-traditional learners benefited from their peers' work.

The study highlighted that lexical knowledge is a complex rather than a linear process and, as Schmitt (2000, p. 5) claims, it involves many aspects of the word (e.g., the meaning(s), the written and the spoken form, the grammatical behavior, etc.). Indeed, the students in this project explored these different aspects of vocabulary knowledge as they provided additional information about the lexical items (e.g., similarity/idiosyncrasy relations between words) in their online dictionary. The opportunity to return to a word many times, and modify its description, allowed students to follow and integrate *very personal trajectories* (for instance, a student could discover a new meaning for a word, while another could focus on a word collocation or an orthographic similarity between the word in the L1 and the target word).

The analysis of the self-evaluation data seemed to confirm Channell's (1988) ideas about the participative role of the learner in second language vocabulary learning, namely that generating the conditions for multiple active manipulation of a word's form and meaning is one way of encouraging the *creation* of learners' own lexical associations. Students' feedback also supported claims of the noticing hypothesis (Fotos, 1993; Robinson, 1995; Schimdt, 1990), which emphasizes the beneficial effect of creating conscious awareness about the link between form and meaning. In the online project learners creatively linked the meaning of words to their beliefs and values and involved different forms of knowledge: their general knowledge and their specific-domain knowledge. As students pointed out, creating the link between form and meaning in authored multimedia vocabulary units, and doing it for the duration of the semester, had a major benefit on their vocabulary learning.

However, while the active role of the L2 learner in making his/her own associations has been recognized to be essential (Nikolova, 2002), further investigations are needed to know which kinds of associations are the most useful in aiding retention (Channell, 1988, p. 94).

The management system of Wiki allows tracing and keeping records of these different manipulations of words. Thus, this electronic tool can provide evidence of the complexity of the individual's development of lexical knowledge as well as of the active role the student played in the vocabulary learning process. This tool could offer important information for studies that seek to analyze the learners' cognitive processes involved in their active re-elaboration of the word.

Additionally, even though many studies (e.g., Al-Seghayer, 2001; Chun & Plass, 1996; Kost, Foss, & Lenzini, 1999; Siribodhi, 1995) have shown that there is a positive impact of image-based annotations on L2 vocabulary acquisition, further research should explore, for instance, whether video can be as effective as pictures to describe a concrete noun (Chun & Plass, 1996).

Further studies involving vocabulary tests would further illuminate aspects of vocabulary acquisition; the use of tests might provide quantitative data on the impact of vocabulary learning strategies used in the integrated environment (classroom and Wiki virtual space) and on learners' "levels of knowledge that may be interpreted as stages in the acquisition of the word" (Read, 1997, p. 315). It is, however, very difficult to design tests that accurately assess the complex multidimensional construct of lexical knowledge.[13] A possible solution might be to integrate vocabulary tests that measure the range of a vocabulary (the student knows *enough* vocabulary to accomplish a specific linguistic activity, in this case "speaking") with self-assessment tools, such as checklists, which can provide information about the state of knowledge of a word (how *well enough* the learner knows the word).

If the promising outcomes evidenced in students' artifacts and comments in this study are confirmed by quantitative data, more sophisticated activities should be planned utilizing the multimedia tools; these additional activities would also be fertile ground for the investigation of the efficacy of vocabulary learning strategies closely related to the online environment.

The outcomes of this project have evident implications in teaching/learning vocabulary not only for Italian, but also for the study of other foreign languages. Students' artifacts and feedback highlighted that a multiliteracies approach can provide them with opportunities to foster their agency and to engage in their learning environment, connecting it to their interests and understandings of the world. The use of the Web 2.0 technology in this project fulfilled the need highlighted by the multiliteracies framework to expand literacy practices. In fact, the multimedia environment provided students with opportunities to become "multiliterate": they developed (1) their recognition literacy (Freebody & Luke, 1990), by identifying the more functional strategies for their vocabulary learning, and (2) their electronic, reflection, and reproductive literacies by constructing their meanings through the use of multiple codes.

Finally, this approach encouraged students to go beyond the more traditional vocabulary learning strategies often adopted in the classroom and promoted in textbooks (such as word lists, translations, use of bilingual dictionary, etc.). Learners need, instead, to explore alternative ways of word retention. In this project they were able to create new multimedia representations of words, making new meaning associations and activating a process of "rereading of the wor[l]d"[14] (NLG, 1996, p. 164) through individual and collective routes.

This all seems to suggest that new technology resources should be an integral part of the learning environment design in order to create contexts for students' critical engagement that can allow them to activate higher orders of thinking and to develop their literacy at multiple levels. The practical application of new literacies required by this learning environment calls for curricular reform and development, which is necessary to ensure that learning is significant for students who are members of the current global and complex society.

Notes

1 Atkinson (1975) developed this method for foreign language vocabulary learning. It consists of two stages: first, the learner associates the target word with a concrete and familiar (key)word based on acoustic similarity; second, he/she produces an imaginal link between the target word and the key word. For instance, in order to learn the Spanish target word *carta* ("postal letter"), the learner can associate it with the English word *cart* (keyword). By recalling the image of a giant postal letter inside a shopping cart the learner can remember the form of the word *carta* as well as the meaning, "postal letter" (Avila & Sadoski, 1996).

2 Non-traditional students are adults who decide to go back to school after the traditional college age of 18–24.

3 These regular courses aim at developing all four language skills (listening, reading, speaking, and writing) as well as grammar and vocabulary competence.

4 The *Profilo della lingua italiana* is the outcome of the European Project "Reference Level Description for National and Regional Languages" promoted by the Council of Europe in 2005. The Project aimed at describing the linguistic and communicative competence of CEFR levels for different languages among which were Italian, French, German, English, and Spanish.

5 For this categorization see the Common European Framework of Reference (Council of Europe, 2001). In spoken interaction the speaker participates in communicative exchanges with at least an interlocutor, while in spoken production he/she mostly produces one-way oral communication.

6 The meanings of a word to be taught for the Intermediate level (CEFR B level) have been selected according to information retrieved from the *Profilo della lingua italiana* word frequency list.

7 Schmitt (2000) identifies two main processes that are involved in vocabulary learning: *explicit learning* and *incidental learning*. The first involves a focused study of the word, while the latter occurs through exposure when the attention is focused on language use rather than on learning itself.

8 Nagy (1997, p. 74) states that there is only a 5–15% probability that a given word would be learned at first exposure. Nation (1990, p. 44) suggests that it requires 5–16, or more, repetitions for a word to be learned. Schmitt (2000) adds that, "if recycling is neglected, many partially known words will be forgotten" (p. 137).

9 Thompson (1987) underlines that "[m]nemonics work by utilizing some well-known principles of psychology: a retrieval plan is developed during encoding, and mental imagery, both visual and verbal is used. They help individuals learn faster and recall better because they aid the integration of new materials into existing cognitive units and because they provide retrieval cues" (p. 211).

10 Schmitt defines *core meaning* as the "the common meaning shared by the members of a society" (2000, p. 27).

11 According to Schmitt (2000, p. 27), Encyclopedic Knowledge might not be fundamental but it is an important part of meaning. This knowledge represents further things that we know about the meaning of a word.

12 Author's adaptation.

13 Existing tests mainly use a sort of rating scale such as the Vocabulary Knowledge Scale (VKS), which follows five steps (Segler et al., 2010): (1) I don't remember having seen this word; (2) I have seen this word before, but I don't know what it means; (3) I have seen this word before, and I think it means . . . (synonym or translation); (4) I know this word, it means . . . (synonym or translation); and (5) I can use this word in a sentence . . . (write a sentence). However, the validity of this scale has been questioned (Read, 1997) because these stages are not linear but interconnected.

14 Author's adaptation.

Bibliography

Ahmed, M. (1989). Vocabulary learning strategies. In P. Meara (Ed.), *Beyond words* (pp. 3–14). London: British Association of Applied Linguistics.

Allen, H.W., & Paesani, K. (2010). Exploring the feasibility of a pedagogy of multiliteracies in introductory foreign language courses. *L2 Journal, 2*, 119–142.

Al-Seghayer, K. (2001). The effect of multimedia annotation modes on L2 vocabulary acquisition: A comparative study. *Language Learning & Technology, 5*(1), 202–232.

Arnett, J. (1995). *Creating an interactive Spanish alphabet program for the primary bilingual classroom: A cooperative multimedia project.* Houston, TX: University of Houston.

Atay, D., & Ozbulgan, C. (2007). Memory strategy instruction, contextual learning and ESP vocabulary recall. *English for Specific Purposes, 26*, 39–51.

Atkinson, R.C. (1975). Mnemotechnics in second-language learning. *America Psychologist, 30*, 821–828.

Atkinson, R.C., & Raugh, M.R. (1975). An application of mnemonic keyword to the acquisition of Russian vocabulary. *Journal of Experimental Psychology: Human Learning & Memory, 104*, 126–133.

Aust, R., Kelley, M.J., & Roby, W. (1993). The use of hyper-reference and conventional dictionaries. *Educational Technology Research and Development, 41*, 63–73.

Avila, E., & Sadoski, M. (1996). Exploring new applications of the keyword method to acquire English vocabulary. *Language Learning, 46*(3), 379–395.

Barcroft, J. (2009). Strategies and performance in intentional L2 vocabulary learning. *The Modern Journal, 87*(4), 546–561.

Boers, F., & Lindstromberg, S. (2008). How cognitive linguistics can foster effective vocabulary teaching. In F. Boers, & S. Lindstromberg (Eds.), *Cognitive linguistic approaches to teaching vocabulary and phraseology* (pp. 1–61). Berlin and New York: Mouton de Gruyter.

Boers, F., Piquer Píriz, A.M., Stengers, H., & Eyckmans, J. (2009). Does pictorial elucidation foster recollection of idioms? *Language Teaching Research, 13*(4), 367–382.

Bowman, A., & Plaisir, J. (1996). Technology approaches to teaching ESL students. *Media and Methods, 32*(3), 26–27.

Brown, D.H. (1996). TESOL and critical literacies: Modern, post, or neo? *TESOL Quarterly, 30*(1), 163–171.

Carlson, R., Kincaid, J.P., Lance, S., & Hodgson, T. (1976). Spontaneous use of mnemonics and grade point average. *Journal of Psychology, 92*(1), 117–122.

Channell, J. (1988). Psycholinguistic considerations in the study of L2 vocabulary acquisition. In R.M. Carter, & M. McCarthy (Eds.), *Vocabulary and language teaching* (pp. 83–96). New York, NY: Longman.

Chun, D., & Plass, J.L. (1996). Effects of multimedia annotations on vocabulary acquisition. *The Modern Language Journal, 80*, 183–198.

Cieslicka, A. (2006). Literal salience in on-line processing of idiomatic expressions by second language learners. *Second Language Research, 22*, 115–144.

Coady, J. (1993). Research on ESL/EFL vocabulary acquisition: Putting it in context. In T. Hucking, M. Haynes, & J. Coady (Eds.), *Second language reading and vocabulary learning* (pp. 3–23). Norwood, NJ: Ablex.

Cohen, A.D. (1987a). Studying learner strategies: How we get the information. In A. Wenden, & J. Rubin (Eds.), *Learner strategies in language learning* (pp. 31–40). Englewood Cliffs, NJ: Prentice Hall.

Cohen, A.D. (1987b). Verbal and imagery mnemonics in second language vocabulary learning. *Studies in Second Language Acquisition, 9*, 43–62.

Cohen, A.D. (1996). Verbal reports as a source of insights into second language learner strategies. *Applied Language Learning, 7*(1), 5–24.

Cohen, A.D., & Aphek, E. (1981). Easifying second language learning. *Studies in Second Language Acquisition, 3*, 221–236.

Cohen, A.D., Weaver, S., & Li, T. (1998). The impact of strategic-based instruction on speaking a foreign language. In A.D. Cohen (Ed.), *Strategies in learning and using second language* (pp. 107–156). London: Longman.

Cope, B., & Gollings, G. (Eds.). (2001). *Multilingual book production: Technology drivers across the book production supply chain, from creator to consumer.* Melbourne, VIC: Common Ground.

Cope, B., & Kalantzis, M. (Eds.). (2000). *Multiliteracies: Literacy learning and the design of social futures.* London: Routledge.

Cope, B., & Kalantzis, M. (2009). "Multiliteracy": New literacies, new learning. *Pedagogies: An International Journal, 4*, 164–195.

Council of Europe. (2001). *The Common European Framework of Reference for Languages: Learning, teaching, assessment.* Cambridge, UK: Cambridge University Press.

Danan, M. (1992). Reversed subtitling and dual coding theory: New directions for foreign language instruction. *Language Learning, 42*, 497–527.

Diao, Y., & Sweller, J. (2007). Redundancy in foreign language reading comprehension instruction: Concurrent written and spoken presentations. *Learning and Instruction, 17*, 78–88.

Dolci, R., & Spinelli, B. (Eds.). (2005). *Educazione linguistica e interculturale in nuovi ambienti di apprendimento.* Venice: Guerra Edizioni.

Dolci, R., & Spinelli, B. (2007). La dimension idioculturelle des micro-communautés d'apprentissage en ligne. *Lidil Revue, 36*, 69–92.

Dörnyei, Z. (2001). *Motivational strategies in the language classroom.* Cambridge, UK: Cambridge University Press.

Estaire, S., & Zanon, J. (1994). *Planning classwork: A task-based approach.* Oxford, UK: Heinemann.

Fang, F.A. (1985). The investigation and evaluation of the teaching methods on medical terminology. Paper presented at the Second National Conference on TESOL, Taipei, Taiwan.

Finkbeiner, M., & Nicol, J. (2003). Semantic category effects in second language word learning. *Applied Psycholinguistics, 24*(3), 369–383.

Fotos, S. (1993). Consciousness raising and noticing through focus on form: Grammar task performance versus formal instruction. *Applied Linguitsics, 14*(4), 385–407.

Freebody, P., & Luke, A. (1990). Literacies programs: Debates and demands in cultural context. *Prospect: Australian Journal of TESOL, 5*(7), 7–16.

Fuchs, C. (2006). *Computer-mediated negotiation across borders: German–American collaboration in language teacher education.* Frankfurt am Main, Germany: Peter Lang.

Fuchs, C., Hauck, M., & Müller, H. (2012). Promoting learner autonomy through multi-literacy skills development in cross-institutional exchanges. *Language Learning & Technology, 16*(3), 82–102.

Gairns, R., & Redman, S. (1986). *Working with words.* Cambridge, UK: Cambridge University Press.

Gee, J.P. (2000). New people in new worlds: Networks, the new capitalism and schools. In B. Cope & M. Kalantzis (Eds.), *Multiliteracies: Literacy learning and the design of social futures* (pp. 43–68). London: Routledge.

Guth, S., & Helm, F. (Eds.). (2010). *Telecollaboration 2.0 for language and intercultural learning.* Bern: Lang.

Hampel, R., & Hauck, M. (2006). Computer-mediated language learning: Making meaning in multimodal virtual learning spaces. *The JALT CALL Journal, 2*(2), 3–18.

Hooper, S., & Rieber, L. (1995). Teaching with technology. In A. Ornstein (Ed.), *Teaching: Theory into practice* (pp. 154–170). Needham Heights, MA: Allyn and Bacon.

Hulstijn, J.H. (1992). Retention of inferred and given word meanings: Experiments in incidental vocabulary learning. In J.L. Arnaud, & H. Béjoint (Eds.), *Vocabulary and applied linguistics* (pp. 113–125). London: Macmillan.

Hulstijn, J.H. (1993). When do foreign-language readers look up the meaning of unfamiliar words? The influence of task and learner variables. *The Modern Language Journal, 77*, 139–147.

Hulstijn, J.H. (1997). Mnemonic methods in foreign language vocabulary learning. In J. Coady & T. Huckin (Eds.), *Second language vocabulary acquisition* (pp. 203–224). Cambridge, UK: Cambridge University Press.

Hulstijn, J.H. (2000). The use of computer technology in experimental studies of second language acquisition: A survey of some techniques and some ongoing studies. *Language Learning & Technology, 3*(2), 32–43.

Hulstijn, J.H., & Laufer, B. (2001). Some empirical evidence for the involvement load hypothesis in vocabulary acquisition. *Language Learning, 51*(3), 539–558.

Keating, G. (2008). Task effectiveness and word learning in a second language: The involvement load hypothesis on trial. *Language Teaching Research, 12*(3), 365–386.

Kelly, P. (1986). Solving the vocabulary retention problem. *ITL Review of Applied Linguistics, 74*, 1–16.

Knight, S. (1994). Dictionary use while reading: The effects on comprehension and vocabulary acquisition for students of different verbal abilities. *Modern Language Journal, 78*(3), 285–299.

Kost, C., Foss, P., & Lenzini, J. (1999). Textual and pictorial glosses: Effectiveness on incidental vocabulary growth when reading in foreign language. *Foreign Language Annual, 32*(1), 89–113.

Kramsch, C., A'Ness, F., & Lam, W.S. (2000). Authenticity and authorship in the computer-mediated acquisition of L2 literacy. *Language Learning & Technology, 4*(2), 78–104.

Kress, G. (2000). Multimodality. In B. Cope, & M. Kalantzis (Eds.), *Multiliteracies: Literacy learning and the design of social futures* (pp. 182–202). Melbourne, VIC: Macmillan.

Kress, G. (2003). *Literacy in the new media age.* London: Routledge.

Kubota, R. (1999). Word processing and WWW projects in a college Japanese language class. *Foreign Language Annals, 32*(2), 205–218.

Lamy, M., & Hampel, R. (2007). *Online communication in language learning and teaching.* New York, NY: Palgrave Macmillan.

Laufer, B. (1992). How much lexis is necessary for reading comprehension? In P. Arnaud, & H. Béjoint (Eds.), *Vocabulary and applied linguistics* (pp. 126–132). London: Macmillan.

Laufer, B., & Hill, M. (2000). What lexical information do L2 learners select in a CALL dictionary and how does it affect word retention? *Language Learning & Technology, 3*(2), 58–76.

Laufer, B., & Ravenhorst-Kalovski, G. (2010). Lexical threshold revisited: Lexical text coverage, learners' vocabulary size and reading comprehension. *Reading in a Foreign Language, 22*, 15–30.

Laufer, B., & Shmueli, K. (1997). Memorizing new words: Does teaching have anything to do with it? *RELC Journal, 28*(1), 89–108.

Mayer, E. (1997). Multimedia learning: Are we asking the right questions? Extensions of a dual-coding theory of multimedia learning. *Journal of Educational Psychology, 32*(1), 1–19.

Mayer, R., & Moreno, R. (2003). Nine ways to reduce cognitive load in multimedia learning. *Educational Psychologist, 38*(1), 43–52.

McDaniel, M.A., & Pressley, M. (1989). Keyword and context instruction of the new vocabulary meanings: Effects on text comprehension and memory. *Journal of Educational Psychology, 81*, 204–213.

Munca, D. (2010). *Web 2.0 as cognitive tools in teaching a foreign language.* Saarbrücken, Germany: Lambert Academic.

Nagy, W. (1997). On the role of context in first- and second-language vocabulary learning. In N. Schmitt, & M. McCarthy (Eds.), *Vocabulary: Description, acquisition, and pedagogy* (pp. 64–83). Cambridge, UK: Cambridge University Press.

Nation, I.S. (1990). *Teaching and learning vocabulary.* New York, NY: Newbury House.

Nation, I.S. (2001). *Learning vocabulary in another language.* Cambridge, UK: Cambridge University Press.

Nation, I.S. (2006). How large a vocabulary is needed for reading and listening? *Canadian Modern Language Review, 63*(1), 59–82.

Navehebrahim, M. (2011). Multiliteracies approach to empower learning and teaching engagement. *Social and Behavioral Sciences, 29*, 863–868.

New London Group (NLG). (1996). A pedagogy of multiliteracies: Designing social futures. *Harvard Educational Review, 66*(1), 60–92.

New London Group (NLG). (2000). A pedagogy of multiliteracies. Designing social futures. In B. Cope, & M. Kalantzis (Eds.), *Multiliteracies: Literacy learning and the design of social futures.* London: Routledge.

Nikolova, O. (2002). Effects of students' participation in authoring of multimedia materials on student acquisition of vocabulary. *Language Learning & Technology, 6*(1), 100–112.

Oxford, R. (1990). *Language learning strategies: What every teacher should know.* Boston, MA: Newbury House.

Oxford, R. (1993). Research on second language learning strategies. *Annual Review of Applied Linguistics, 13*, 175–187.

Oxford, R. (1996). Employing a questionnaire to assess the use of language learning strategies. *Applied Language Learning, 7*(1), 25–45.

Paivio, A. (1971). *Imagery and verbal processes.* New York, NY: Holt, Rinehart & Winston.

Paivio, A. (1979). *Imagery and verbal processes.* Hillsdale, NJ: Erlbaum.

Paivio, A. (1986). *Mental representations: A dual coding approach.* New York, NY: Oxford University Press.

Palmberg, R. (1988). Computer games and foreign language vocabulary learning. *ELT Journal, 42*, 247–252.

Peter, E. (2007). Manipulating L2 learners' online dictionary use and its effect on L2 word retention. *Language Learning Technology, 11*(2), 36–58.

Politzer, R., & McGroarty, M. (1985). An exploratory study of learning behaviors and their relationship to gains in linguistic and communicative competence. *TESOL Quarterly, 19*(1), 103–123.

Prensky, M. (2001). Digital natives, digital immigrants, part II: Do they really think differently? *On the Horizon, 9*(6). Retrieved from www.marcprensky.com/writing/Prensky%20-%20Digital%20Natives,%20Digital%20Immigrants%20-%20Part2.pdf.

Prince, P. (2012). Towards an instruction programme for L2 vocabulary: Can a story help? *Language Learning & Technology, 16*(3), 103–120.

Pusack, J., & Otto, S. (1997). Taking control of media. In M. Bush, & R. Terry (Eds.), *Technology enhanced language learning* (pp. 1–64). Lincolnwood, IL: National Texbook Company.

Read, J. (1997). Vocabulary and testing. In N. Schmitt, & M. McCarthy (Eds.), *Vocabulary: Description, acquisition, and pedagogy* (pp. 303–320). Cambridge, UK: Cambridge University Press.

Richardson, W. (2009). *Blogs, wikis, podcasts, and other powerful web tools for classrooms.* Thousand Oaks, CA: Corwin Press.

Robinson, P. (1995). Review article: Attention memory and the "noticing" hypothesis. *Language Learning, 45*(2), 283–331.

Royce, T. (2002). Multimodality in the TESOL classroom: Exploring visual–verbal synergy. *TESOL Quarterly, 36*(2), 191–205.

Sanaoui, R. (1995). Adult learners' approaches to learning vocabulary in second languages. *Modern Language Journal, 79,* 15–28.

Saravanan, V. (2012). Curriculum design, development, innovation and change. *Social and Behavioral Sciences, 47,* 1276–1280.

Schmidt, R. (1990). The role of consciousness in second language learning. *Applied Linguistics, 11,* 129–158.

Schmitt, N. (2000). *Vocabulary in language teaching.* Cambridge, UK: Cambridge University Press.

Schmitt, N. (2008). Instructed second language vocabulary learning. *Language Teaching Research, 12*(3), 329–363.

Schmitt, N., & McCarthy, M. (Eds) (1997). *Vocabulary: Description, acquisition, and pedagogy.* Cambridge, UK: Cambridge University Press.

Schouten-van Parreren, C. (1989). Vocabulary learning through reading: Which conditions should be met when presenting words in texts? *AILA Review, 6,* 5–85.

Segler, T.M., Pain, H., & Sorace, A. (2010). Second language vocabulary acquisition and learning strategies in ICALL environments. *Computer Assisted Language Learning, 15*(4), 409–422.

Siribodhi, T. (1995). Effects of three interactive multimedia CALL programs on the vocabulary acquisition of elementary level EFL studemts (Doctoral dissertation, University of Kansas, 1995). *Dissertation Abstracts International, 59*(09), 3552A.

Spinelli, B., & Parizzi, F. (2010). *Il Profilo della lingua Italiana Livelli del QCER A1, A2, B1, B2.* Firenze, Italy: La Nuova Italia.

Thompson, I. (1987). Memory in language learning. In A. Wenden, & J. Rubin (Eds.), *Learning strategies in language learning.* New York, NY: Prentice Hall.

Underwood, J. (1989). HyperCard and interactive video. *CALICO Journal, 6*(3), 7–20.

Unsworth, L. (2001). *Teaching multiliteracy across the curriculum.* Basingstoke, UK: Open University Press.

Warschauer, M., & Shetzer, H. (2000). An electronic literacy approach to network-based language teaching. In M. Warschauer, & R. Kern (Eds.), *Network-based language teaching: Concepts and practice* (pp. 171–185). Cambridge, UK: Cambridge University Press.

Webb, S. (2008). The effects of context on incidental vocabulary learning. *Reading in a Foreign Language, 20*(2), 232–245.

Webb, S., & Rodgers, M. (2009). The lexical coverage of movies. *Applied Linguistics, 30,* 407–427.

Wiersma, W., & Jurs, S.G. (2009). *Research method in education.* Boston, MA: Pearson.

Willis, J. (2001). Foundational assumptions for information technology and teacher education. *Contemporary Issues in Technology and Teacher Education, 1*(3), 305–320.

9

CREATING AN EFFECTIVE LEARNING ENVIRONMENT IN AN ADVANCED CHINESE LANGUAGE COURSE THROUGH FILM, POSTER PRESENTATIONS, AND MULTILITERACIES

Sujane Wu

Students in advanced Chinese language courses in US collegiate settings often feel overwhelmed by, and struggle with, newly introduced vocabulary and formal usage of words (*shumian yu* 書面語 in Chinese).[1] Often they are not able to successfully complete the assigned reading of Chinese texts (e.g., a newspaper article or a literary critique) due to many unfamiliar characters and a high level of formality in words and grammar (Chang, 2006; Lee-Thompson, 2008; Shen & Jiang, 2013). While dealing with new words and grammar is common to all language learners, it is especially relevant in Chinese as foreign language (CFL) classes for students whose native writing systems are different (i.e., using the Roman alphabet) (Everson, 2009; Ke, 1996, 1998; Lee-Thompson, 2008; Shen, 2000, 2005; Shen & Jiang, 2013). All CFL instructors encourage students to learn new vocabulary in context and overcome the challenges of confronting unfamiliar characters; but learners in the upper-level courses, working with Chinese texts written for educated native speakers, are heavily burdened with memorizing and accurately reproducing Chinese characters, decoding unfamiliar characters and identifying word boundaries as well as their meanings (Everson, 2009, 2011; Lee-Thompson, 2008). Consequently, this struggle takes away time and effort they should be spending on speaking and writing (Ke, 1998; Shen, 2000). This struggle also causes frustration and distracts them from critically engaging the text in a meaningful way.

This problem also exacts a toll on instructors who teach advanced Chinese courses. While all CFL instructors strive to help advanced learners retain what they have previously learned and guide them to meaningfully transfer prior knowledge to new content and contexts (Chang, 2006), those teaching advanced courses are often frustrated by being unable to go beyond mere linguistic proficiencies (e.g., vocabulary, grammar, sounding out characters and tones) to provide an effective environment where learners can engage in a more intellectual, substantial, and stimulating interaction.

In order to understand how to alleviate the burdens and frustration felt by both learners and instructors, we need to look at the following issues that are frequently seen in the college-level world language classroom, including CFL:

1. Accurate retrieval of information from texts is overemphasized (Alderson & Urquhart, 1984; Kern, 2000).
2. Receptive skills (reading/listening) are emphasized more than productive skills (writing/speaking) (Kumagai, 2007; Ling, 2007; Shen, 2000).
3. Course contents are often not intellectually challenging or stimulating (Iwasaki & Kumagai, 2008; Kumagai & Iwasaki, 2011; Zhang, 2011).
4. Cultural and social perspectives embedded in texts are undervalued (Iwasaki & Kumagai, 2008; Kramsch, 1993; Kumagai & Iwasaki, 2011; Zhang, 2011).
5. Students' diverse backgrounds are often overlooked (Elder, 2000).

In its 2007 report, the MLA Ad Hoc Committee on Foreign Languages argues that the goal of language programs is to produce a "specific outcome" for all educated world language learners: "translingual and transcultural competence." The report further points out that the current goal of advanced language training to replicate "the competence of an educated native speaker" is "rarely reach[ed]" and should be replaced with a goal of translingual and transcultural competence that:

> places value on the ability to operate between languages. Students are educated to function as informed and capable interlocutors with educated native speakers in the target language. They are also trained to reflect on the world and themselves through the lens of another language and culture. (MLA, 2007, pp. 3–4)

Such an insightful statement calls for reflection on teaching and learning in advanced CFL courses. How can CFL educators and learners begin to solve the aforementioned issues? And how can CFL educators help their learners to develop a "translingual and transcultural competence"?

The MLA's proposal of restructuring language education is also supported by Kalantzis and Cope (2008) as they argue for "new kinds of learning." They assert that literacy should not be just about rules and accuracy. It should also be about being able to read a text and know where and how to "search for clues about its meaning without immediately feeling alienated and excluded from it" (p. 203). They further elaborate this line of thinking and remark that:

> It [literacy] is also about understanding how this text works in order to participate in its meanings (its own particular "rules"), and about working

out the particular context and purposes of the text (for herein you will find more clues to its meaning to the communicator and to you). Finally, literacy is about actively communicating in an unfamiliar context and learning from your successes and mistakes. (Kalantzis & Cope, 2008, p. 203)

Kalantzis and Cope's "new kinds of learning"are elaborated in the New London Group's (NLG) 1996 proposal. The NLG proposes "a much broader view of literacy than portrayed by traditional language-based approaches" (p. 60). It summarizes this new approach in one word—*multiliteracies*—to address the world's increasingly diversified cultural and linguistic environments, and the changing communication channels of media and technologies (Kalantzis & Cope, 2008, p. 196). The idea behind multiliteracies is to foster students' understanding of and ability to "negotiat[e] the multiple linguistic and cultural differences" that exist in our society (NLG, 1996, p. 60) and to train students to critically interpret and make connections between the meanings of written words and other modes of representation: multimodal literacy. The multiliteracies approach thus focuses on the meaning-making process with the notion that knowledge and meaning are constantly being made and remade in various ways. It also highlights the importance that the linguistic mode should interface with visual, audio, gestural, and spatial information to create meaning (Kalantzis & Cope, 2008, p. 203; NLG, 1996, p. 65).

In order to help advanced CFL learners develop their translingual and transcultural competence, instructors must emphasize writing and speaking literacies in addition to the receptive skills (reading/listening), and use the recommendations from the MLA report to restructure their courses to help learners explore Chinese culture and society as well as different perspectives (Zhang, 2011, p. 201), and guide them to "operate between languages" (MLA, 2007, p. 3). In this chapter I suggest that film is an effective teaching and learning resource, especially if used with an approach that embodies the idea of multiliteracies (NLG, 1996): poster presentations.

Effective Learning Through Film

It is often acknowledged that film, mass media, and multimedia offer rich teaching resources for language instructors. And film in particular, which is "multimodal by nature" (Chan & Herrero, 2010, p. 8), can be "used to challenge students' imaginations and to help them consider alternative ways of seeing, feeling, and understanding things" (MLA, 2007, p. 4; Zhang, 2011, pp. 206–207). Film and other media have become "an essential part" of our everyday life (Quinlisk, 2003, p. 39), and they offer a space for viewers to reflect on different social and cultural perspectives and attitudes, including one's own (Ning, 2009; Quinlisk, 2003; Zhang, 2011). Therefore, the various modes of representation in film and other media, including spoken, written, and visual, can be used in many language learning contexts to develop learners' social and cultural literacies (Quinlisk, 2003, p. 35; Goldoni, 2008). Working with media, in particular with film, allows learners to "not only develop skills of inquiry and communication but develop an understanding of some of the social and cultural practices that affect their access to the target language community as well" (Quinlisk, 2003, p. 39). The use of film in a world language class promotes learners' active learning and participation as they engage in specifically designed activities to learn about people's lives and customs of the target society and the relationship with their own culture.

Film is "full of cross references" (NLG, 1996, p. 82). Audiences make sense of the meaning of a film through intertextuality. The intertextuality, as the NLG advocates:

> draws attention to the potentially complex ways in which meanings (such as linguistic meanings) are constituted through relationships to other texts (real or imaginary), text types (discourse or genres), narratives, and other modes of meaning (such as visual design, architectonic or geographical positioning). (1996, p. 82)

And students, by using poster presentations to showcase their analyses of Chinese films, exploit the multimodal literacies for their use of both visual (i.e., still shots from the film) and textual forms (i.e., key points of their arguments) to present their ideas in a public space in an engaging way.

Use of Poster Presentation

Poster presentation is a method commonly used by instructors in classroom settings and by experts to present their research at professional conferences in fields such as engineering, natural science, and social science. In the humanities it has been adopted by instructors in the field of Teaching English as a Second Language (TESOL) to assess learners' oral proficiency (Furmanovsky & Sheffner, 1997; Lambert, 2008; Pudwill & Cullen, 2003). However, in the CFL field, poster presentation are rarely employed.

In many classrooms nowadays, PowerPoint presentations are a common way to promote a multimodal approach to language learning. Yet I would argue that poster presentations in world language courses has several noteworthy benefits that surpass those of PowerPoint presentations. A poster presentation offers learners a natural, authentic context to *repeatedly* express their viewpoints (Lambert, 2008); also, since learners make presentations in a public setting, it gives them a chance to communicate with a wider, diverse audience. In other words, a poster presentation provides an opportunity for learners to negotiate meanings with the audience without a prescribed, memorized text; it helps both the presenters and their audience to engage in a more dynamic, dialogic discussion (Lambert, 2008; White, 2011); finally, it encourages learners to use all the multimodal resources (language—written, spoken; visual images—pictures, different fonts, colors, use of space, etc.) that can fit on a 36' × 24' poster board in order to communicate meaning effectively.

Objectives of Poster Presentation

From the standpoint of Chinese language students who strive to participate in the target language community and to interact with diverse groups of people beyond the classroom (including native speakers, language instructors, and learners at different levels), the poster presentation in a public space offers an ideal environment for learning in a social setting, where the students and the audience can both actively participate in a meaningful conversation.

The main objective in the design of a poster presentation project is to help students become competent communicators in a diverse community, as advocated by the NLG (1996) and the MLA Ad Hoc Committee (2007). The second objective is to use the *poster* as a space and context for multimodal sign-making in which students articulate their critical interpretations and analyses of the film of their choice multimodally. Students are asked to present their projects at least *twice* in a given time duration, providing them a chance to reflect and reshape their presentations to make them better. Third, students discover how to interact with an audience *without a prepared text*. Even though students may use small notecards during their presentations, they are strongly discouraged from merely reading aloud from the cards. They are also discouraged from memorizing their presentations. They are reminded that their poster should be their prompt. Moreover, since the audience can interrupt and ask questions anytime, they must be prepared to adjust their remarks as in a real dialogue. And, finally, the use of visual forms (e.g., screen shot images from the films, maps, etc.) in their posters helps students present their ideas more effectively and attractively.

In sum, the poster presentation project aims to enhance not only the linguistic meaning-making process, but also to highlight the non-verbal modes of meaning. The meanings conveyed through language and other modes of representation are constantly being remade by different users in different times and spaces in order to achieve their own social and cultural purposes (NLG, 1996, p. 64). Poster presentation, therefore, is one of many ways to employ multiple communication channels and media (p. 60), to create an effective learning environment and to foster students' critical engagement with their chosen films and with a culturally and linguistically diverse audience.

A poster presentation project on film is at the center of an advanced Chinese course I designed in 2010, which is guided by the notions of multimodality and intertextuality. In the following sections, I will first describe the goals and curriculum structure of the course and explain how the study of films and the poster presentation project provides an opportunity to achieve these goals. Then I will explain in detail the implementation of the project, its outcomes, and students' reflections articulated in the post-project survey.

The Course: *Advanced Readings in Chinese: Modern Literary Texts*

The course as taught during the fall semesters of 2010 and 2011 was for students who had completed six semesters of Chinese at a college level or its equivalent. The class met twice a week, 80 minutes per class for 14 weeks. Its objectives as stated in the course syllabus (in Chinese) were as follows:

1. To cultivate problem-solving skill: Students acquire the confidence and competence to critically understand the written texts without knowing each and every Chinese character and compound word.
2. To increase communicative competencies: Students learn to communicate orally in a more natural way and with an authoritative voice to a diverse audience, including other CFL learners and native speakers.
3. To negotiate multiple views and ideas: Students learn how to express their own views in writing using evidence to support them, and to negotiate their interpretations with those of the audience during their poster presentations at the end of the semester.

Participants of Diverse Backgrounds

Participants were 23 students (total for the two years) at a liberal arts college in the northeastern United States. They ranged from first-year college students through fourth year. They came from diverse backgrounds: most were native English speakers, but some had bilingual or even trilingual backgrounds. Some spoke one of the Chinese dialects (e.g., Cantonese or Taiwanese) at home, and some were international students (including one from Malaysia and one from Lebanon). Some had studied abroad in China or Taiwan, but others had not lived in any Chinese-speaking area. The students brought to the classroom a wide range of learning experiences and different linguistic and cultural backgrounds. This created a very diverse learning environment with a certain degree of tension among the students. The tension came from the "issue of differences"— the increasingly varied linguistic and cultural differences emerging in our society and in our classroom (NLG, 1966, p. 61). With regard to these differences, I worked to break down barriers and instructed students to view their diverse backgrounds as resources rather than conflicts.

Textbooks Used in the Course: Shifting From Literature to Film

The title of the course, *Advanced Readings in Chinese: Modern Literary Texts* indicates that this advanced language course is designed as a part of the typical two-tiered structure of foreign language programs and departments in collegiate settings. That is, the beginning level mainly focuses on linguistic exercises and communicative language skills, whereas the advanced level emphasizes literary texts with a more traditional approach to reading and writing (e.g., Byrnes, Maxim, & Norris, 2010; Kern, 2004; Maxim, 2014; MLA, 2007; Swaffar & Arens, 2005; Urlaub, 2014; see Chapter 1, this volume).

Two textbooks were used in this advanced Chinese class. The course was not originally created using film as teaching material until the availability in 2007 of the textbook, *Readings in contemporary Chinese cinema: A textbook of advanced modern Chinese* (hereafter, *Cinema*) by Chih-p'ing Chou, Wei Wang, and Joanne Chiang. In the preface, the authors describe their views, shared by many Chinese language instructors, on the usefulness of film as teaching material in the CFL classroom. However, they did not design this *Cinema* textbook as "a [line-by-line] reader for the movie" as typically done, because a line-by-line reader would take students too long to finish and would be pedagogically unsound and less stimulating (Chou et al., 2007, p. vii).[2]

The textbook authors chose ten films from the last three decades by directors from China, Hong Kong, and Taiwan. The authors provide a synopsis as well as a critique for each film, although for a few films the synopsis and critique are combined into one essay. Besides the authors' synopsis and critique for each film, extracted segments of the film dialogue are also provided. As is typically done, the texts are supplemented by linguistic information (i.e., new vocabulary with English glossaries and sentence-pattern examples and explanations), as well as exercises to assess comprehension (Chou et al., 2007, p. vii). The textbook does not offer any explicit learning objectives and pedagogical suggestions for instructors, nor are any relevant visual images included. Nonetheless, the textbook gives an instructor a convenient and flexible base to design the curriculum by modifying and expanding its contents in order to meet the needs of the course. When the textbook is used with the actual films, it is particularly suitable to develop multiliteracies because it provides an effective means to train learners' abilities not only to understand written texts, but also to critically interpret signs, symbols, and images as well as other semiotic resources, such as audio, oral, gestural, and spatial designs of meaning (NLG, 1996, p. 83).

The second textbook used for this course is *The Routledge advanced Chinese multimedia course: Crossing cultural boundaries* by Kunshan Lee, Hsin-hsin Liang, Liwei Jiao, and Julian Wheatley (2010; hereafter, *RACMC*). This book consists of 12 lessons divided into four thematic units, each unit comprised of three lessons, ranging from popular culture, social change, and cultural traditions to history and politics as well. The authors state: "[It] aims to develop language skills in the course of focusing on thinking about the Chinese and their culture" and "emphasizes the link between cultural literacy and high levels of language competence" (Lee, 2010, p. vii). This book is complemented by audio CDs and a multimedia website that are integrated into the design of the curriculum.[3] The audio CDs are based on printed lessons and help enhance students' listening comprehension; whereas the website offers video clips of relevant interviews to illustrate different perspectives on a variety of issues.

Thematic Units of the Course

To enhance pedagogical effectiveness and allow students to learn from the linguistic, social, and cultural diversities within their learning community, I chose a thematic approach using the *Cinema* textbook as a point of departure. Four films out of ten from the *Cinema* textbook were selected and supplemented by sections from the *RACMC* textbook. Other forms of visual representation, such as film advertisements, DVD covers, and written sources such as film reviews, were incorporated into the learning process in order to cultivate students' competence in examining cultural values, morality, patterns of interaction in social and cultural practices, and verbal and non-verbal communications (Quinlisk, 2003, p. 37; Goldoni, 2008). The course was divided into three units based on their thematic significance and similarity:

- Unit 1: The conflicts between the old and the new: generation gaps and social changes.
- Unit 2: Cultural traditions: the transformation of Chinese architecture and food.
- Unit 3: The relationship between individual and political or economic change.

These three units worked well as a coherent sequence that helped students use previously learned linguistic forms and content knowledge. Moreover, the three thematic approaches encouraged students to critically examine the many aspects of Chinese society and culture.

Brief Description of Each Unit

To give an overview of the structure, I will provide a brief description of each unit. For Unit 1, I selected two films from the *Cinema* textbook: *Shower* 洗澡 (*Xizao*, 1999) directed by Zhang Yang from China, and *Eat, Drink, Man, and Woman* 飲食男女 (*Yinshi nannü*, 1994) directed by Ang Lee from Taiwan.[4] This unit uses bathing and food as metaphors to focus on the changes and choices each individual must make in order to move forward and integrate with society.

To complement *Eat, Drink, Man, and Woman*, Unit 2 began with a focus on food using a lesson in the *RACMC* textbook on Chinese food culture and its transformation. After viewing the video clips provided by the textbook authors on their website and analyzing the texts in the textbook, students conducted interviews with native Chinese speakers in the community regarding their views on

Chinese food culture as well as the social connotations of its transformations. Another lesson used for Unit 2 is on Chinese architecture in transition, which is also from the *RACMC* textbook. This lesson discusses two examples of very contemporary Western style architecture—the National Center for Performing Arts (a.k.a. the Eggshell and National Grand Theater) and the National Indoor Stadium in Beijing (a.k.a. the Bird's Nest), built for the 2008 Beijing Olympics. The textbook authors suggest that students contribute to the debate about whether or not the radical designs would undermine Chinese traditional values. For this unit, I used the activities of interviews with native speakers in the community and debates among learners to acknowledge and analyze different perspectives.

Unit 3 discussed two films that are also treated in the *Cinema* textbook: *Farewell My Concubine* 霸王別姬 (*Bawang bieji*, 1993) directed by Chen Kaige, and *To Live* 活著 (*Huozhe*, 1994) directed by Zhang Yimou. These two films were used to explore how political and economic changes affect the lives of individuals.

As mentioned earlier, the course design reinforced the important role that prior knowledge played in language learning. The knowledge learned in Unit 1 and Unit 2 would become a potential bridge for the understanding of Unit 3 and enable students to participate in an informed discussion about the struggles that each individual faced during the political turmoil featured in the films in Unit 3. As Quinlisk (2003) argues for the development of media literacy, the use of film was "not only as a way to incorporate mass media as a source of linguistic input but also as a tool for learning to interpret multiple layers of messages and to separate mediated images of people, places, things, ideas, and values from those of the real world" (p. 35).

A Sample Lesson From the Course: Reading Shower

The lesson on the film *Shower* is a good example to illustrate the sequence of learning and how students prepared their poster presentations. *Shower* was one of two films used as primary materials in Unit 1, and it was complemented by a synopsis, a critique, and excerpts from the dialog provided by the *Cinema* textbook. Additional materials, including the cover images from the DVD, film reviews, and a brief description of the film from the internet were also used. This lesson had three objectives:

- To "prepare learners to interpret multiple forms of language use (oral and written) in multiple contexts" (Kern, 2004, p. 7), and look into the relationship among different genres (e.g., film, reviews, DVD covers) and modes of representation.
- To foster critical understanding of an unfamiliar target culture by comparing it to parallels from the learners' own cultures (Zhang, 2011).
- To create an environment in which meaningful conversations engage the intellectual content (Kern, 2004, p. 7).

The themes of this unit were (1) to explore the conflicts between the old and the new societies and values, and (2) to consider the compromises made by individuals and communities. While conflicts between the old and the new exist almost everywhere in the modern world, they are particularly intense in China since the late 20th century. In the film *Shower*, the traditional values of family and communal responsibilities are challenged by modernization. The film *Shower* engages students' life experiences with the issue from their own cultures and encourages them to make connections to the Chinese society and culture. By studying the film's audio, visual, and written materials, students were encouraged to critically analyze what were valued and devalued in modern Chinese society (Chen, 2011; Zhang, 2011).

The following section describes in detail using the film *Shower* to illustrate how students were guided to pay attention to the use of multimodality in constructing meaning and to notice intertextuality among various texts (both linguistic and otherwise) used in the lesson. (See Appendix A for a chart of the instructional procedures.)

Prior to viewing the film *Shower*, the class discussed different cultural representations and perspectives in the film's title 洗澡 (*Xizao*). The Chinese term *xizao* 洗澡 is a compound word meaning to take "a bath" in a traditional way or "a shower" in modern day practice.[5] The English translation "Shower," however, disguises the significant social and cultural meanings of the "bathing"[6] from its title. The students were asked to consider the loss of meaning in translation.

Then students were instructed to examine the images and written texts on the front and back covers of the DVD. On the front cover, the text claims that the film has caused great dispute among viewers. Students were asked to use their knowledge of Chinese history, society, and culture to speculate about the reasons why the film has generated the controversy. Also, by looking closely at the image on the front cover, in which three shirtless men are standing inside a blue-color shower room laughing, students were led to surmise that the story might be a comedy.

Next, the students discussed the back cover of the DVD, which contains a short description of the story in Chinese and English, and more images from the film. After reading the description of the story, the students were asked to closely inspect the images on the back cover to explain the connections between them, and to try to predict the ending of the story.[7] This pre-viewing activity was meant to stimulate their imaginations about the film, and to encourage them to interpret the embedded denotative and connotative social and cultural meanings represented in the texts and images.

The students then watched the film on their own and studied the synopsis provided in the *Cinema* textbook. While watching, they were instructed to focus on the three main characters—a father and two sons—in terms of how they are portrayed visually and through dialogs, their lifestyles, and their relationship to one another and to the bath house. The three main characters symbolize three aspects of today's China: The father, who owns and manages a traditional bath house in Beijing, symbolizes the old and traditional China; the elder son named Daming, who is pursuing his career in the modern city of Shenzhen far away, symbolizes the modernization and economic development of contemporary China; and the younger son, who is mentally challenged, but works hard helping his father maintain the bath house, symbolizes the hardworking but powerless common people. The students were also instructed to learn vocabulary and phrases in context while preparing for the analysis of the symbolic meanings of "cleansing oneself" and the differences between taking a shower and taking a bath in the film (and in traditional Chinese culture). They were asked to pay special attention to specific segments, such as the first scene in the film where Daming walks into an automatic "shower booth" which strikingly resembles a miniature car-washing facility, to "take a shower"; and another scene where the father makes a comment about the differences between "showering" and "bathing" when Daming insists on taking a shower, not a bath. In class we discussed the meanings of the aforementioned scenes while viewing the still images and analyzed the use of music and sound in the film (e.g., fast-paced music accompanying the automatic showering) and their effects.

Following the discussion described above was a critical reading of a variety of texts, including a critique on the culture of the traditional bath house (provided in the textbook) and two film reviews from websites. Swaffar (2004) discusses the benefits of using film reviews in advanced language classrooms as follows:

> Reading several reviews with differing assessments will help students learn how to look for the basis for judgments in this relatively formal genre to identify the accepted value of the reviewer and her presumed audience. Such an exercise, then, provides practice in identifying how individual statements are made within formulaic genres in particular cultural contexts. (p. 35)

She argues that film reviews, as a genre with conventional structure, provide "excellent, fairly transparent windows into perceptions about different segments within a larger cultural community" to foster students' cultural literacy (p. 35). After reading the reviews, the students were asked to present orally their own critiques, using the vocabulary and structures they learned from the readings. By reading and offering their own reviews of the film, the students entered into a "broader social analysis of powerful cultural stories" (Quinlisk, 2003, p. 36).

Composing essays is the most difficult competence to be developed in the CFL curriculum because writing competence usually takes longer and requires more effort to develop (Ling, 2007). Therefore, in the CFL curriculum writing competence is always treated as a supplementary skill to reading competence. In the recent decade, researchers have argued that writing and reading should be taught as an integrated skill in CFL classes for the reason that writing can also improve learners' reading comprehension and vice versa (Shen, 2000). Thus, in terms of the interconnected relationship between reading and writing (i.e., literacy), writing as a communication skill deserves its own place and attention in CFL curriculum (Ling, 2007; Shen, 2000). Needless to say, the more guidance students receive when they write, the better they get. Writing and rewriting help students to develop their writing competence and organize their thoughts in a more logical way.

Subsequently, the learning process for this film concluded with summative writing activity. Each student wrote an essay in which she had to address, but was not limited to, the following topics (the topics were given in Chinese):

1. What cultural values are emphasized or de-emphasized, and how are they illustrated visually and/or conveyed linguistically?
2. How do the stories of the characters, especially the three main characters in the film, differ from or are similar to people you know from your own life experience?
3. Why and how is China's economic development in conflict with traditional values?

In addition to the writing, students presented what they wrote orally in the next class. The goal of this summative writing and speaking activities was to prepare students for their poster presentations at the end of the semester.

Implementation of the Poster Presentation Project

The students started to work on the poster presentation project after they had studied two movies. They worked on them for about seven weeks. About halfway through the semester (week 7) after the students had engaged in class discussion on how to critically interpret different modes of representation (e.g., the discussion on the film *Shower* above), I provided a list of films from which each student could select one film for her own poster presentation project. Some of the films on the list were treated in the *Cinema* textbook, but they had not been shown or discussed in class. The films on the list, directly or indirectly, reflect the themes of the three units addressed in the course, and also offer students different perspectives with which to understand Chinese society (Chou et al., 2007). (See Appendix B for a list of the films.)

After each student chose a film, she watched it on her own schedule. A week later the students had to submit a written summary of the story and decide on a tentative topic for their poster project. They also had to explain the reason why they chose the particular topic and list the relevant social and cultural contexts required to understand the film. They were reminded again to pay attention to the different modes of representation used in the film (such as use of spoken language, visuals, music, and gestures, etc.) in addition to the plot of the story.

The next step was to give students a hands-on training on how to find Chinese resources in the library for their project. Each student had to find at least one film review and one analytic essay concerning the film and/or its director. If the film had not been the subject of an analytic essay, they were allowed to use two film reviews for their project. In addition to finding and reading a review and an essay in Chinese language, the students read English reviews and/or essays in order to examine different perspectives on the film. By comparing and contrasting different viewpoints offered by different genres (thus, with different social purposes and for a different audience) and from different linguistic/cultural contexts (probably with different sociocultural assumptions and, again, for a different audience), I intended that students would gain a broader, nuanced understanding of the film. Another effect of using English reviews and/or essays was to provide students with easier access to the background and context information about the film. Reading reviews in English is a good way to reduce students' anxiety and increase their confidence, so they are able to more actively engage in the content of the film and the texts.

After the library session, the students began writing their reports based on the resources they found. They were required to write two drafts before their actual presentations. The content of their written reports had to at least include the following:

1. A topic and statement of how the topic reflects the social and cultural perspectives in China, and of how the topic relates to any of the three major themes discussed in the course.
2. Their own analysis and interpretation of the film with explicit description of verbal and non-verbal evidence from the film.
3. The arguments that have been made in the resources they consulted and how these resources support or oppose their own viewpoints.

Here are some examples of topics the students chose for their projects. Using the film *24 City* (Jia Zhangke, 2008), one student chose to address the impact of urban development and how common people were forced to be displaced and relocated in China. Her project was related to the theme addressed in Unit 3. Another student chose a topic from Unit 1, conflicts between the old and the new, and analyzed the father–son relationship through the film *Sunflower* (Zhang Yang, 2005) directed by the same director as *Shower*. Other topics included: the impact of the Cultural Revolution on Chinese personal life; the phenomena of migrant populations and laborers in Beijing; and the changing views on marriage and family brought by China's modernization.

Following the written report was poster-making. For their posters, students were required to use images (screen shots) from the film and to include key points from their analysis and resources, as if they were presenting at a professional conference. I made a sample poster to facilitate a discussion on criteria for what makes a good poster.[8] Students were encouraged to think about the relationship between words and images. They recognized that an image should not be merely an illustration of the text; rather, images should be as important as the text on a poster and add their own meaning. Through discussion they also learned that flow between words and images should be taken into consideration when making a poster. This kind of discussion helped students explore the composition features required for a good poster and decide on evaluation criteria for their own project. Creating their own evaluation criteria allowed them to take more responsibility for their own learning.

For the next class students were asked to bring a draft copy of their posters on 8.5' × 11' paper, and used this draft to get feedback from their peers. This was the first round of peer review regarding the effectiveness of their use of text and images according to the criteria they themselves articulated during the previous class meeting. When they came back for the next session, they brought a revised second draft of their posters and practiced their presentations in groups, receiving further feedback from their peers. In this rehearsal class the students helped one another to create an effective learning environment by discussing how they could improve their presentations by using eye contact, speaking pace, or demeanor differently.

The culmination of the poster project was on presentation day when the students showcased their critical readings of their chosen films and how they took into account Chinese social and cultural perspectives. The format of Presentation Day was as follows:

- The 60 minute class time was divided into three periods (20 minutes each).
- The nine students were divided into three groups with each group assigned to one of the 20 minute periods.
- Each student presented at least twice, each time for 10 minutes, to a different subset of the students. Three presentations went on simultaneously.
- During their allotted time, presenters stood by their posters and described their work to their audience. The presentations included a brief synopsis of the film, the key ideas of their analysis, and a conclusion, and then they responded to questions from the audience.

The audience was comprised not only of classmates but visitors responding to publicity and direct invitation. These included all Chinese language instructors, students from other Chinese courses, and Chinese students in residence, as well as other native Chinese speakers from the community. All audience members were asked to fill out evaluation forms (which were created based on the criteria set by the students themselves). (See Appendix C: Guidelines for implementation of the poster presentation project.)

Analysis of Mary's Poster About the Film *24 City*[9]

On presentation day, Mary's poster attracted many visitors for its eye-catching title and subheadings, the use of background colors that contrasted with the grayscale screen shots, and the presenter's gestures and poise. Figure 9.1 shows the image of the poster and the section titles with English translations.[10]

贾樟柯的《二十四城记》：一部纪念过去的伪纪录片

[Jia Zhangke's *24 City*: The Past Recollected through a Pseudo-documentary Lens]

1. 电影的历史背景

[The Historical Background of the Film *24 City*]

2. 导演介绍，拍摄影片的过程

[The Director and the Process of Film Making]

3. 以伪纪录片结构来表达真假的穿行

[Exploring the Continuum between Reality and Fiction through a Pseudo-documentary Film]

4. 以诗歌来表达价值观

[Revealing Social, Cultural Values through Poetry]

5. 以视觉性的镜头来展现出集体的回忆

[Representing Collective Memory through Visual Images]

6. 结论：《二十四城记》如何纪念420厂的往事

[Conclusion: How the Film *24 City* Commemorates the Factory's Past]

7. 参考书目[Works Cited]

FIGURE 9.1   Mary's poster with Chinese texts and English translation (including its subheadings).

The English synopsis from the DVD back cover serves as the basis for Mary's exploration of the film. The synopsis says:

> *24 City* chronicles the dramatic closing of a once-prosperous state-owned aeronautics factory and its conversion into a sprawling luxury apartment complex. Bursting with poetry, pop songs and striking visual detail, the film weaves together unforgettable stories from three generations of workers whose lives have revolved around the factory—some real, some played by actors (including Joan Chen)—into a vivid portrait of the human struggle behind China's economic miracle. (*24 City* DVD back cover, 2008)[11]

Mary discusses how Jia Zhangke's film provides cultural and social perspectives on China's economic development. The entire content of the poster suggests that her intensive reading of the texts and images from the DVD covers had been refined by the class discussions (e.g., on the film *Shower*) earlier in the semester. On the poster, Mary states (in Chinese):

> 我们来自西方的<u>视者</u>[观众]很难以<u>思考</u>[想象]中国的经济发展在民生中所造成的变迁是多么地深刻广泛。不过，贾樟柯的作品能够<u>给我们赋予</u>[赋予我们]一点印象。
>
> [It is difficult for a Western audience to imagine what a huge impact economic development has imposed on the Chinese people. Jia Zhangke's film provides a rough picture of this effect.][12]

Examining the poster more closely, one may notice that Mary designed her poster based on the structure of a research paper. The organization of her poster also suggests that, as a Psychology major, she is familiar with the poster presentation in an academic setting. She successfully transferred her prior knowledge of academic poster presentations to her language learning environment. She divided the contents into three sections: the left column (subheadings 1–2) serves as the introduction; the middle column contains her three key findings (subheadings 3–5), and the right column her conclusion and references (subheadings 6–7). Each subheading is accompanied by a screen shot.

Mary's poster also suggests that she pays attention to the connections between text and image, which speaks to the criterion presented earlier: that is, the images should not merely be used as illustrations of the text; rather, they convey meanings of their own. For example, the still image placed with subheading 5 [Representing Collective Memory through Visual Images] in the poster (Figure 9.1) shows two men with seemingly emotionless faces—but the emotionlessness is itself an emotional expression. And their eyes seem to stare aimlessly into the camera lens and are thereby also staring at the viewers. However, when examining the image more closely, one can see that the man on the right has his arm around the shoulder of the other man, and both are standing in front of an unadorned brick-like wall. In order to understand the reason behind the selection of this particular still image to represent subheading 5, we need to examine Mary's texts:

> 影片也含有许多视觉性的镜头。观看者[观众]能够看到厂子里的机械动作[运作]、厂子所造的飞机零件、勤劳的工人、以及工厂的拆迁。最充满人情味的情景展示在厂子周围所建立的友谊。420厂旁边的家属区里面有老年人打麻将，还有女士一起练习唱戏。受采访的老同事勾肩搭背地重温往事，讲从前的生活。

> [The film includes many static images. The audience is shown a series of images such as machines operating in the factory, workers making parts for military aircraft, diligent workers' faces as well as the half-demolished Factory 420. The friendship among the workers in this community is portrayed warmly in the scenes around the factory—workers of the older generations are playing Majiang (a.k.a. Mah-jongg) in a residential hall near Factory 420; women are singing Chinese opera together; two former co-workers, one man with his arm around the shoulder of the other man, are recollecting their past.][13]

From this text, we can sense that she chose the image carefully even though there were many other scenes that she could have used to illustrate this section. It is important to note that in the film there is no conversation between these two men, and the scene that follows this image shows the two men smiling as one is gently tickling the other's neck. By focusing on the men's gestures and emotionless facial expression, she had created a provocative atmosphere; the audience could not help but look into these two men's eyes and wonder what they were thinking and looking at. The selection of this particular image demonstrates Mary's visual competence as well as her understanding of the multimodal meaning-making process; she was able to create a particular emotion by taking advantage of the intermodal effects.

Because of the unsaturated color used in the film (as shown in the screen shots), Mary chose to use colored backgrounds (blue, green, yellow, and pink) to make the images stand out, allowing the drab images to evoke the aged factory. Mary emphasizes that the success of Jia Zhangke's film comes from his mixture of documentary and fiction (see subheading 3), and that he paints a picture of the displacement and ambivalence of the working class people in China by mixing the perspectives of the actors and non-actors. She argues in section 3 from her poster that Jia's *24 City* uses interviews with the former workers at Factory 420 to represent the attitudes and perspectives of both the director and those of the people who spent their entire working lives in the factory.

Summary of the Post-Presentation Survey

In the post-presentation survey distributed to the class after the completion of the project, the students reflected on their own learning, challenges, and rewards. Most of their comments were positive. Below are the students' reflections in which they demonstrate that a poster presentation project is a powerful way to inform their own language learning and enhance their language competence.

Most of the students agreed that the project was a valuable activity, as it refined their speaking, listening, reading, and writing abilities. In respect to reading improvement, the students highlighted the importance of the research component of this project, which allowed them to engage a wide range of Chinese materials and learn to organize their thoughts in the target language. However, reading many unfamiliar texts and deciding what could be useful information were also considered a challenge, but they thought it worked to their benefit. As for the writing activities, the students commented that writing a long essay in the initial stage and then condensing it to a shorter version for the poster increased their ability to write for different audiences and in different formats. Some students reported that the activity was more fun than just writing an essay on a film. They thought the poster presentation also pushed them to sharpen their public speaking skills by presenting their work to native speakers of the target language. All students found the question and answer session very challenging, yet stimulating, because they had few ways to anticipate or prepare for the questions they were asked, particularly for questions raised by fast-speaking native language users.

In addition to the aforementioned advantages, all students remarked that the poster presentation project created an opportunity for social interaction and engagement with learners of different fluency levels as well as with native speakers. Such diverse groups rarely have a shared space and occasion to exchange perspectives on Chinese culture and society using the Chinese language. In sum, students appreciated the fact that a poster presentation project was a good alternative to a final research paper, and that presenting their ideas in one poster was enjoyable and stimulating.

Conclusion

The poster presentation project has helped the students in the advanced-level Chinese courses develop multiliteracies through intensive engagement with the primary source, their chosen films, and extensive reading of secondary materials of various types with different social purposes, and in multiple languages (i.e., Chinese and English). They read the DVD covers (both images and texts) designed to capture the potential audience's attention; film reviews that conveyed reviewers' assessments of the quality of the films and their recommendations to the audience; and scholarly essays that interpret the significance of the films within the wider social/cultural/literary contexts. This process allowed students to examine the main text (a film) from multiple views and interpretations based on cultural/linguistic differences as well as genre differences. It also pushed them to negotiate meanings created by others, and to create their own meaning using multimodal channels (Kalantzis & Cope, 2008). The poster presentation project aims to go beyond linguistic elements by cultivating the students' ability to look into a deeper layer of Chinese culture, society, values, and ideology in an effective learning environment. Unlike a typical PowerPoint presentation, a poster presentation on film highlights the significance of multimodality and intertextuality in communicating meanings. It engages learners in alternative ways of viewing the world and themselves. And it embodies the case put forth by the 2007 MLA report that language teaching be transcultural and translingual, and that it should operate between languages (p. 3).

A variety of academic disciplines, especially the sciences, and the professional world have long used poster presentations to teach multifaceted skills from research, critical reading and writing, to extracting key points, summarizing, and public speaking. As I have demonstrated in this chapter, combining film analysis with poster presentation constitutes a new pedagogical approach to the teaching of Chinese as a foreign/world language, one that can be easily exported to other levels of CFL teaching and to the teaching of other languages as well.

Notes

1 In Chinese, *shumian yu* 書面語 are words and expressions used only for written composition. They are stylistically different from those used in spoken language (口語 *kouyu*).

2 According to the *Cinema* textbook authors (Chou, Wang, and Chiang), "a reader for the movie" means that "every word and every line of the movie is transcribed onto the page, then appended with English annotations or translations of vocabulary words and grammar structures."

3 The website is 《二十一世纪的中国》 (*Chinese Society in the New Millennium*). See www.duke.edu/web/chinesesoc/.

4 For the names of Chinese directors in this chapter, I use Chinese order to refer to a person, which begins with the last name, then first name. Here, Zhang 張 is the last name, and Yang 揚 is the first name. Since Ang Lee (Chinese order is Li An 李安) is well known by Western audiences, I follow the customary way to refer to him.

5 The two characters 洗 (*xi*) and 澡 (*zao*) are synonyms, which originally meant "cleansing" or washing away something.

6 Such as in the case that Chinese people usually bathe at night before bed, not in the morning. It also has a connotation of purifying one's body and spirit.

7 For example, the synopsis from the back cover says, "the Elder son ... find[s] the charm of the bathing pool and its importance to the neighborhood." The bath house was also a place for social interaction.

8 I consulted Smith College's website for poster-making guidelines and samples of posters for science students when I first implemented this project in fall 2010. Even though the website is for science students' presentations, it was helpful to get a sense of how the basic requirements are structured. See www.science.smith.edu/posters/Home.html.

9 The student's name is a pseudonym.

10 This poster was made by a student in the fall 2010 class. Also, through email correspondence, dated November 26, 2014, with The Cinema Guild, Inc., the US distributor of the film granted me permission to use for educational purposes the still images appearing in the photo of the poster. The still images are from the film *24 City*. Two of the images in the poster are from the distributor's website: www.cinemaguild.com/theatrical/24_press.htm.

11 The DVD was distributed in the US in 2010 by The Cinema Guild, Inc. The text can also be found on the company's websites. See www.cinemaguild.com/theatrical/24_press.htm, and www.cinemaguild.com/homevideo/pr_24city.htm.

12 The rough English translation is mine. Note that the Chinese text in square brackets [...] is my revision of the student's errors of some idiomatic usages. I do, however, show her original sentences here as much as possible.

13 This paragraph is an excerpt from subheading 5 of the student's poster.

References

Alderson, J.C., & Urquhart, A.H. (Eds.). (1984). *Reading in a foreign language.* New York, NY: Longman.

Byrnes, H., Maxim, H.H., & Norris, J.M. (2010). Realizing advanced foreign language writing development in collegiate education: Curricular design, pedagogy, assessment. *Modern Language Journal, 94* (Monograph Series, Issue Supplement s1), 1–235.

Chan, D., & Herrero, C. (2010). Using film to teach languages: A teachers' toolkit. Cornerhouse Education. Retrieved December 2, 2014 from www.cornerhouse.org/resources/.

Chang, C. (2006). Effects of topic familiarity and linguistic difficulty on the reading strategies and mental representations of nonnative readers of Chinese. *Journal of Language and Learning, 4*(2), 172–198.

Chen, L. (2011). Teaching Chinese film in an advanced language class. In the special section: China through the cinematic lens. *ASIANetwork EXCHANGE, 18*(2), 30–45.

Chou, C., Wang, W., & Chiang, J. (2007). *Readings in contemporary Chinese cinema: A textbook of advanced modern Chinese.* Princeton, NJ: Princeton University Press.

Elder, C. (2010). Outing the native speaker: The problem of diverse learner backgrounds in "foreign" language classrooms—An Australian case study. *Language, Culture and Curriculum, 13*(1), 86–108.

Everson, M. (2009). Literacy development in Chinese as a foreign language. In M. Everson, & Y. Xiao (Eds.), *Teaching Chinese as a foreign language: Theories and application* (pp. 97–111). Cambridge, MA: Cheng & Tsui.

Everson, M. (2011). Best practices in teaching logographic and non-Roman writing systems to L2 learners. *Annual Review of Applied Linguistics, 31*, 249–274.

Furmanovsky, M., & Sheffner, M. (1997). Using posters in content courses. *The Internet TESL Journal, 3*(1). Retrieved October, 15, 2014 from http://iteslj.org/Lessons/Sheffner-Posters.html.

Goldoni, F. (2008). Designing a foreign language curriculum in postsecondary education drawing from the multiliteracy, functionalist, and genre-based approaches. *Vigo International Journal of Applied Linguistics (VIAL), 5*, 63–86.

Iwasaki, N., & Kumagai, Y. (2008). Towards critical approaches in an advanced level Japanese course: Theory and practice through reflection and dialogues. *Japanese Language and Literature, 42*, 123–156.

Jia, Z. (2008). Director. *24 City.* Distributed by The Cinema Guild, Inc., United States, www.cinemaguild.com/theatrical/24_press.htm.

Kalantzis, M., & Cope, B. (2008). Language education and multiliteracies. In S. May, & N.H. Hornberger (Eds.), *Encyclopedia of language and education, 2nd edition, Vol. 1: Language policy and political issues in education* (pp. 195–211). New York, NY: Springer.

Ke, C. (1996). An empirical study on the relationship between Chinese character recognition and production. *Modern Language Journal, 80*, 340–350.

Ke, C. (1998). Effects of language background on the learning of Chinese characters among foreign language students, *Foreign Language Annals, 31*(1), 91–100.

Kern, R. (2000). *Literacy and language teaching.* New York, NY: Oxford University Press.

Kern, R. (2004). Literacy and advanced foreign language learning: Rethinking the curriculum. In H. Byrnes, & H.H. Maxim (Eds.), *Advanced foreign language learning: A challenge to college programs* (pp. 2–18). Boston, MA: Heinle & Heinle.

Kramsch, C. (1993). *Context and culture in language teaching.* Oxford, UK: Oxford University Press.

Kumagai, Y. (2007). Tension in a Japanese language classroom: An opportunity for critical literacy? *Critical Inquiry in Language Studies, 4*(2–3), 85–116.

Kumagai,Y., & Iwasaki, N. (2011).What it means to read "critically" in a Japanese language classroom: Students' perspective. *Critical Inquiry in Language Studies, 8*(2), 125–152.

Lambert, I. (2008). Assessing oral communication: Poster presentations. *Language Research Bulletin, 23*. ICU,Tokyo. Retrieved October, 15, 2014 from http://web.icu.ac.jp/lrb/vol_23_files/Lambert.pdf.

Lee, K.C., Liang, H., Jiao, L., & Wheatley J.K. (2010). 《文化纵横观》: *The Routledge advanced Chinese multimedia course: Crossing cultural boundaries.* New York, NY: Routledge.

Lee-Thompson, L. (2008). Learning strategies applied by American learners of Chinese as a foreign language. *Foreign Language Annals, 41*(4), 702–721.

Ling,V. (2007). Studies on L2 acquisition of the Chinese script published in America. In A. Guder, X. Jiang, & Y. Wan (Eds.), *The cognition, learning and teaching of Chinese characters* (pp. 51–83). Beijing, China: Beijing Language & Culture University Press.

Maxim, H.H. (2014). Curricular integration and faculty development:Teaching language-based content across the foreign language curriculum. In J. Swaffar, & P. Urlaub (Eds.), *Transforming postsecondary foreign language teaching in the United States* (pp. 79–101). *New York, NY: Springer.*

Modern Language Association (MLA) Ad Hoc Committee on Foreign Languages. (2007). Foreign languages and higher education: New structures for a changed world. *Profession 2007,* 234–245.

New London Group (NLG). (1996). A pedagogy of multiliteracies: Designing social futures. *Harvard Educational Review, 66*(1), 60–92.

Ning, C. (2009). Engaging a "truly foreign" language and culture: China through Chinese film. *Educational Perspectives, 42*(1–2), 29–35. Retrieved from http://files.eric.ed.gov/fulltext/EJ858387.pdf.

Pudwill, L., & Cullen, B. (2003). Poster presentations for engineering students. *The Language Teacher, 27*(1). Retrieved October 15, 2014 from www.jalt-publications.org/tlt/articles/2003/01/pudwill.

Quinlisk, C. (2003). Media literacy in the ESL/EFL classroom: Reading images and cultural stories. *TESOL Journal, 12*(3), 35–40.

Shen, H. (2000).The interconnection of reading text based writing and reading comprehension among college intermediate learners of Chinese as a foreign language. *Journal of the Chinese Language Teachers Association, 36*, 29–47.

Shen, H. (2005). An investigation of Chinese-character learning strategies among non-native speakers of Chinese. *System, 33*, 49–68.

Shen, H., & Jiang, X. (2013). Character reading fluency, word segmentation accuracy, and reading comprehension in L2 Chinese. *Reading in a Foreign Language, 25*(1), 1–25.

Swaffar, J. (2004). A template for advanced learner tasks: Staging genre reading and cultural literacy through the précis. In H. Byrnes, & H.H. Maxim (Eds.), *Advanced foreign language learning: A challenge to college programs* (pp. 19–45). Boston, MA: Heinle & Heinle.

Swaffar, J., & Arens, K. (2005). *Remapping the foreign language curriculum: An approach through multiple literacies.* New York, NY: Modern Language Association.

Urlaub, P. (2014). On language and content: The stakes of curricular transformation in collegiate foreign language education. In J. Swaffar, & P. Urlaub (Eds.), *Transforming postsecondary foreign language teaching in the United States* (pp. 1–15). New York, NY: Springer.

White, E.J. (2011). Bakhtinian dialogic and Vygotskian dialectic: Compatabilities and contradictions in the classroom? *Educational Philosophy and Theory.* Retrieved from http://researchcommons.waikato.ac.nz; doi: 10.1111/j.1469-5812.2011.00814.x.

Zhang, L. (2011). Teaching Chinese cultural perspectives through film. *L2 Journal, 3*(2), 201–231. Produced by eScholarship Repository. Retrieved October 22, 2014 from http://repositories.cdlib.org/uccllt/12/vol3/iss2/art5/.

Zhang,Y. (1999). Director. *Shower.* Distributed by Guangzhou Beauty Media Group, China.

Appendix A: Instructional Procedures for the Film Shower

	Source materials	Text types	Subjects
Day 1: Pre-viewing	• The DVD covers	• Movie title in Chinese and English translation • Short description of the story • Still images from the film	• Cultural differences conveyed in the movie title • Interconnection between linguistic meaning and visual meaning • Prediction of the ending
Day 2: Viewing the film	• The film • The *Cinema* textbook	• Selected images from the film • Read the synopsis in the textbook (including learning new vocabulary, phrases, and sentence patterns in context)	• Portraits of the main characters (the father and two sons) • The symbolism of the main characters and the bath house in Beijing
Day 3: Post-viewing (1)— Other people's critique and reviews	• The *Cinema* textbook • Website	• Critique on the traditional bath house provided in the textbook • Two film reviews (in Chinese) from the web	• The structures of a review and a critique • Criteria of film reviews
Day 4: Post-viewing (2)— Providing one's own critique	• All of the above	• Students' own film reviews (written and oral)	• Cultural values • Comparison between the characters' and one's own life experiences • The impact of economic development on personal life and traditional values

Appendix B: Films Used for Poster Presentation Project in Fall 2010

Director 導演	Chinese title (Year)	English title
Chen, Joan 陳沖	天浴 (1998)	Xiu Xiu: The Sent Down Girl
Cheng, Fen Fen 鄭芬芬	聽説 (2009)	Hear Me
Feng, Xiaogang 馮小剛	一聲嘆息 (2000)	A Sigh
Jia, Zhangke 賈樟柯	二十四城記 (2008)	24 City
To, Johnnie 杜琪峰 and Wai, Ka-fai 韋家輝	孤男寡女 (2000)	Needing You
Wang, Xiaoshuai 王小帥	十七歲的單車 (2001)	Beijing Bicycle
Yang, Edward 楊德昌	一一 (2000)	Yi Yi: A One and a Two
Zhang, Yang 張揚	向日葵 (2005)	Sunflower
Zhang, Yimou 張藝謀	一个都不能少 (1999)	Not One Less

Appendix C: Guidelines for Implementation of the Poster Presentation Project

Step 1: Selecting and Viewing Film

- Select the film from a list of films (see Appendix B) provided.
- Watch the film of one's own choice.

Step 2: Reading and Writing

- Library session (search one film review and one analytic essay in Chinese and English).
- Write the first draft essay.
- Give and receive feedback from peers.
- Revise the second draft essay.

Step 3: Making the Poster

- Analyze a sample poster and decide the evaluation criteria.
- Create a draft poster in a 8.5' × 11' paper for peer review.
- Rehearse the presentation using the second draft poster.

Step 4: Presenting

- Present the poster.
- Attend others' presentations.
- Provide comments.

Step 5: Reflecting on the Project

- Respond to the survey.
- Discuss the challenges and rewards.

AFTERWORD

Ana López-Sánchez and Yuri Kumagai

The call for transformation that the MLA Ad Hoc Committee on Foreign Languages issued in 2007 generated considerable discussion and concern, as attested by the number of publications responding to the document. These publications, including two rather recent volumes (Paesani, Allen, & Dupuy, 2015; Swaffar & Urlaub, 2014), suggest that the language and cultural studies community continues to be in "response-mode," seeking to advance frameworks that can bring about the desired changes. Literacy- and multiliteracies-based frameworks, in particular, have emerged as particularly strong contenders for the rearticulation. This book aligns with those who advocate the adoption of the *pedagogy of multiliteracies* (New London Group (NLG), 2000) to transform language and cultural studies departments. As discussed in Chapter 1, "Advancing Multiliteracies in World Language Education," the multiliteracies framework was designed to generate active and dynamic transformation (Cope & Kalantzis, 2009) in general educational settings and the world at large; change would come by reformulating curricula to include a multiplicity of texts previously excluded from the educational space, and by teaching those texts through pedagogical practices that empower students to become agents of change. The multiliteracies framework for world language departments delineated in these pages is based on the same premises and objectives.

Below, we briefly highlight the ways in which the pedagogical practices and proposals in the book can be transformative: for learners, for individual practitioners, for departments, and for the field at large.

A Framework for Curricular Integration and Transformation

The most often invoked reason to adopt the multiliteracies framework and, indeed, a major way in which it can be transformative for language and cultural studies departments, is its ability to bring integration and coherence to curricula. The majority of the chapters in this volume, while not advancing overarching four-year integrated curricula, show how language and content can be brought together at different levels of the curriculum. A major way in which this integration is accomplished is through the use of genres (e.g., narratives, news reports, film reviews). For example, in Chapter 2, "Developing Multiliteracies Through Genre in the Beginner German Classroom," Warren and Winkler introduce (short) travel narratives and dialogues that are culturally situated, and guide students through an analysis of the moves (or stages) and language of the genres, and into the production of this type of narrative. Chapter 3, "Redesigning the Intermediate Level of the Spanish Curriculum Through a Multiliteracies Lens," by López-Sánchez and Chapter 5, "Reading Words to Read Worlds: A Genre-Based Critical Multiliteracies Curriculum in Intermediate/Advanced Japanese Language Education," by Kumagai and Iwasaki, identify, respectively, the movie review, and reporting texts, specifically newspaper articles, as appropriate genres for the intermediate and intermediate/advanced levels of the curriculum. Class activities aim to identify the resources necessitated to produce these genres, and create awareness of the specific context of culture and situation.

As an advocate of a multiliteracies framework, the volume, naturally, devotes a number of its chapters to the teaching of multimodal, (i.e., non-written) genres: bimodal advertisements, the video presentation, and the poster presentation. Focusing on the analysis and/or the production of these genres, Sagnier's "Multiliteracies and Multimodal Discourses in the Foreign Language Classroom" (Chapter 4), Kumagai et al.'s "Fostering Multimodal Literacies in the Japanese Language Classroom: Digital Video Projects" (Chapter 6), and Wu's "Creating an Effective Learning Environment in an Advanced Chinese Language Course Through Film, Poster Presentations, and Multiliteracies," (Chapter 9) present instructional sequences that direct the learners' attention to the different semiotic systems and toward an understanding of how meaning is created by orchestrating various modes. The pedagogical sequences proposed in these and in the "written" (alphabetical) genre chapters can easily be replicated or adapted for the instruction of other genres.

Language and cultural studies departments have been regarded—in particular, in relation to the lower levels of the curriculum—as skill-training spaces that do not contribute to the larger mission of higher education, of fostering critical thinking. The implementation of a multiliteracies framework guarantees that activities that encourage critical thinking, through Critical Framing and Analyzing activities, are present at all levels—and further transforms the departments. Two chapters in the book, in particular, have the development of a critical stance in the learners at their core: Chapter 7, "Implementing Multiliteracies in the Korean Classroom Through Visual Media," by Brown et al. and Chapter 5 (see above), by Kumagai and Iwasaki, guide learners to recognize how specific language and other semiotic systems (visual images, gestures, clothing) in TV dramas, talk shows, and newspapers, are being used to construct reality in a certain way (e.g., to construct "foreigners" in Korean popular culture). In turn, by recognizing the mechanisms that construct reality in certain ways, learners can contest and possibly transform that ideology, reconstructing (or redesigning) it in different ways.

Below we discuss some other features that, we believe, define multiliteracies approaches and that further connect the chapters in this book.

A Pedagogy for "Designers"

Language learning has been mainly conceived as the acquisition of linguistic resources, and a process that is only complete when the learner can replicate the competence of an idealized "native" speaker. The view that we have espoused in the book, informed by the NLG's proposals, sees the learner and the learning process in a completely different light as captured in the notion of the "learner-as-designer". In multiliteracies-based frameworks, learners are afforded a freer, more agentive position and given the space to make their own unique meaning, ably incorporating designs that they have been exposed to, without simply reproducing them. As shown in many of the chapters in the book, students created an array of new meanings and texts, from the (redesigned) modeled genres (Chapters 2, 3, and 5), which, however, bore the students' unique voice and subjectivity, to new hybrid genres that better expressed their views, opinions, and multilingual subjectivities (Chapters 6, 7, 8, and 9).

A Pedagogy of Collaboration

Traditionally, in second language acquisition (SLA) and in foreign language teaching, learning is considered an individual act whereby the learner receives and internalizes knowledge provided by a teacher for later use. This understanding is in stark contrast with the sociocultural perspective on learning and on literacy (informed by Vygotskian theory) that we draw on and advocate in this book, which posits that "knowledge is developed as part and parcel of collaborative interactions with others of diverse skills, backgrounds, and perspectives" (NLG, 2000, p. 30).

The proposals presented in this book all provide students with multiple opportunities to engage in the co-construction of knowledge. Any reading/ viewing, analysis (or "deconstruction"), and writing/designing of texts is done collaboratively (i.e., in pairs, small groups, or in a whole class), in an effort to maximize assistance from peers and instructors. Some of the chapters also emphasize the co-construction of knowledge in non-traditional areas, such as grammar and vocabulary learning. López-Sánchez (Chapter 3) advocates the use of

"Concept-Based Instruction," where an understanding of complex grammatical concepts such as aspect and mood is, partly, jointly constructed between teacher and learners. In Spinelli's "Empowering Students in the Italian Classroom to Learn Vocabulary Through a Multiliteracies Framework" (Chapter 8), vocabulary lists and expressions are generated, and (multimodally) defined in a collaborated manner in a Wiki. When collaboration in the class is not a possibility, scaffolding is provided through, for example, handouts with prompts or support materials in English, leading learners to progress gradually from more guided tasks to independent work.

A Pedagogy for "Social Agents"

The *pedagogy of multiliteracies* considers both teachers and learners as "designers of social futures," thus assigning them both far greater agency than do traditional pedagogies. The learners in the multiliteracies classroom are viewed not as mere "passive receivers of knowledge," but as social agents, and are positioned as active creators of meaning. The instructional space becomes an arena where they deconstruct, reconstruct, and transform genres (Chapters 2 and 3), engage in critical analysis (Chapter 4), recognize themselves as "cultural and linguistic mediators" (Chapter 5), negotiate identities and redesign self-images (Chapters 6 and 7), gain a sense of ownership of their own learning (Chapter 8), and become confident multimodal meaning makers (Chapter 9).

In turn, the scholar-instructors in this book acted not as authoritative figures, but as facilitators and expert members who managed and monitored the trajectory of students' learning. In other words, they were enablers, empowering students through their teaching practices. And they may be enablers, and social actors in other ways, since the teaching practices that they have shared in this book may become, as Sagnier (Chapter 4) puts it, "seeds of change" that bring about curricular transformation in world languages and cultural studies programs.

Final Remarks

Compiling this edited book has offered us an invaluable opportunity to work collaboratively with innovative scholar-practitioners, who are teaching at a range of collegiate institutions across the US, under different and yet similar conditions and circumstances, and who engaged both common and separate (knowledge) traditions. It has also been a great, rare chance to engage European and Asian languages scholarship in a dialogue. As shown in this book, we have a lot to learn from each other. We hope this book can play a role in bringing together all world languages practitioners in a concerted effort to advance our departments' educational mission and to make our students' learning more meaningful.

References

Cope, B., & Kalantzis, M. (2009). Multiliteracies: New literacies, new learning. *Pedagogies: An International Journal, 4*(3), 164–195.

New London Group (NLG). (2000). A pedagogy of multiliteracies: Designing social futures. In B. Cope, & M. Kalantzis (Eds.), *Multiliteracies: Literacy learning and the design of social futures* (pp. 9–37). New York, NY: Routledge.

Paesani, K.W., Allen, H.W., & Dupuy, B. (2015). *A multiliteracies framework for collegiate foreign language teaching.* Englewood Cliffs, NJ: Prentice Hall.

Swaffar, J.K., & Urlaub, P. (2014). *Transforming postsecondary foreign language teaching in the United States.* New York, NY: Springer.

CONTRIBUTORS

Lucien Brown is Assistant Professor of Korean Linguistics at the University of Oregon. His research focuses on honorifics, politeness, and social aspects of language learning and teaching. He is the author of *Korean honorifics and politeness in language learning* (2011), co-author of *Korean: A comprehensive grammar* (Routledge, 2011), and co-editor of *The handbook of Korean linguistics* (2015).

Noriko Iwasaki is Senior Lecturer (the UK equivalent of Associate Professor) in Language Pedagogy in the Department of Linguistics at SOAS, University of London. She currently serves as Deputy Chair of the Association of Japanese Language Teachers in Europe, e.V. Her research interests include language pedagogy, second language acquisition and psycholinguistics. She has published articles in such journals as *Applied Linguistics, Foreign Language Annals, Japanese Language and Literature,* and *Language* and *Cognitive Processes.*

Keiko Konoeda is a PhD candidate in Education at the University of Massachusetts Amherst and Lecturer of Japanese in the Asian Studies Program at Bates College. She has published in *Readings in Language Studies* (Vol. 1, 2009) and *Occasional Papers by the Association of Teachers of Japanese* (Vol. 11, 2012). Her interests include Bakhtinian theory of language, learner multimodal media production, critical media literacy, and narrative inquiry.

Yuri Kumagai is Senior Lecturer of Japanese at Smith College, Massachusetts. She specializes in critical literacy and multiliteracies in foreign language education. Her articles appear in journals such as *Critical Inquiry in Language Studies, Critical Studies in Education,* and *Writing Systems.* She has co-edited (with S. Sato) four books (in Japanese) on topics related to language pedagogy and co-authored a textbook (with N. Iwasaki), *The Routledge intermediate/advanced Japanese reader: A genre-based approach to reading as a social practice*, (2015).

Keunyoung Lee is a PhD student in Korean Linguistics in the Department of East Asian Languages and Literatures at the University of Oregon. Prior to beginning the PhD program, she received her Master's degree in Linguistics with a Language Teaching Specialization (LTS) from the University of Oregon, and joined the Department of East Asian Languages and Literatures in 2012. Her research interests lie in Korean syntax, second language acquisition, and language teaching.

Ana López-Sánchez is Assistant Professor of Spanish at Haverford College, Pennsylvania. She is an applied linguist working in the area of curriculum development and language pedagogy. Previously, she worked and published in the area of cross-cultural pragmatics; she is currently writing a book on Spanish FL pedagogy and education, and a textbook on writing.

Miyuki Nishimata (Fukai) is Instructor/Academic Director of Summer Programs of the Kyoto Consortium for Japanese Studies, a study abroad program located in Kyoto, Japan. She has been involved in research projects that investigate blogging, podcasting, and literacy activities from the perspectives of sociocultural theory and critical literacy. She has published articles in journals such as *Japanese Language and Literature* and *Japanese Language Education around the Globe*, as well as chapters in books on classroom projects and assessment.

Christine Sagnier is Director of the French Language Program at Princeton University and a specialist in applied linguistics and second language acquisition. Her research explores issues in applied linguistics in cognitive psychology, psycholinguistics and sociocultural theory. She has published articles in European research journals and a book, *Metacognition and social interactions in foreign language learning: A sociocognitive perspective* (2013). Her interests include human learning and cognition, Vygotskian theories on language and learning, discourse analysis, multiliteracies, social semiotics, and visual communication.

Shinji Sato is Senior Lecturer and Director of the Japanese Language Program at Princeton University. His research interests include language policy and teaching, and the critical examination of commonplace ideas in language education. He has co-edited several books on language education in Japan. His book chapter, "Communication as intersubjective activity: When native/non-native speakers' identity appears in computer-mediated communication," appears in *The native speaker concept: Ethnographic investigations of native speaker effects* (2009).

Barbara Spinelli is Senior Lecturer at Columbia University, New York, and Assistant Professor of Second Language Acquisition at the University for Foreigners in Perugia, Italy. She collaborates with the Centre for Language Assessment and Certifications as a teacher trainer and is involved in language testing and European research projects. Her main research areas are: network-based language learning, curriculum design, and plurilingual and intercultural education. She has published articles in ISL journals. She is the co-author of the *Profilo della lingua italiana: Livelli di riferimento del QCER A1, A2, B1, B2* (2010).

Mackenzie Warren has an MA in German Studies with a concentration in Second Language Acquisition from Georgetown University, Washington, DC. Her research focuses on L2 writing and teaching through the lens of systemic functional linguistics. She currently works as the Institutional Marketing Associate for Global Communications at Oxford University Press.

Claudia Winkler is ABD in German Studies at Georgetown University, Washington, DC. She has published articles on new media in the *Women in German Yearbook* (Vol. 29, 2013) and on *Heimat* in *German Politics and Society* (Vol. 31, 2013). She currently works as the senior project associate for the Religious Freedom Project at Georgetown University's Berkley Center for Religion, Peace & World Affairs.

Sujane Wu is Associate Professor of Chinese Language and Literature at Smith College, Massachusetts. Her primary specialization is traditional Chinese poetry and painting. She has taught all levels of Chinese language in the US for more than 20 years. She has developed various projects in both literature and language courses that explore the intertextual relationship where words and images co-construct meanings. Her work also integrates the use of Chinese and English as multi-literacies practice. She has also translated many literary works from Chinese to English.

INDEX